This Side of Paradise

Youth, Love & Self-Discovery
in the Dazzling Dawn of the Jazz Era

A Modern Translation
Adapted for the Contemporary Reader

F. Scott Fitzgerald

Translated by Tim Zengerink

Table of Contents

Preface
Message to the Reader

Rebuilding the Greatest Library in Human History

Thousands of years ago, the Library of Alexandria was the heart of global knowledge — a sanctuary where the wisdom of every known civilization was gathered and shared freely.

And then, it was lost.

Now, we're rebuilding it — and you are invited to join us.

At the Library of Alexandria, we've set out to make every book available to every person on Earth — not just in print, but in every language, every format, and for every reader.

Here's how we do it:

- **Deluxe Print Editions at True Printing Cost** - Order any book as a high-quality paperback, elegant hardcover, or stunning boxset — and only pay what it costs to print. No markups. No middlemen.
- **Unlimited Access to the Greatest Works** - Enjoy thousands of timeless classics — from Plato to Shakespeare to Tolstoy — in beautiful, modern eBook and audiobook editions. Read and listen without limits — for every reader, everywhere.
- **Modern Translations for Every Language & Dialect** - We're reimagining the classics in clear, accessible language — and translating them into every dialect imaginable. Everyone deserves to understand humanity's greatest ideas.

When you visit **LibraryofAlexandria.com**, you're not just accessing books — you're joining a global movement to restore, preserve, and share the wisdom of civilization.

Join us today at LibraryofAlexandria.com

Together, we'll ensure the light of human wisdom never fades again.

With gratitude,

The Modern Library of Alexandria Team

Visit:
www.libraryofalexandria.com
Or scan the code below:

Introduction

A Portrait of Youth and the Roaring Twenties

F. Scott Fitzgerald's debut novel, *This Side of Paradise*, published in 1920, marked the arrival of a bold new voice in American literature and encapsulated the exuberance, uncertainty, and restless spirit of a generation coming of age in the aftermath of World War I. A semi-autobiographical work, the novel draws heavily from Fitzgerald's own life, charting the journey of Amory Blaine, a young man navigating love, ambition, disillusionment, and the search for self-identity in a rapidly changing world. With its unique structure, modern sensibilities, and sparkling prose, *This Side of Paradise* became a cultural sensation, heralding the Jazz Age and cementing Fitzgerald's place as one of its defining chroniclers.

When *This Side of Paradise* was first published, it captured the imagination of a post-war generation that was questioning traditional values and seeking new forms of expression. The novel was an immediate success, propelling Fitzgerald to literary fame almost overnight and famously winning him back the love of Zelda Sayre, who agreed to marry him after the book's publication. Beyond its romantic backstory, however, the novel is a profound exploration of youth's aspirations and anxieties. It portrays a generation caught between the old social structures of the Gilded Age and the modern, liberated attitudes that would define the 1920s.

At its heart, *This Side of Paradise* is the story of a young man's inner journey. Amory Blaine, the protagonist, is a Princeton student who struggles to reconcile his desire for wealth and success with his deeper longing for love, purpose, and meaning.

Through Amory's romantic entanglements, friendships, and intellectual pursuits, Fitzgerald examines the complexities of growing up and the painful process of self-discovery. The novel's episodic structure—combining traditional narrative with letters, poetry, and dramatic dialogue—reflects the fragmented and experimental spirit of the time, making it both a literary and cultural milestone.

The title of the novel is drawn from a line in the poem "Tiare Tahiti" by Rupert Brooke: *"Well, this side of Paradise! ... There's little comfort in the wise."* The choice of title underscores the book's central theme: the tension between youthful idealism and the sobering realities of adulthood. For Amory, life is a quest for a "paradise" that often seems just out of reach—a search for fulfillment, beauty, and significance that is constantly challenged by the compromises and disappointments of the real world.

Fitzgerald's prose in *This Side of Paradise* is vibrant and lyrical, capturing both the excitement and the melancholy of youth. He writes with a keen awareness of the fleeting nature of time, the intensity of first love, and the desire to leave a mark on the world. These themes would become hallmarks of his later work, particularly in *The Great Gatsby*, but here they are explored through the raw, passionate lens of a young writer finding his voice. The novel is not just a coming-of-age story but also a manifesto for a generation eager to break free from the constraints of the past.

The historical context of *This Side of Paradise* adds further depth to its themes. The early 20th century was a time of profound social and cultural change in America. The devastation of World War I had shaken traditional beliefs and values, paving the way for new ideas about love, gender roles, and individual freedom. The novel reflects this shift, particularly in its portrayal of modern relationships. Amory's romantic experiences with characters like Rosalind Connage highlight the changing dynamics of love and courtship, as women became more independent and assertive in their choices.

Moreover, the novel's exploration of class and ambition resonates with the broader American Dream narrative. Amory is keenly aware of social hierarchies and the allure of wealth and status, yet he also grapples with the emptiness that can accompany material success. This tension between external achievement and inner fulfillment is a theme that would recur throughout Fitzgerald's career, reflecting his own ambivalence about the high society he both admired and critiqued.

This Side of Paradise is also notable for its literary experimentation. Fitzgerald blends multiple genres and forms, incorporating poetry, autobiographical elements, and dramatic interludes to create a rich and varied narrative texture. This innovative approach mirrors the fragmented nature of modern life and the restless energy of youth. It also sets the novel apart from the more traditional coming-of-age stories of its time, giving it a freshness and vitality that continue to appeal to readers today.

Themes of Love, Loss, and Self-Discovery

One of the central themes of *This Side of Paradise* is the search for identity. Amory Blaine is a character in flux, constantly reinventing himself as he navigates the complexities of youth and early adulthood. His journey is marked by moments of intense passion, intellectual curiosity, and emotional upheaval. Through Amory's experiences, Fitzgerald explores the universal question: Who am I, and what do I want from life? This theme is particularly poignant in the context of the post-war era, when traditional values were being questioned, and young people were seeking new ways to define themselves.

Love plays a pivotal role in Amory's development, serving as both a source of inspiration and a catalyst for growth. His relationships with women like Isabelle Borgé and Rosalind

Connage are characterized by intense emotions, misunderstandings, and the inevitable pain of unfulfilled desires. These romantic experiences are not merely plot points but windows into Amory's evolving understanding of himself and the world around him. Through these relationships, Fitzgerald examines the changing roles of men and women in modern society, as well as the challenges of balancing personal ambition with genuine emotional connection.

The theme of ambition is closely intertwined with the novel's exploration of class and social status. Amory is deeply aware of the privileges and limitations imposed by his background. While he is determined to rise above his middle-class roots and achieve success, he also struggles with the superficiality and emptiness of the upper-class world he aspires to join. This tension between social climbing and authentic selfhood is a recurring motif in Fitzgerald's work, reflecting his own experiences as a writer who achieved fame but often felt alienated from the glamorous circles he depicted.

Disillusionment is another key theme in *This Side of Paradise*. As Amory matures, he becomes increasingly aware of the gap between his youthful dreams and the realities of life. The novel's final chapters, in particular, highlight his sense of loss and resignation as he confronts the limitations of his ambitions and the transience of love and beauty. This sense of disillusionment is emblematic of the Lost Generation—a term often used to describe the post-war youth who felt adrift in a world that no longer adhered to traditional values or offered clear paths to fulfillment.

Fitzgerald's treatment of these themes is both personal and universal. While the novel is deeply rooted in the specific cultural context of the 1920s, its exploration of youth, love, and self-discovery transcends its time. Readers of all generations can relate to Amory's struggles, his moments of triumph and despair, and his ultimate realization that life is a complex, often contradictory journey.

Fitzgerald's Literary Style and Cultural Impact

Fitzgerald's style in *This Side of Paradise* is characterized by its lyrical beauty, sharp wit, and emotional resonance. His prose captures the fleeting, almost dreamlike quality of youth, evoking a world of summer evenings, romantic escapades, and intellectual debates. At the same time, his writing is grounded in keen social observation, offering incisive commentary on the class structures, gender roles, and cultural shifts of his time.

One of the most striking aspects of the novel is its structure. Divided into two books—*"The Romantic Egotist"* and *"The Education of a Personage"*—the narrative traces Amory's journey from idealistic youth to disillusioned young man. This progression is not linear but rather episodic, reflecting the fragmented and often chaotic nature of personal growth. Fitzgerald enhances this effect by incorporating a variety of narrative techniques, including letters, diary entries, and even poetry. This experimental approach was innovative for its time and contributed to the novel's fresh and modern feel.

The cultural impact of *This Side of Paradise* cannot be overstated. Upon its release, the novel was hailed as a defining portrait of a new generation—one that was more liberated, cynical, and self-aware than its predecessors. Fitzgerald's depiction of flappers, jazz, and modern romance resonated with readers who were eager to see their own experiences and aspirations reflected in literature. The novel's success not only launched Fitzgerald's career but also helped to shape the cultural narrative of the 1920s, establishing the Jazz Age as a distinct literary and cultural moment.

In addition to its cultural significance, *This Side of Paradise* offers valuable insights into Fitzgerald's development as a writer. Many of the themes, characters, and stylistic elements that would later define his work are already present in this debut novel. Amory Blaine, with his blend of charm, ambition, and vulnerability, can be seen as a precursor to characters like Jay Gatsby and Dick Diver. Similarly, the novel's exploration of wealth, class, and the pursuit of happiness foreshadows the more mature and complex treatments of these themes in Fitzgerald's later works.

Ultimately, *This Side of Paradise* is a novel that celebrates both the beauty and the heartbreak of youth. It is a story of dreams pursued and lost, of love found and abandoned, and of the enduring quest for self-understanding. Through Amory's journey, Fitzgerald invites readers to reflect on their own experiences of growing up, falling in love, and confronting the realities of the world. The novel's enduring appeal lies in its ability to capture the universal longing for a life of significance and connection—a longing that is as powerful today as it was a century ago.

Book One:
The Romantic Egotist

Chapter 1. Amory, Son Of Beatrice

Amory Blaine inherited from his mother every quality, except for a few scattered, indefinable traits, that made him worthwhile. His father was an ineffective, tongue-tied man who loved Byron's poetry and had a habit of falling asleep while reading the Encyclopedia Britannica. He became rich at thirty when his two older brothers, who were successful Chicago stockbrokers, died, and in his initial excitement at feeling the world was now his, he traveled to Bar Harbor where he met Beatrice O'Hara. As a result, Stephen Blaine passed down to future generations his height of just under six feet and his tendency to hesitate during critical moments, both of these characteristics showing up in his son Amory. For many years he remained in the background of his family's life, a passive figure whose face was nearly hidden by dull, fine hair, constantly busy "looking after" his wife, constantly troubled by the thought that he didn't and couldn't understand her.

But Beatrice Blaine! Now there was a woman! Early photographs taken on her father's estate at Lake Geneva, Wisconsin, or in Rome at the Sacred Heart Convent—an educational luxury that in her time was reserved only for daughters of the extraordinarily wealthy—revealed the exquisite refinement of her features, the perfect artistry and elegance of her clothing. She received a brilliant education—her youth spent in renaissance splendor, she was well-versed in the latest rumors of the Old Roman Families; recognized by name as a fabulously rich American girl to Cardinal Vitori and Queen Margherita and more sophisticated celebrities that one would have needed considerable culture even to know about. In England she learned to favor whiskey and soda over wine, and her casual conversation was enhanced in two ways during a winter spent in Vienna. All told, Beatrice O'Hara received the kind of education that will never be possible again; a schooling measured by the quantity of things and people one could look down upon while remaining charming; a refinement rich in all arts and customs, yet empty of all ideas, in the final days when the master gardener pruned the lesser roses to create one flawless bloom.

During her quieter periods, she went back to America, where she encountered Stephen Blaine and became his wife—this happened mainly because she felt somewhat tired and melancholy. Her sole child was carried through a difficult pregnancy and was born on a spring day in eighteen ninety-six.

When Amory turned five, he had already become a wonderful companion for his mother. He was a boy with reddish-brown hair and striking, beautiful eyes that he would eventually grow into, along with a quick and creative mind and a love for dressing up in costumes. From age four to ten, he traveled across the country with his mother in his grandfather's private railroad car, journeying from Coronado, where his mother grew so restless that she suffered a nervous breakdown at an upscale hotel, all the way down to Mexico City, where she contracted a mild case of tuberculosis that was almost commonplace at the time. This illness actually pleased her, and she later incorporated it into her personal mystique—particularly after having several strong drinks to boost her spirits.

While other wealthy children of varying fortune were rebelling against their governesses on Newport's beaches, or receiving spankings, tutoring, or having adventure stories like "Do and Dare" or "Frank on the Mississippi" read to them, Amory was biting compliant hotel staff at the Waldorf, overcoming his instinctive dislike of chamber music and symphonies, and receiving a uniquely tailored education from his mother.

"Amory."

"Yes, Beatrice." (Such an old-fashioned name for his mother; she encouraged it.)

"Honey, don't even think about getting out of bed just yet. I've always believed that getting up early when you're young makes you anxious. Clothilde is bringing your breakfast up to you."

"All right."

"I'm feeling so old today, Amory," she would sigh, her face becoming a perfect portrait of sadness, her voice beautifully controlled, her hands as expressive as Bernhardt's. "My nerves are frayed—completely frayed. We have to leave this frightening place tomorrow and go look for sunshine."

Amory's sharp green eyes would peer out from beneath his messy hair as he looked at his mother. Even at such a young age, he harbored no false impressions about who she really was.

"Amory."

"Oh, yes."

"I want you to take a really hot bath, as hot as you can stand, and just let your nerves unwind. You can bring a book to read in the tub if you'd like."

She introduced him to sections of the "Fetes Galantes" before he turned ten; by eleven he could speak smoothly, though somewhat nostalgically, about Brahms and Mozart and Beethoven. One afternoon, while alone at the hotel in Hot Springs, he tried his mother's apricot cordial, and finding the taste agreeable, he became quite drunk. This was enjoyable for a time, but in his excitement he attempted to smoke a cigarette, and fell victim to a crude, common reaction. While this incident appalled Beatrice, it also privately entertained her and became part of what a later generation would have called her "routine."

"This son of mine," he heard her tell a room full of amazed, admiring women one day, "is completely sophisticated and quite charming—but fragile—we're all fragile; here, you know." Her hand was brilliantly silhouetted against her lovely chest; then lowering her voice to a whisper, she told them about the apricot cordial. They delighted in her words, for she was a skilled storyteller, but many were the keys turned in cabinet locks that night to prevent little Bobby or Barbara from possibly getting into mischief....

These family trips were always conducted with great ceremony and formality; they included two housemaids, the family's private automobile, or Mr. Blaine when he could accompany them, and very frequently a doctor. When Amory came down with whooping cough, four irritated medical specialists stood around his bed, hunched over and glowering at one another; when he contracted scarlet fever, the total number of people caring for him, including doctors and nurses, reached fourteen. Nevertheless, since family loyalty runs deeper than mere convenience, he recovered from his illnesses.

The Blaines weren't tied to any particular city. They were known as the Blaines of Lake Geneva; they had plenty of family members who could take the place of friends, and they enjoyed an impressive reputation that stretched from Pasadena all the way to Cape Cod. However, Beatrice became increasingly inclined to prefer only people she had just met, since there were particular tales—like the story of her personal rules and all the changes she'd made to them over time, along with recollections from her years living overseas—that she felt compelled to tell again and again at regular intervals. Much like Freudian dreams, these stories had to be released, or they would flood back and overwhelm her emotional state. Yet Beatrice held critical views about American women, particularly the drifting group of former Westerners.

"They have accents, my dear," she explained to Amory, "not Southern accents or Boston accents, not an accent tied to any particular place, just an accent"—her voice grew distant and thoughtful. "They adopt these old, worn-out London accents that have seen better days and need someone to use them. They speak like an English butler might sound after spending several years with a Chicago opera company." Her words became nearly incomprehensible—"Imagine—there comes a time in every Western woman's life—when she feels her husband has become successful enough for her to have—an accent—they're trying to impress me, my dear—"

Though she viewed her body as a collection of weaknesses, she regarded her soul as equally troubled, and therefore significant in her existence. She had previously been a Catholic, but after realizing that priests paid far more attention to her when she was either losing or rediscovering her faith in the Church, she maintained a charmingly uncertain stance. Frequently she criticized the middle-class nature of American Catholic priests, and felt confident that if she had lived near the grand European cathedrals, her soul would still burn as a delicate flame upon Rome's magnificent altar. Nevertheless, aside from doctors, priests remained her preferred pastime.

"Oh, Bishop Wiston," she would announce, "I don't want to discuss myself. I can picture the parade of emotional women rushing to your door, begging you to be understanding"—then after a pause filled by the clergyman—"but my state of mind is strangely different."

Only to bishops and those of higher rank did she reveal her romantic involvement with a member of the clergy. When she had first come back to her homeland, there had been a non-religious, Swinburnian young man in Asheville, whose passionate kisses and unsentimental conversations had captured her strong interest— they had talked through the situation from both sides with an intellectual romance that was completely free of excessive sentiment. In the end, she had chosen to marry for social standing, and the young non-believer from Asheville had experienced a spiritual transformation, converted to the Catholic Church, and had now become—Monsignor Darcy.

"Indeed, Mrs. Blaine, he is still delightful company—quite the cardinal's right-hand man."

"I know that Amory will come to him someday," whispered the beautiful woman, "and Monsignor Darcy will understand him just as he understood me."

When Amory turned thirteen, he had grown rather tall and slender, and felt closer than ever to his Celtic mother. He had worked with tutors from time to time—the plan was for him to "keep up" with his studies, picking up "where he left off" at each new location. However, since no tutor could ever figure out exactly where he had stopped, his mind remained in excellent condition. What a few more years of this lifestyle might have done to him remains uncertain. Nevertheless, four hours out from shore on a voyage to Italy with Beatrice, his appendix ruptured, likely from eating too many meals while lying in bed. After a flurry of urgent telegrams sent to Europe and America, the massive ship slowly turned around and headed back to New York to drop Amory off at the dock, much to the astonishment of the other passengers. You have to admit that even if it wasn't exactly living, it was certainly spectacular.

After the surgery, Beatrice suffered a nervous breakdown that looked suspiciously like alcohol withdrawal, and Amory was left behind in Minneapolis, where he would spend the next two years living with his aunt and uncle. It was there that the rough, unrefined atmosphere of Western civilization first hit him—catching him completely off guard, you might say.

A Kiss for Amory

His lip curled when he read it.

"I'm hosting a bobbing party," the invitation read, "on Thursday, December seventeenth, at five o'clock, and I would really love for you to come.

Sincerely yours,

R.S.V.P. Myra St. Claire."

He had spent two months in Minneapolis, and his main challenge had been hiding from "the other guys at school" just how much better he believed himself to be than them, though this belief rested on unstable ground. One day he had shown off in French class (he was taking senior-level French) to the complete bewilderment of Mr. Reardon, whose accent Amory scorned with contempt, and to the amusement of his classmates. Mr. Reardon, who had spent a few weeks in Paris a decade earlier, got his payback by grilling Amory on verb conjugations whenever he had his textbook open. But when Amory tried showing off another time in history class, the results were quite catastrophic, since the boys in that class were his own age, and they spent the entire following week making snide remarks to each other:

"Oh—I believe, don't you know, the American revolution was largely an affair of the middle classes," or

"Washington came from very good bloodline—oh, quite good—I believe."

Amory cleverly attempted to recover by deliberately making mistakes. Two years earlier, he had started writing a history of the United States which, although it only reached the Colonial Wars, had been declared by his mother to be absolutely captivating.

His main weakness was in sports, but once he realized that athletic ability was the key to power and popularity at school, he started making intense, determined efforts to succeed in winter sports. Despite his ankles hurting and wobbling no matter how hard he tried, he bravely skated around the Lorelie rink every afternoon, wondering when he would finally be able to handle a hockey stick without it mysteriously getting caught up in his skates.

The invitation to Miss Myra St. Claire's hair-cutting party spent the morning in his coat pocket, where it had an intense physical encounter with a dusty piece of peanut brittle. During the afternoon he pulled it out with a sigh, and after some thought and a rough draft in the back of Collar and Daniel's "First-Year Latin," he wrote a response:

My dear Miss St. Claire:

Your truly charming invitation for Thursday evening was absolutely delightful to receive this morning. I will be charmed and enchanted indeed to present my compliments on Thursday evening.

Faithfully,

Amory Blaine.

On Thursday, he walked thoughtfully along the icy, snow-cleared sidewalks and spotted Myra's house at half past five, a delay he imagined his mother would have approved of. He stood on the doorstep with his eyes casually half-shut and carefully planned his entrance. He would walk across the room at just the right pace toward Mrs. St. Claire and speak with precisely the right tone:

"My dear Mrs. St. Claire, I'm terribly sorry for being late, but my maid"—he stopped mid-sentence, realizing he was about to repeat someone else's words—"but my uncle and I had to meet with someone—Yes, I've already met your delightful daughter at dance class."

Then he would shake hands with all the prim little women, giving that subtle, somewhat foreign bow, and nod to the guys who would be standing around, frozen into stiff groups for mutual protection.

A butler (one of three in Minneapolis) opened the door with a sweeping motion. Amory walked inside and removed his cap and coat. He was somewhat surprised not to hear the sharp chatter of conversation coming from the next room, and he concluded the gathering must be quite formal. He liked that—just as he liked the butler.

"Miss Myra," he said.

To his surprise, the butler smiled in a terrifying way.

"Oh, yeah," he said, "she's here." He didn't realize that his inability to speak with a proper cockney accent was damaging his reputation. Amory looked at him with cold disapproval.

"But," the butler continued, his voice rising without reason, "she's the only one who's here. The party has left."

Amory gasped in sudden horror.

"What?"

"She's been waiting for Amory Blaine. That's you, isn't it? Her mother says that if you showed up by five-thirty you two were to go after them in the Packard."

Amory's despair became crystal clear when Myra herself appeared, wrapped up to her ears in a polo coat, her face obviously sulky, her voice only managing to sound pleasant with great effort.

"'Hey, Amory."

"'Hey, Myra." He had described the state of his vitality.

"Well—you made it here, at least."

"Well—I'll tell you. I suppose you don't know about the car accident," he made up.

Myra's eyes opened wide.

"Who was it addressed to?"

"Well," he continued desperately, "my uncle and aunt and I."

"Was anyone killed?"

Amory stopped for a moment and then nodded.

"Your uncle?"—alarm.

"Oh, no just a horse—a sort of gray horse."

At this point the Irish butler snickered.

"He probably flooded the engine," he suggested. Amory would have tortured him without a moment's hesitation.

"We're leaving now," Myra said coolly. "You see, Amory, the sleds were scheduled for five o'clock and everyone was here, so we couldn't wait—"

"Well, I couldn't help it, could I?"

"So mama told me to wait until half past five. We'll catch the bobsled before it reaches the Minnehaha Club, Amory."

Amory's composure completely fell apart. He imagined the cheerful group making their way through the snowy streets with jingling sounds, the limousine pulling up, the awful public spectacle of him and Myra getting out in front of sixty judgmental eyes, and his apology—a genuine one this time. He let out an audible sigh.

"What?" asked Myra.

"Nothing. I was just yawning. Are we definitely going to catch up with them before they arrive?" He was nurturing a small hope that they might slip into the Minnehaha Club and meet the others there, be discovered in casual seclusion by the fire and completely recover his lost composure.

"Oh, absolutely Mike, we'll catch them for sure—let's hurry."

He became aware of his stomach. As they entered the machine, he quickly applied a diplomatic coating to the rather crude plan he had devised. His strategy was built on some complimentary gossip he had picked up at dancing school, suggesting that he was "really handsome and had an English quality about him."

"Myra," he said, speaking more quietly and selecting his words with care, "I'm deeply sorry. Can you ever forgive me?" She looked at him seriously, taking in his earnest green eyes and his mouth, which to her thirteen-year-old sensibilities, shaped by the polished romantic ideals of her time, represented the perfect embodiment of romance. Yes, Myra could forgive him quite easily.

"Why—yes—sure."

He looked at her once more, then lowered his gaze. He had eyelashes.

"I'm terrible," he said sadly. "I'm different. I don't know why I make mistakes. Because I don't care, I suppose." Then, recklessly: "I've been smoking too much. I've got tobacco heart."

Myra imagined an entire night of excessive smoking, with Amory looking pale and staggering from the effects of nicotine-damaged lungs. She let out a small gasp.

"Oh, Amory, don't smoke. You'll stunt your growth!"

"I don't care," he continued in a gloomy tone. "I have to. It's become a habit of mine. I've done many things that if my family found out"—he paused, allowing her imagination time to conjure up terrible possibilities—"I attended the burlesque show last week."

Myra was completely overwhelmed. He looked at her again with those green eyes. "You're the only girl in this town that I really like," he said in a burst of emotion. "You just get it."

Myra wasn't certain that she actually was, but it had a fashionable ring to it, even if it seemed somewhat inappropriate.

Thick dusk had settled outside, and when the limousine took a sharp turn, she was thrown against him; their hands made contact.

"You shouldn't smoke, Amory," she whispered. "Don't you know that?"

He shook his head.

"Nobody cares."

Myra hesitated.

"I care."

Something stirred within Amory.

"Oh, yes, you do! You have a crush on Froggy Parker. I think everyone knows that."

"No, I haven't," she said very slowly.

A silence fell, while Amory felt a thrill run through him. There was something captivating about Myra, tucked away here warmly from the faint, cold air outside. Myra, a small figure wrapped in clothing, with wisps of blonde hair escaping from beneath her skating cap.

"Because I have a crush too—" He stopped mid-sentence, hearing the distant sound of young people laughing, and as he looked through the frosted glass down the lamp-lit street, he could see the dark shapes of the approaching group. He had to move fast. With a sudden, awkward motion, he reached across and grabbed Myra's hand—specifically her thumb.

"Tell him to go straight to the Minnehaha," he whispered. "I want to talk to you—I have to talk to you."

Myra spotted the group up ahead and caught a quick glimpse of her mother, then—forget about proper etiquette—looked into the eyes next to her. "Take this side street, Richard, and head straight to the Minnehaha Club!" she called through the speaking tube. Amory leaned back into the cushions with a relieved sigh.

"I can kiss her," he thought. "I'll bet I can. I'll bet I can!"

Overhead the sky was half crystal-clear, half hazy, and the night air was cold and alive with intense energy. From the Country Club steps, the roads extended into the distance, appearing as dark lines across the white covering; massive piles of snow bordered each side like the trails left by enormous moles. They stayed for a moment on the steps, gazing at the bright holiday moon.

"Pale moons like that one"—Amory gestured vaguely—"make people mysterious. You look like a young witch who's taken off her cap and has her hair all tousled"—her hands reached up to touch her hair—"Oh, leave it alone, it looks perfect."

They floated up the stairs and Myra guided them into the small cozy room he had always imagined, where a warm fire crackled in front of a large, comfortable couch you could sink into. Years later, this room would become an important setting for Amory, a place where many emotional dramas would unfold. Right now they chatted briefly about bobbing parties.

"There are always some shy guys," he said, "sitting at the back of the sled, kind of lurking and whispering and pushing each other around. Then there's always some crazy cross-eyed girl"—he gave a terrifying imitation—"who's always talking tough, you know, to the chaperone."

"You're such a funny boy," Myra said, puzzled.

"What do you mean?" Amory immediately focused his attention, finally on familiar territory.

"Oh—you're always talking about crazy things. Why don't you come skiing with Marylyn and me tomorrow?"

"I don't like girls during the day," he said curtly, and then, realizing this sounded rather blunt, he added: "But I like you." He cleared his throat. "I like you first and second and third."

Myra's eyes grew distant and dreamy. What an incredible story this would be to share with Marylyn! Here she was on the couch with this gorgeous boy—the small fire crackling nearby—the feeling that they were completely alone in this enormous building—

Myra gave in. The mood was just too perfect.

"I like you the first twenty-five," she admitted, her voice shaking, "and Froggy Parker twenty-sixth."

Froggy had dropped twenty-five positions in just one hour. He hadn't even realized it yet.

But Amory, being right there, quickly leaned over and kissed Myra's cheek. He had never kissed a girl before, and he touched his lips thoughtfully, as if he had tasted some exotic fruit. Then their lips met gently like young wildflowers swaying in the breeze.

"We're terrible," Myra said softly with delight. She slid her hand into his, letting her head fall against his shoulder. A sudden wave of revulsion washed over Amory, filled with disgust and hatred for the entire situation. He desperately wanted to escape, to never see Myra again, to never kiss anyone; he became aware of his face and hers, of their intertwined hands, and he longed to crawl out of his own body and find somewhere safe to hide from view, tucked away in a corner of his mind.

"Kiss me again." Her voice emerged from a vast emptiness.

"I don't want to," he heard himself saying. There was another pause.

"I don't want to!" he repeated passionately.

Myra jumped to her feet, her cheeks flushed pink from wounded pride, the large bow at the back of her head quivering in response.

"I hate you!" she shouted. "Don't you ever dare to speak to me again!"

"What?" Amory stammered.

"I'm going to tell mama you kissed me! I really will! I really will! I'll tell mama, and she won't let me play with you anymore!"

Amory stood up and stared at her helplessly, as if she were some unfamiliar creature whose existence on earth he had never noticed before.

The door burst open without warning, and Myra's mother stood in the doorway, struggling with her reading glasses on a handle.

"Well," she began, adjusting it kindly, "the man at the front desk told me you two kids were up here—How are you doing, Amory."

Amory observed Myra and anticipated the explosion—but it never happened. The sulky expression disappeared, the bright flush faded away, and Myra's voice became as calm as a peaceful summer lake when she responded to her mother.

"Oh, we started so late, mama, that I thought we might as well—"

He could hear shrieks of laughter coming from below and caught the bland smell of hot chocolate and tea cakes as he quietly followed the mother and daughter downstairs. The sound of the phonograph mixed with the voices of many girls humming along to the music, and a subtle warmth began to grow and spread through him:

"Casey Jones—climbed up to the cabin
Casey Jones—with his orders in his hand.
Casey Jones—climbed up to the cabin
Took his farewell journey to the promised land."

Snapshots of The Young Egotist

Amory lived in Minneapolis for almost two years. During his first winter there, he wore moccasins that started out yellow, but after being treated with oil repeatedly and getting dirty, they turned into their final color—a grimy, greenish-brown shade. He also wore a gray plaid mackinaw jacket and a red knit cap. His dog, Count Del Monte, chewed up and ate the red cap, so his uncle bought him a gray replacement that came down over his face. The problem with this new cap was that when you breathed into it, your breath would freeze inside; one day the thing actually froze to his cheek. He rubbed snow on his cheek to treat it, but it still turned a bluish-black color anyway.

The Count Del Monte once ate an entire box of laundry bluing, but it caused him no physical harm. Later on, though, he went completely insane and ran frantically down the street, crashing into fences, tumbling into gutters, and following his bizarre path right out of Amory's life. Amory wept on his bed.

"Poor little Count," he cried. "Oh, poor little Count!"

After several months, he began to suspect that the Count was putting on an elaborate emotional performance.

———————

Amory and Frog Parker believed that the greatest line in all of literature appeared in Act III of "Arsene Lupin."

They sat in the front row during the Wednesday and Saturday afternoon performances. The line was:

"If someone can't become a great artist or a great soldier, the next best thing is to become a great criminal."

———————

Amory fell in love again and wrote a poem. This was it:

"Marylyn and Sallee,
Those are the girls for me.
Marylyn stands above
Sallee in that sweet, deep love."

He was curious about whether McGovern from Minnesota would earn a spot on the first or second All-American team, how to perform the card-pass trick, how to execute the coin-pass maneuver, chameleon neckties, how babies came into the world, and whether Three-fingered Brown was truly a superior pitcher compared to Christie Mathewson.

Among other things he read: "For the Honor of the School," "Little Women" (twice), "The Common Law," "Sapho," "Dangerous Dan McGrew," "The Broad Highway" (three times), "The Fall of the House of Usher," "Three Weeks," "Mary Ware, the Little Colonel's Chum," "Gunga Din," The Police Gazette, and Jim-Jam Jems.

He possessed all of Henty's historical prejudices and had a special fondness for Mary Roberts Rinehart's upbeat murder mysteries.

———————

School destroyed his ability to speak French properly and made him dislike the classic writers that everyone was supposed to read. His teachers thought he was lazy, couldn't be trusted, and only had shallow intelligence.

He gathered locks of hair from numerous girls. He wore rings belonging to several of them. Eventually he could no longer borrow any more rings, due to his anxious habit of chewing them until they were misshapen. This behavior, it appeared, typically triggered jealous suspicions in the next person who wanted to borrow them.

Throughout the summer months, Amory and Frog Parker attended the Stock Company every week. Afterwards, they would walk home through the warm August evening air, wandering down Hennepin and Nicollet Avenues among the lively crowds. Amory couldn't understand how people failed to see that he was destined for greatness, and when strangers in the crowd looked his way with curious glances, he put on his most romantic expression and walked as if floating on the invisible cushions of air that seem to lift every fourteen-year-old off the pavement.

Always, after he got into bed, there were voices—vague, fading, captivating—just outside his window, and before he drifted off to sleep he would indulge in one of his favorite daydreams, the one about becoming a great halfback, or the one about the Japanese invasion, when he was honored by being made the youngest general in the world. It was always the process of becoming he dreamed about, never the actual achievement. This, too, was quite typical of Amory.

Code Of the Young Egotist

Before he was called back to Lake Geneva, he had shown up looking shy but secretly radiant, wearing his first pair of long pants, complemented by a purple pleated tie and a "Belmont" collar with edges that met perfectly, purple socks, and a handkerchief with purple trim visible in his breast pocket. Beyond his appearance, though, he had developed his first personal philosophy, a set of principles to guide his life, which could best be described as a form of aristocratic self-centeredness.

He had come to understand that his own well-being was tied to that of a particular, ever-changing individual who carried the name Amory Blaine—a label that would forever connect him to his history. Amory saw himself as a lucky young man, someone with unlimited potential for both good and bad. He didn't think of himself as having a "strong character," but instead counted on his ability to pick things up quickly and what he considered his intellectual superiority from reading many profound books. He took pride in knowing he could never become a mechanical or scientific genius. No other peaks seemed beyond his reach.

Physically.—Amory believed that he was extremely handsome. He was right. He imagined himself as an athlete with potential and a graceful dancer.

Socially.—Here his condition was, perhaps, most dangerous. He believed he possessed personality, charm, magnetism, poise, the ability to dominate all men of his time, and the talent for captivating all women.

Mentally.—Complete, unquestioned superiority.

Now I need to make a confession. Amory had a rather Puritan conscience. Not that he gave in to it—later in life he almost completely destroyed it—but at fifteen it made him think he was much worse than other boys... lack of principles... the urge to control people in nearly every way, even for bad purposes... a certain coldness and absence of warmth, sometimes reaching the level of cruelty... a constantly changing sense of what was right... a wicked selfishness... a confused, secretive fascination with everything related to sex.

There was also a strange thread of vulnerability woven throughout his character... a cutting remark from an older boy (older boys typically despised him) could easily knock him off balance into brooding sensitivity or fearful foolishness... he was at the mercy of his own emotions and he sensed that while he could be reckless and bold, he lacked courage, determination, and self-worth.

Vanity, balanced by self-doubt if not genuine self-awareness, a view of people as puppets responding to his desires, an ambition to surpass as many peers as possible and reach some undefined pinnacle of success... this was the foundation upon which Amory entered his teenage years.

Preparing For the Great Adventure

The train gradually slowed with the lazy pace of midsummer as it approached Lake Geneva, and Amory spotted his mother waiting in her electric car on the gravel station driveway. It was an old electric vehicle, one of the earliest models, painted in gray. Seeing her sitting there with her slender, upright posture, and her face where beauty and grace came together, softening into a dreamy, nostalgic smile, suddenly filled him with immense pride in her. As they exchanged a reserved kiss and he climbed into the electric car, he felt a sudden anxiety that he might have lost the necessary charm to live up to her expectations.

"Dear boy—you're so tall... look behind and see if there's anything coming..."

She glanced left and right, then carefully accelerated to two miles per hour, pleading with Amory to keep watch for her; and at one particularly busy intersection she had him get out and run ahead to wave her forward like a traffic officer. Beatrice could be described as an extremely cautious driver.

"You're tall—but you're still very handsome—you've gotten past that awkward phase, or is that at sixteen; maybe it's fourteen or fifteen; I can never recall; but you've moved beyond it."

"Don't embarrass me," murmured Amory.

"But, my dear boy, what strange clothes! They look like they're a matching set—don't they? Is your underwear purple, too?"

Amory made a rude grunting sound.

"You need to go to Brooks' and get some really nice suits. Oh, we'll have a talk tonight or maybe tomorrow night. I want to tell you about your heart—you've probably been neglecting your heart—and you don't realize it."

Amory realized how shallow the recent influences of his own generation had been. Apart from a slight feeling of shyness, he sensed that the old cynical bond with his mother remained completely intact. However, during the first few days he roamed around the gardens and walked along the shoreline in a state of extreme loneliness, discovering a sluggish satisfaction in smoking "Bull" tobacco at the garage with one of the drivers.

The sixty acres of the estate were scattered with both old and new summer houses, along with numerous fountains and white benches that appeared unexpectedly from their leafy hiding spots; there was a large and ever-growing family of white cats that roamed through the many flower gardens and would suddenly appear as silhouettes at night against the darkening trees. It was along one of these shaded pathways that Beatrice finally cornered Amory, after Mr. Blaine had, as he always did, withdrawn for the evening to his private library. After scolding him for avoiding her, she led him into a lengthy private conversation in the moonlight. He couldn't come to terms with her beauty, which had given birth to his own, her elegant neck and shoulders, the poise of a privileged woman of thirty.

"Amory, sweetheart," she said gently, "I went through such an odd, unsettling experience after I left you."

"Did you, Beatrice?"

"When I had my last breakdown"—she talked about it like it was some kind of brave, heroic accomplishment.

"The doctors told me"—her voice took on a confidential tone—"that if any living man had consumed alcohol as consistently as I have, he would have been completely destroyed physically, my dear, and would be dead—long dead and buried."

Amory flinched and wondered what Froggy Parker would have thought if he had heard this.

"Yes," Beatrice went on dramatically, "I had dreams—incredible visions." She pressed her palms against her eyes. "I saw bronze rivers washing against marble coastlines, and magnificent birds soaring through the sky, multicolored birds with shimmering feathers. I heard unusual music and the blast of exotic trumpets—what?"

Amory had snickered.

"What, Amory?"

"I said go on, Beatrice."

"That was everything—it simply kept coming back again and again—gardens that displayed brilliant colors that would make this seem completely bland, moons that spun and rocked back and forth, more pale than winter moons, more golden than harvest moons—"

"Are you feeling completely better now, Beatrice?"

"Quite well—as well as I will ever be. I am not understood, Amory. I know I can't express it to you, Amory, but—I am not understood."

Amory felt deeply touched. He wrapped his arm around his mother, softly pressing his head against her shoulder.

"Poor Beatrice—poor Beatrice."

"Tell me about yourself, Amory. Did you have two terrible years?"

Amory thought about lying, but then chose not to.

"No, Beatrice. I enjoyed them. I adapted myself to the middle class. I became conventional." He surprised himself by saying that, and he pictured how Froggy would have stared in amazement.

"Beatrice," he said suddenly, "I want to go away to school. Everyone in Minneapolis is going away to school."

Beatrice looked alarmed.

"But you're only fifteen."

"Yes, but everyone goes away to school at fifteen, and I want to, Beatrice."

On Beatrice's suggestion, they dropped the subject for the rest of their walk, but a week later she delighted him by saying:

"Amory, I've decided to let you do what you want. If you still want to, you can go to school."

"Yes?"

"To St. Regis's in Connecticut."

Amory felt a sudden rush of excitement.

"It's being arranged," Beatrice went on. "It would be better if you left. I would have preferred for you to attend Eton, and then Christ Church, Oxford, but that seems impossible now—and for now we'll let the university matter handle itself."

"What are you going to do, Beatrice?"

"God knows. It seems to be my destiny to waste away my years in this country. I don't regret being American for even a moment—in fact, I think that kind of regret is typical of very common people, and I'm certain we are the great nation of the future—but"—and she sighed—"I feel my life should have drifted away peacefully near an older, more refined civilization, a land of lush greens and autumn browns—"

Amory didn't respond, so his mother went on:

"I'm sorry you haven't had the chance to travel overseas, but even so, since you're a man, it's probably better that you mature here under the fierce eagle—is that the correct expression?"

Amory agreed that it was. She wouldn't have appreciated the Japanese invasion.

"When do I go to school?"

"Next month. You'll need to head East a bit early to take your exams. After that you'll have a week off, so I'd like you to travel up the Hudson and make a visit."

"To whom?"

"To Monsignor Darcy, Amory. He wants to see you. He went to Harrow and then to Yale—became a Catholic. I want him to talk to you—I feel he can be such a help—" She gently stroked his reddish-brown hair. "Dear Amory, dear Amory—"

"Dear Beatrice—"

———

So early in September, Amory, equipped with "six sets of summer underwear, six sets of winter underwear, one sweater or T-shirt, one jersey, one winter overcoat, etc.," headed off to New England, the land of schools.

There were Andover and Exeter, carrying the legacy of New England's past—large, university-like democratic institutions; St. Mark's, Groton, St. Regis'—drawing students from Boston's elite and New York's prominent Knickerbocker families; St. Paul's, famous for its impressive ice rinks; Pomfret and St. George's, wealthy and impeccably dressed; Taft and Hotchkiss, which groomed the affluent children of the Midwest for social achievement at Yale; Pawling, Westminster, Choate, Kent, and countless others; all producing their polished, traditional, distinguished graduates, year after year; their intellectual focus centered on college admission tests; their unclear mission outlined in numerous brochures as "To provide a Complete Mental, Moral, and Physical Education as a Christian Gentleman, to prepare the young man for confronting the challenges of his time and era, and to establish a strong foundation in the Arts and Sciences."

At St. Regis, Amory spent three days taking his exams with dismissive self-assurance, then returned to New York for his obligatory visit. The big city, which he barely saw, left little impact on him, apart from the impression of cleanliness he got from the tall white buildings viewed from a Hudson River steamboat in the early morning. His thoughts were so filled with fantasies of athletic achievements at school that he saw this visit merely as a somewhat tedious introduction to the great adventure ahead. This, though, turned out not to be the case.

Monsignor Darcy's house was an old, sprawling building situated on a hill that looked out over the river, and there its owner lived, between his journeys to every corner of the Roman Catholic world, much like an exiled Stuart monarch awaiting the call to rule his homeland. Monsignor was forty-four at that time, and energetic—a bit too heavy for perfect proportions, with hair the shade of spun gold, and a dazzling, all-encompassing personality. When he entered a room dressed in his complete purple ceremonial robes from head to foot, he looked like a Turner sunset, and drew both admiration and notice. He had authored two novels: one of them fiercely anti-Catholic, written just before his conversion, and five years afterward another, in which he had tried to transform all his sharp criticisms against Catholics into even more sophisticated hints against Episcopalians. He was deeply ritualistic, remarkably theatrical, loved the concept of God enough to remain celibate, and genuinely cared for his fellow man.

Children loved him because he had a childlike nature; young people enjoyed his company because he remained youthful at heart and wasn't easily scandalized. Born in the right place and time, he might have become a Richelieu—instead, he was a highly moral, deeply religious (though not especially devout) minister who made a great show of working behind the scenes, and who valued life completely, even if he didn't always find complete happiness in it.

He and Amory connected instantly—the cheerful, commanding church leader who could captivate an embassy reception, and the green-eyed, serious young man, wearing his first full-length pants, both recognized in their hearts a father-son bond within thirty minutes of talking together.

"My dear boy, I've been waiting to see you for years. Take a big chair and we'll have a chat."

"I just got back from school—St. Regis's, you know."

"So your mother says—a remarkable woman; have a cigarette—I'm sure you smoke. Well, if you're like me, you hate all science and mathematics—"

Amory nodded enthusiastically.

"I hate all of them. I only like English and history."

"Of course. You'll hate school for a while, too, but I'm glad you're going to St. Regis's."

"Why?"

"Because it's a gentleman's school, and democracy won't affect you so soon. You'll encounter plenty of that in college."

"I want to go to Princeton," Amory said. "I'm not sure why, but I picture all Harvard guys as weaklings, the way I used to be, and all Yale guys as wearing those big blue sweaters and smoking pipes."

Monsignor chuckled.

"I'm one, you know."

"Oh, you're different—I think of Princeton as being lazy and good-looking and aristocratic—you know, like a spring day. Harvard seems sort of indoors—"

"And Yale is November, crisp and energetic," finished Monsignor.

"That's it."

They quickly fell into a close relationship that would last forever.

"I supported Bonnie Prince Charlie," Amory declared.

"Of course you were—and for Hannibal—"

"Yes, and for the Southern Confederacy." He was quite skeptical about becoming an Irish patriot—he suspected that being Irish was somewhat ordinary—but Monsignor convinced him that Ireland was a romantic lost cause and Irish people were quite charming, and that it should definitely be one of his main prejudices.

After a busy hour that included several more cigarettes, and during which Monsignor discovered, to his surprise but not to his shock, that Amory had not been raised as a Catholic, he announced that he had another guest. This guest turned out to be the Honorable Thornton Hancock, from Boston, former minister to The Hague, author of a scholarly history of the Middle Ages and the last member of a distinguished, patriotic, and brilliant family.

"He comes here to find peace," the Monsignor said in confidence, speaking to Amory as an equal. "I serve as his refuge from the exhaustion of doubt, and I believe I'm the only person who understands how his seemingly steady mind is actually lost and yearns for something solid like the Church to hold onto."

Their first lunch together became one of the most memorable experiences of Amory's early years. He practically glowed with energy and radiated an unusual brightness and appeal. Monsignor drew out Amory's finest thoughts through careful questions and thoughtful prompts, and Amory responded with a clever brilliance, discussing countless impulses, desires, aversions, beliefs, and anxieties. The two of them dominated the conversation, while the older man—with his more reserved, less open, though certainly not less warm personality—seemed happy to listen and enjoy the warm glow that flowed between them. Monsignor had the ability to bring a sense of warmth and light to many people's lives; Amory possessed this same quality in his youth and, to some degree, when he grew much older, but it would never again feel quite so naturally mutual between them.

"He's a brilliant young man," thought Thornton Hancock, who had witnessed the magnificence of two continents and conversed with Parnell and Gladstone and Bismarck—and later he said to Monsignor: "But his education shouldn't be entrusted to a school or college."

For the following four years, Amory focused his sharpest thinking on becoming popular, navigating the complex social hierarchy of university life, and understanding American high society through events like Biltmore tea parties and golf courses at Hot Springs.

In all, it was a wonderful week that turned Amory's mind inside out, confirmed a hundred of his theories, and crystallized his joy of life into a thousand ambitions. Not that the conversation was academic—heaven forbid! Amory had only the vaguest idea of who Bernard Shaw was—but Monsignor drew just as much from "The Beloved Vagabond" and "Sir Nigel," making sure that Amory never once felt out of his depth.

But the trumpets were announcing Amory's first battle with his own generation.

"You're not sorry to leave, naturally. For people like us, home is wherever we're not," said Monsignor.

"I am sorry—"

"No, you're not. No single person in the world is essential to you or to me."

"Well—"

"Good-by."

The Egotist Down

Amory's two years at St. Regis', while alternately difficult and successful, held as little genuine importance in his personal development as the American preparatory school, dominated as it is by the universities, holds for American society overall. We lack an Eton to foster the self-awareness of a ruling class; instead, we possess sterile, weak, and harmless prep schools.

He made a terrible first impression, was widely viewed as both conceited and arrogant, and everyone disliked him. He played football with great intensity, switching between moments of reckless brilliance and a tendency to protect himself from danger as much as propriety would allow. In a moment of wild panic, he retreated from a fight with a boy of equal size, earning widespread ridicule, and a week later, driven by desperation, he started a fight with a much larger boy, from which he emerged severely beaten but feeling somewhat proud of himself.

He felt bitter toward everyone who had authority over him, and this attitude, along with his lazy lack of interest in his schoolwork, frustrated every teacher he encountered. He became disheartened and saw himself as an outcast; he started brooding in secluded spots and reading after the lights went out. Terrified of being by himself, he gathered a small group of friends around him, but since these weren't the popular students at school, he simply used them as reflections of himself, as audiences in front of whom he could perform the show-off behavior that was absolutely necessary to him. He felt unbearably isolated and desperately miserable.

There were a few small sources of comfort. Whenever Amory felt overwhelmed, his pride was always the last thing to disappear, so he could still feel a pleasant warmth when "Wookey-wookey," the deaf elderly housekeeper, told him he was the most handsome boy she had ever seen. He had taken satisfaction in being the lightest and youngest player on the varsity football team; he felt pleased when Doctor Dougall informed him at the conclusion of an intense discussion that he could, if he wanted to, achieve the highest grades in school. However, Doctor Dougall was mistaken. It was simply not in Amory's nature to earn the top marks in school.

Miserable, restricted by limitations, disliked by both professors and fellow students—that described Amory's first semester. However, when Christmas arrived, he had gone back to Minneapolis, keeping his thoughts to himself yet oddly triumphant.

"Oh, I was pretty cocky at first," he said to Frog Parker in a condescending tone, "but I did really well—I was the lightest guy on the team. You should go away to school, Froggy. It's amazing."

Incident of the Well-Meaning Professor

On the final evening of his first semester, Mr. Margotson, the head teacher, sent a message to the study hall instructing Amory to come to his office at nine o'clock. Amory had a feeling that he was about to receive some guidance, but he decided to be polite since Mr. Margotson had always treated him with kindness.

His summoner greeted him with a serious demeanor and gestured toward a chair. He cleared his throat several times and wore a deliberately kind expression, the way someone does when they know they're dealing with a sensitive situation.

"Amory," he started. "I called you here about something personal."

"Yes, sir."

"I've been watching you this year and I—I like you. I believe you have what it takes to become a—a really good man."

"Yes, sir," Amory managed to say. He despised it when people spoke about him as though he were a confirmed failure.

"But I've noticed," the older man continued without really seeing, "that the other boys don't seem to like you very much."

"No, sir." Amory licked his lips.

"Oh—I thought you might not realize exactly what they were objecting to. I'm going to explain it to you, because I believe that when a young man understands his problems, he's better equipped to handle them—to meet the expectations others have of him." He cleared his throat again with careful hesitation, and went on:

"They seem to feel that you're rather too bold—"

Amory couldn't take it anymore. He got up from his chair, barely keeping his voice steady as he began to speak.

"I know—oh, don't you think I know." His voice rose. "I know what they think; do you think you have to tell me!" He paused. "I'm—I've got to go back now—hope I'm not being rude—"

He quickly left the room. Outside in the cool air, as he walked toward his house, he felt triumphant about his refusal to accept help.

"That damn old fool!" he shouted frantically. "As if I didn't know!"

He decided, however, that this was a good excuse not to return to study hall that night, so, comfortably settled in his room, he ate Nabisco crackers and finished "The White Company."

Incident of The Wonderful Girl

There was a bright star in February. New York revealed itself to him on Washington's Birthday with the brilliance of a long-awaited event. His earlier glimpse of it as a vivid whiteness against a deep-blue sky had created an image of magnificence that competed with the dream cities in the Arabian Nights; but this time he experienced it under electric lights, and romance sparkled from the chariot-race sign on Broadway and from the women's eyes at the Astor, where he and young Paskert from St. Regis had dinner. When they walked down the theater aisle, welcomed by the anxious twanging and discord of out-of-tune violins and the rich, heavy scent of paint and powder, he moved within a world of luxurious pleasure. Everything captivated him. The play was "The Little Millionaire," starring George M. Cohan, and there was one breathtaking young brunette who made him sit with tears of joy in his eyes, lost in the ecstasy of watching her dance.

"Oh—you—wonderful girl,
What a wonderful girl you are—"

sang the tenor, and Amory silently but passionately agreed.

"All—your—wonderful words
 Thrill me through—"

The violins rose and trembled on the final notes, the girl collapsed like a crumpled butterfly on the stage, and thunderous applause filled the theater. Oh, to fall in love like that, to the dreamy, enchanting melody of such music!

The final scene took place on a rooftop garden, and the cellos sang mournfully to the musical moon, while lighthearted adventure and bubbly, frothy comedy danced back and forth in the stage lights. Amory burned with desire to become a regular at rooftop gardens, to meet a girl who would look like that—or better yet, that exact girl; whose hair would be bathed in golden moonlight, while beside him sparkling wine would be served by a waiter speaking in an incomprehensible language. When the curtain dropped for the final time he let out such a deep sigh that the audience members in front of him turned around and stared and spoke loudly enough for him to hear:

"What a remarkable-looking boy!"

This distracted him from the performance, and he found himself wondering whether the people of New York truly saw him as attractive.

Paskert and he walked quietly toward their hotel. Paskert was the first to break the silence. His wavering fifteen-year-old voice interrupted Amory's thoughts with a melancholy tone:

"I'd marry that girl tonight."

There was no need to ask which girl he was talking about.

"I'd be proud to take her home and introduce her to my family," Paskert continued.

Amory was clearly impressed. He wished he had been the one to say it instead of Paskert. It sounded so sophisticated.

"I wonder about actresses; are they all pretty bad?"

"No way, absolutely not," said the street-smart young man with conviction, "and I know that girl is as good as they come. I can tell."

They continued walking, blending into the Broadway crowd, lost in thought as music drifted from the cafes around them. New faces appeared and disappeared like countless lights, some pale, others wearing makeup, all looking exhausted yet kept going by a tired kind of excitement. Amory stared at them, completely captivated. He was mapping out his future. He would live in New York and become a regular at every restaurant and cafe, dressed in formal evening wear from early evening until dawn, sleeping through the boring morning hours.

"Yes, sir, I'd marry that girl tonight!"

Heroic In General Tone

October of his second and final year at St. Regis stood out as a peak moment in Amory's memory. The game against Groton began at three o'clock on a crisp, energizing afternoon and stretched well into the sharp autumn twilight, with Amory playing quarterback, shouting desperately, making seemingly impossible tackles, and calling plays in a voice that had worn down to a rough, angry whisper, yet he still managed to take pleasure in the blood-soaked bandage wrapped around his head and the intense, magnificent heroism of diving, colliding bodies and sore limbs. During those moments, courage poured forth like wine from the November dusk, and he became the timeless hero, united with the sea-warrior at the bow of a Viking ship, one with Roland and Horatius, Sir Nigel and Ted Coy, battered and worn down to fighting form and then hurled by his own determination into the gap, pushing back the assault, hearing from a distance the roar of the crowd... eventually bruised and exhausted, but still elusive, rounding the end, twisting, shifting speed, stiff-arming defenders...

falling behind the Groton goal line with two players grabbing his legs, scoring the game's only touchdown.

The Philosophy of The Slicker

From his position of mocking superiority as a senior and his various achievements, Amory looked back with bitter amazement at where he had stood just one year earlier. He had transformed as completely as Amory Blaine was capable of transforming. Amory plus Beatrice plus two years in Minneapolis—these elements had shaped who he was when he first arrived at St. Regis'. However, those Minneapolis years hadn't created a thick enough veneer to hide the "Amory plus Beatrice" combination from the searching gaze of a boarding school, so St. Regis' had very painfully stripped Beatrice's influence out of him, and started laying down fresh and more traditional foundations over the core Amory. Yet both St. Regis' and Amory remained unaware that this essential Amory hadn't actually changed within himself. The very traits that had once caused him to suffer—his moodiness, his inclination to put on airs, his laziness, and his fondness for acting like a fool—were now simply accepted as normal, viewed as recognized quirks in a star quarterback, a talented actor, and the editor of the St. Regis Tattler: it baffled him to watch easily influenced younger students copying the exact same vanities that had recently been shameful weaknesses.

After the football season ended, he settled into a dreamy state of contentment. On the night of the pre-holiday dance, he quietly slipped away and went to bed early, savoring the pleasure of listening to the violin music drift across the grass and flow through his window. Many evenings he would lie there, awake and dreaming of hidden cafes in Montmartre, where elegant women engaged in romantic mysteries with diplomats and soldiers of fortune, while orchestras performed Hungarian waltzes and the atmosphere was dense and exotic with intrigue, moonlight, and adventure. When spring arrived, he read "L'Allegro" by request and found himself inspired to write lyrical pieces about Arcadia and the pipes of Pan. He repositioned his bed so the morning sun would wake him at dawn, allowing him to dress and venture out to the ancient swing that hung from an apple tree near the sixth-form house. Settling into the swing, he would pump his legs higher and higher until he achieved the sensation of soaring into the open air, into a magical realm of piping satyrs and nymphs who bore the faces of fair-haired girls he encountered on the streets of Eastchester. When the swing reached its peak, Arcadia seemed to lie just beyond the crest of a particular hill, where the brown road faded from view in a golden speck.

He read extensively throughout the spring of his eighteenth year: "The Gentleman from Indiana," "The New Arabian Nights," "The Morals of Marcus Ordeyne," "The Man Who Was Thursday," which he enjoyed despite not fully grasping it; "Stover at Yale," which became something of a guidebook for him; "Dombey and Son," because he felt he ought to read more substantial literature; the complete works of Robert Chambers, David Graham Phillips, and E. Phillips Oppenheim, along with selections from Tennyson and Kipling. Among all his coursework, only "L'Allegro" and the precise, logical nature of solid geometry managed to capture his otherwise indifferent attention.

As June approached, he realized he needed someone to talk with in order to organize his thoughts, and he was surprised to discover a fellow thinker in Rahill, who served as president of the sixth form. Through numerous conversations—whether walking along the main road, lying flat on their stomachs at the edge of the baseball field, or staying up late at night with their cigarettes glowing in the darkness—they worked through various school-related issues, and during these discussions they developed the concept of the "slicker."

"Do you have any tobacco?" Rahill whispered one night, poking his head through the doorway five minutes after lights-out.

"Sure."

"I'm coming in."

"Take a couple of pillows and lie in the window seat, why don't you."

Amory sat up in bed and lit a cigarette while Rahill got comfortable for a conversation. Rahill's favorite topic was discussing what would happen to their sixth form classmates in the future, and Amory never grew tired of describing these potential outcomes for him.

"Ted Converse? That's simple. He'll fail his exams, spend all summer tutoring at Harstrum's, get into Sheffield with about four conditions, and drop out halfway through his freshman year. Then he'll head back West and cause trouble for a year or so; eventually his father will force him to enter the paint business. He'll get married and have four sons, all of them idiots. He'll always believe St. Regis's ruined him, so he'll send his sons to day school in Portland. He'll die of locomotor ataxia when he's forty-one, and his wife will donate a baptismal font or whatever it's called to the Presbyterian Church, with his name on it—"

"Wait a minute, Amory. That's way too depressing. What about you?"

"I belong to a higher class. You do as well. We are philosophers."

"I'm not."

"Of course you are. You've got a really sharp mind." But Amory understood that nothing theoretical, no abstract concept or broad principle, could ever motivate Rahill until he encountered its specific, practical details firsthand.

"Haven't," Rahill insisted. "I let people take advantage of me here and don't get anything in return. I'm at the mercy of my friends, damn it—I do their assignments, bail them out of trouble, make pointless summer visits to see them, and I'm always stuck entertaining their little sisters; I keep my cool when they act selfishly and then they think they're paying me back by voting for me and calling me the 'big man' of St. Regis's. I want to get to a place where everyone does their own work and I can tell people exactly where they can go. I'm sick of being nice to every loser in this school."

"You're not a slicker," Amory said suddenly.

"A what?"

"A slicker."

"What the hell is that?"

"Well, it's something that—that—there are many of them. You're not one, and I'm not either, though I am closer to being one than you are."

"Who is one? What makes you one?"

Amory thought it over.

"Well, I guess the sign of it is when a guy smooths his hair back with water."

"Like Carstairs?"

"Yes—absolutely. He's a smooth operator."

They spent two evenings working out a precise definition. The slicker was attractive or well-groomed; he possessed intelligence, specifically social intelligence, and he employed every method within the bounds of honesty to advance himself, gain popularity, earn admiration, and avoid trouble. He dressed well, maintained a particularly tidy appearance, and got his name from the way his hair was always worn short, saturated with water or hair tonic, parted down the middle, and slicked back according to current fashion trends. The slickers of that year had chosen tortoise-shell glasses as symbols of their status, which made them so simple to identify that Amory and Rahill never overlooked a single one. The slicker appeared to be spread throughout the school, consistently a bit more knowledgeable and cunning than his peers, managing some team or another, and keeping his intelligence carefully hidden.

Amory considered the slicker a highly useful way to categorize people until his third year of college, when the definition became so vague and unclear that it needed to be broken down into many subcategories, eventually becoming just one characteristic among many. Amory's private role model possessed all the typical slicker traits, but also had bravery, exceptional intelligence, and remarkable abilities—Amory also acknowledged that this person had an eccentric side that completely contradicted what a true slicker should be.

This marked the first genuine departure from the false pretenses of academic tradition. The smooth operator represented a clear path to success, fundamentally different from the preparatory school "big shot."

"THE SLICKER"

Possesses a sharp understanding of social hierarchies and what matters in society.

Dresses impeccably. Acts as though clothing and appearance don't matter—but fully understands that they do.

Participates only in activities where he can excel and stand out.

Attends college and achieves success in terms of worldly accomplishments.

Hair perfectly groomed and slicked back.
"THE BIG MAN"

Tends toward foolishness and lacks awareness of social expectations.

Believes clothing is unimportant and tends to be careless about his appearance.

Participates in everything out of a sense of obligation.

Arrives at college facing an uncertain future. Feels lost without his familiar social circle and constantly claims that his school years were the best time of his life. Returns to his old school to give speeches about what St. Regis's graduates are accomplishing.

Hair is not slicked back.

Amory had made up his mind about Princeton, even though he would be the only student from St. Regis' entering that year. Yale held a certain romance and appeal from the stories he'd heard around Minneapolis, and from St. Regis' alumni who had been "tapped for Skull and Bones," but Princeton attracted him most, with its vibrant atmosphere and its enticing reputation as the most enjoyable country club in America. Overshadowed by the intimidating college entrance exams, Amory's high school years faded into memory. Years later, when he returned to St. Regis', he seemed to have forgotten his sixth-form successes, and could only see himself as the awkward boy who had rushed through hallways, mocked by his intense classmates driven by practical thinking.

Chapter 2. Spires And Gargoyles

At first Amory only noticed the abundance of sunlight streaming across the long, green lawns, sparkling on the glass windowpanes, and flowing around the tops of spires and towers and fortress-like walls. Slowly he became aware that he was actually walking up University Place, feeling self-conscious about his suitcase, developing a new habit of staring straight ahead whenever he passed someone. Multiple times he could have sworn that men turned to look at him with judgment. He wondered dimly if something was wrong with his clothes, and wished he had shaved that morning on the train. He felt awkwardly stiff and clumsy among these white-flanneled, hatless young men, who had to be juniors and seniors, based on the confident ease with which they walked.

He discovered that 12 University Place was a massive, run-down mansion that appeared to be empty at the moment, even though he knew it typically housed about twelve first-year students. Following a quick confrontation with his landlady, he ventured out to explore the area, but he had barely walked a block when he became painfully aware that he seemed to be the only person in town wearing a hat. He rushed back to 12 University, left his derby hat behind, and stepped outside bareheaded, wandering slowly down Nassau Street. He paused to examine a collection of sports photographs displayed in a shop window, which included a large picture of Allenby, the football team captain, and then found himself drawn to a candy store with a sign reading "Jigger Shop" above its window. The name rang a bell, so he strolled inside and settled onto a tall stool.

"Chocolate sundae," he told a Black person.

"Double chocolate jiggah? Anything else?"

"Why—yes."

"Bacon bun?"

"Why—yes."

He ate four of these, enjoying their pleasant taste, and then had another double-chocolate drink before feeling relaxed. After taking a quick look at the pillowcases, leather pennants, and Gibson Girl pictures decorating the walls, he left and walked down Nassau Street with his hands in his pockets. He was gradually learning to tell the difference between upperclassmen and new students, even though freshman caps wouldn't appear until the following Monday. Those who seemed too obviously and nervously comfortable were freshmen, because as each train brought a new group, they were immediately absorbed into the crowd of hatless, white-sneakered, book-carrying students whose purpose seemed to be wandering endlessly up and down the street, producing thick clouds of smoke from brand-new pipes. By afternoon Amory noticed that the newest arrivals were now mistaking him for an upperclassman, and he tried deliberately to look both pleasantly bored and casually judgmental, which was as close as he could describe the common facial expression.

At five o'clock, he felt the urge to hear his own voice, so he went back to his house to check if anyone else had shown up. After climbing the shaky stairs, he looked around his room with resignation, deciding that it was pointless to try for any more creative decorating beyond class banners and tiger pictures. There was a knock at the door.

"Come in!"

A thin face with gray eyes and an amused smile appeared in the doorway.

"Do you have a hammer?"

"No—sorry. Maybe Mrs. Twelve, or whatever she calls herself, has one."

The stranger walked into the room.

"Are you a patient in this mental hospital?"

Amory nodded.

"Terrible barn for the rent we pay."

Amory had to admit that it was true.

"I thought about the campus," he said, "but they say there are so few freshmen that they feel lost. They have to sit around and study just to have something to do."

The gray-eyed man chose to introduce himself.

"My name's Holiday."

"My name is Blaine."

They shook hands with the trendy, exaggerated downward motion. Amory smiled broadly.

"Where did you go to prep school?"

"Andover—where did you?"

"St. Regis's."

"Oh, did you? I had a cousin there."

They talked extensively about the cousin, and then Holiday

47

mentioned that he needed to meet his brother for dinner at six o'clock.

"Come along and have a bite with us."

"All right."

At the Kenilworth, Amory encountered Burne Holiday—the one with gray eyes turned out to be Kerry—and while eating a bland meal of watery soup and pale vegetables, they observed the other first-year students, who either sat in small clusters appearing quite uncomfortable, or gathered in large groups that seemed completely at ease.

"I hear Commons is pretty bad," said Amory.

"That's what people are saying. But you have to eat there—or pay regardless."

"Crime!"

"Imposition!"

"Oh, at Princeton you have to accept everything during your first year. It's like a damn preparatory school."

Amory agreed.

"He's got a lot of energy, though," he insisted. "I wouldn't have gone to Yale for a million dollars."

"Me either."

"Are you going out for anything?" Amory asked the older brother.

"Not me—Burne here is trying out for the Prince—the Daily Princetonian, you know."

"Yes, I know."

"Are you going out for anything?"

"Why—yes. I'm going to give freshman football a try."

"Play at St. Regis's?"

"Some," Amory admitted with self-deprecation, "but I'm getting so damn skinny."

"You're not thin."

"Well, I used to be stocky last fall."

"Oh!"

After dinner they went to the movies, where Amory was captivated by the smooth-talking remarks of a man sitting in front of him, along with all the wild yelling and shouting.

"Yoho!"

"Oh, sweetheart—you're so big and strong, but oh, so gentle!"

"Clinch!"

"Oh, Clinch!"

"Kiss her, kiss that lady, quick!"

"Oh-h-h—!"

A group started whistling "By the Sea," and the crowd joined in loudly. This was followed by an unclear song that involved a lot of stomping, and then by a long, rambling lament.

"Oh-h-h-h-h
She works in a Jam Factory
And—that-may-be-all-right
But you can't-fool-me
For I know—DAMN—WELL
That she DON'T-make-jam-all-night!
Oh-h-h-h!"

As they made their way out, exchanging curious but detached looks with others, Amory realized he enjoyed going to the movies and wanted to appreciate them the way the row of upperclassmen sitting in front of them had, with their arms draped casually over the backs of their seats, making sharp and witty remarks, displaying an attitude that blended clever criticism with good-natured amusement.

"Want a sundae—I mean a drink?" asked Kerry.

"Sure."

They ate a heavy dinner and then, still strolling leisurely, made their way back to 12.

"Wonderful night."

"It's amazing."

"Are you men going to unpack?"

"I suppose so. Come on, Burne."

Amory chose to remain sitting on the front steps for a bit, so he said good night to them.

The vast canopy of trees had faded into shadowy figures at the final moments of dusk. The early moon had bathed the curved branches in pale blue light, and drifting through the night, moving in and out of the delicate streams of moonlight, came a melody— a song carrying more than a touch of melancholy, endlessly fleeting, endlessly sorrowful.

He recalled how a graduate from the 1890s had shared a story about one of Booth Tarkington's favorite pastimes: positioning himself in the center of campus during the early morning hours and singing tenor melodies to the stars above, stirring up conflicting feelings among the students lying in their beds, depending on whatever emotions they happened to be experiencing at the time.

Now, far down the shadowy stretch of University Place, a group dressed in white broke through the darkness, and marching figures in white shirts and white pants moved rhythmically up the street with their arms linked and their heads tilted back:

"Going back—going back,
Going—back—to—Nassau—Hall,
Going back—going back—
To the—Best—Old—Place—of—All.
Going back—going back,
From all—this—earthly—ball,
We'll—clear—the—track—as—we—go—back—
Going—back—to—Nassau—Hall!"

Amory shut his eyes as the spectral parade approached. The melody climbed so high that everyone else fell silent except the tenor voices, which carried the tune triumphantly beyond the critical moment before passing it to the ethereal choir. Then Amory opened his eyes, somewhat worried that seeing would ruin the beautiful illusion created by the music.

He sighed with anticipation. Leading the white team was Allenby, the football captain, lean and confident, seemingly aware that this year the college's hopes depended on him, that his one hundred sixty pounds were expected to weave through the heavy blue and crimson defensive lines to secure victory.

Captivated, Amory observed each row of interlocked arms as it drew alongside him, the faces unclear above the polo shirts, the voices merging into a song of victory—and then the parade moved through the dim Campbell Arch, and the voices became quieter as it curved eastward across the campus.

The minutes ticked by and Amory remained seated in complete silence. He felt frustrated by the regulation that prevented first-year students from being outside after curfew, since he longed to wander through the dim, fragrant pathways, where Witherspoon loomed like a somber guardian over Whig and Clio, her classical offspring, where the dark Gothic serpent of Little wound its way down to Cuyler and Patton, which then cast their enigma across the tranquil hillside that descended toward the lake.

Princeton during the day gradually came into focus in his mind—West and Reunion, carrying the scent of the 1860s, Seventy-nine Hall, brick-red and proud, Upper and Lower Pyne, refined Elizabethan ladies somewhat reluctant to dwell among merchants, and above everything else, reaching upward with bright blue ambition, the magnificent dreaming towers of Holder and Cleveland.

From the beginning, he fell in love with Princeton—its relaxed beauty, its partially understood importance, the wild moonlit celebrations of rush week, the attractive, wealthy crowds at major sporting events, and beneath it all the atmosphere of competition that filled his class. Starting from the day when the wild-eyed and worn-out freshmen in their jerseys gathered in the gymnasium and chose someone from Hill School as class president, a Lawrenceville celebrity as vice-president, and a hockey star from St. Paul's as secretary, continuing right through to the end of sophomore year, it never stopped—that intense social hierarchy, that reverence, rarely spoken of, never truly acknowledged, for the mythical "Big Man."

First it came down to schools, and Amory, the only one from St. Regis', observed as groups formed, expanded, and reformed around him; students from St. Paul's, Hill, and Pomfret claimed certain unspoken reserved tables in the dining hall, changed clothes in their designated sections of the gym, and unconsciously surrounded themselves with a protective circle of slightly less prestigious but socially ambitious classmates to shield them from the friendly yet somewhat bewildered public high school students. From the instant he understood this dynamic, Amory came to despise social barriers as fake divisions created by the powerful to support their weaker followers and exclude those who were nearly as strong.

Having made up his mind to become one of the campus elite, he showed up for freshman football practice. However, during the second week, while playing quarterback and already earning mentions in small articles in the Princetonian, he injured his knee badly enough to sideline him for the remainder of the season. This setback forced him to step back and reassess his circumstances.

"12 Univee" was home to a dozen assorted question marks. The group included three or four unremarkable and rather bewildered boys from Lawrenceville, two wannabe wild men from a New York private school (Kerry Holiday dubbed them the "plebeian drunks"), a Jewish young man, also from New York, and, as a consolation for Amory, the two Holidays, whom he liked immediately.

The Holidays were rumored to be twins, but in reality the dark-haired one, Kerry, was a year older than his blond brother, Burne.

Kerry was tall, with humorous gray eyes, and a sudden, charming smile; he immediately became the mentor of the house, cutting down those who got too big for their britches, keeping conceit in check, and dispensing rare, satirical humor. Amory laid out the foundation of their future friendship with all his ideas about what college should and actually did mean. Kerry, not yet inclined to take things seriously, gently teased him for being so curious at such an inappropriate time about the complexities of the social system, but he liked him and found him both interesting and amusing.

Burne, with his fair hair, quiet demeanor, and focused intensity, only appeared in the house like a fleeting figure, slipping in silently at night and departing again in the early morning to work on his studies in the library—he was competing for the Princetonian, battling fiercely against forty other candidates for the highly sought-after first position. In December he fell ill with diphtheria, and someone else won the competition, but when he returned to college in February, he courageously pursued the prize once more. As a result, Amory's interactions with him were limited to brief three-minute conversations while walking to and from lectures, so he was unable to understand Burne's single consuming passion and discover what motivated him beneath the surface.

Amory was far from satisfied. He missed the status he had earned at St. Regis', the recognition and admiration he had enjoyed there, yet Princeton energized him, and there were many opportunities ahead designed to awaken the strategic mind lying dormant within him, if only he could find a way in. The exclusive upper-class clubs, about which he had questioned a reluctant alumnus during the previous summer, sparked his interest: Ivy, aloof and breathtakingly aristocratic; Cottage, a striking blend of brilliant risk-takers and well-dressed womanizers; Tiger Inn, robust and athletic, energized by an authentic refinement of preparatory school values; Cap and Gown, opposed to drinking, mildly religious and politically influential; ostentatious Colonial;

scholarly Quadrangle; and the dozen other clubs, differing in history and standing.

Anything that made an underclassman stand out too much was branded with the damning label of "showing off." The movies flourished on sharp criticism, but the students who created them were usually showing off; discussing clubs was showing off; taking a strong stance on anything, such as drinking parties or abstaining from alcohol, was showing off; in other words, drawing personal attention to yourself wasn't acceptable, and the person with real influence was the one who stayed neutral, until club elections in sophomore year when everyone would be locked into some group for the remainder of their college years.

Amory discovered that writing for the Nassau Literary Magazine wouldn't bring him any benefits, but serving on the board of the Daily Princetonian would offer anyone significant advantages. His unclear ambition to pursue memorable acting with the English Dramatic Association disappeared when he realized that the most creative minds and abilities were focused on the Triangle Club, a musical comedy group that took an elaborate Christmas tour each year. Meanwhile, experiencing an unusual sense of isolation and restlessness in Commons, with fresh aspirations and goals awakening within him, he allowed the first semester to pass caught between jealousy of the developing successes and confused frustration with Kerry about why they weren't immediately welcomed into the class elite.

Many afternoons they relaxed in the windows of 12 Univee and observed the class walking back and forth to Commons, noticing followers already gravitating toward the more popular students, watching the isolated student with his rushed pace and lowered gaze, feeling envious of the confident security of the large social groups.

"We're the damn middle class, that's what!" he grumbled to Kerry one day as he sprawled across the sofa, methodically smoking through a pack of Fatimas with thoughtful deliberation.

"Well, why not? We came to Princeton so we could feel superior to the small colleges—have an advantage over them, more self-confidence, dress better, make an impression—"

"Oh, it's not that I have a problem with the flashy social hierarchy," Amory confessed. "I enjoy having a group of impressive people at the top, but damn, Kerry, I need to be one of them."

"But right now, Amory, you're nothing more than a sweaty middle-class person."

Amory remained silent for a moment.

"I won't be long," he said at last. "But I can't stand having to work for anything I want to achieve. It will leave its mark on me, you understand."

"Honorable scars." Kerry suddenly stretched his neck to look down the street. "There's Langueduc, if you want to see what he looks like—and Humbird is right behind him."

Amory jumped up energetically and headed toward the windows.

"Oh," he said, examining these distinguished men, "Humbird appears to be a real stunner, but this Langueduc—he's the rough-and-tumble type, isn't he? I'm suspicious of that kind. All diamonds appear large when they're uncut."

"Well," said Kerry, as the excitement died down, "you're a literary genius. It's your decision."

"I wonder"—Amory stopped speaking—"if I could be. I genuinely think so sometimes. That sounds terrible, and I wouldn't say it to anyone except you."

"Well—go ahead. Let your hair grow and write poems like this guy D'Invilliers in the Lit."

Amory lazily reached for a stack of magazines on the table.

"Have you read his latest work?"

"Never miss them. They're rare."

55

Amory looked through the magazine.

"Hello!" he said in surprise, "he's a freshman, isn't he?"

"Yeah."

"Listen to this! My God!"

"'A serving lady speaks:
Black velvet drapes its folds across the day,
White candles, trapped within their silver holders,
Wave their slender flames like shadows in the wind,
Pia, Pompia, come—come away—'"

"Now, what the hell does that mean?"

"It's a pantry scene."

"'Her toes are rigid like a stork in flight;
She lies upon her bed on white sheets,
Her hands pressed against her smooth chest like a saint,
Beautiful Cunizza, step into the light!'"

"My God, Kerry, what the hell is this all about? I swear I don't understand him at all, and I'm a literary person myself."

"It's pretty difficult," Kerry said, "but you have to think about hearses and sour milk when you read it. That's not as passionate as some of the others."

Amory threw the magazine onto the table.

"Well," he sighed, "I'm really confused about what I want. I know I'm not a typical guy, but I can't stand anyone else who isn't either. I can't figure out whether I should develop my intellect and become a great playwright, or just reject all that highbrow literature and be a smooth Princeton socialite."

"Why make a decision?" Kerry suggested. "It's better to just go with the flow, like I do. I'm planning to ride Burne's success to become prominent myself."

"I can't just coast through life—I need to feel engaged. I want to have influence, even if it's helping someone else, or become chairman at Princeton or president of Triangle. I want people to look up to me, Kerry."

"You're thinking too much about yourself."

Amory straightened up when he heard this.

"No. I'm thinking about you, too. We need to get out there and socialize with our classmates right now, while it's still fun to be a snob. I'd love to bring some nobody to the prom in June, for example, but I wouldn't do it unless I could be completely smooth about it—introduce her to all the popular social climbers, and the football captain, and all that basic stuff."

"Amory," Kerry said with frustration, "you're just going in circles. If you want to make a name for yourself, get out there and work toward something; if you don't, then just relax." He yawned. "Come on, let's get some fresh air. We'll head down and watch football practice."

———————

Amory slowly came to accept this perspective, determined that the following fall would mark the beginning of his career, and gave himself over to observing Kerry find happiness at 12 Univee.

They filled the Jewish student's bed with lemon pie; they extinguished the gas throughout the entire house every night by blowing into the gas jet in Amory's room, leaving Mrs. Twelve and the local plumber completely puzzled; they moved all the belongings of the working-class drunks—pictures, books, and furniture—into the bathroom, which confused the pair when they groggily discovered the switch upon returning from their Trenton drinking spree; they felt tremendously disappointed when the working-class drunks chose to treat it as a prank; they played red-dog and twenty-one and jackpot from dinner until sunrise, and when one man's birthday came around, they convinced him to purchase enough champagne for a wild celebration. Since the host of the party had stayed sober, Kerry and Amory accidentally caused him to fall down two flights of stairs and spent the entire following week visiting him at the infirmary, feeling ashamed and remorseful.

"Tell me, who are all these women?" Kerry asked one day, complaining about how much mail Amory was receiving. "I've been checking the postmarks recently—Farmington and Dobbs and Westover and Dana Hall—what's going on?"

Amory grinned.

"All from the Twin Cities." He listed them one by one. "There's Marylyn De Witt—she's attractive, has her own car which is really convenient; there's Sally Weatherby—she's putting on too much weight; there's Myra St. Claire, she's an ex-girlfriend, easy to make out with if you're into that—"

"What approach do you use with them?" Kerry asked. "I've tried everything, and those crazy jokers aren't even intimidated by me."

"You're the 'nice boy' type," Amory suggested.

"That's exactly the problem. Mother always thinks the girl is safe when she's with me. Honestly, it's irritating. When I try to hold someone's hand, they just laugh at me and let me do it, as if their hand isn't even part of their body. The moment I take hold of a hand, they seem to mentally detach it from the rest of themselves."

"Pout," Amory suggested. "Tell them you're rebellious and let them try to reform you—go home angry—come back in thirty minutes—shock them."

Kerry shook his head.

"No way. I wrote a really heartfelt letter to a girl from St. Timothy last year. At one point I got carried away and wrote: 'My God, how I love you!' She took nail scissors, cut out the 'My God' part, and showed the rest of the letter to everyone at school. It doesn't work at all. I'm just 'good old Kerry' and all that nonsense."

Amory smiled and attempted to imagine himself as "good old Amory." He failed entirely.

February brought a steady drizzle of snow and rain, the whirlwind of freshman midterm exams came and went, and life at 12 University Avenue remained engaging, though perhaps lacking clear direction. Each day Amory treated himself to a club sandwich, cornflakes, and julienne potatoes at "Joe's," usually joined by Kerry or Alec Connage. Connage was a reserved, somewhat distant sophisticate from Hotchkiss who lived in the adjacent room and found himself in the same forced isolation as Amory, since his entire graduating class had chosen Yale. "Joe's" wasn't much to look at and had questionable cleanliness standards, but it offered the invaluable option of running an unlimited tab, which Amory found quite useful. His father had been dabbling in mining investments and, as a result, while his allowance remained generous, it fell considerably short of what he had anticipated.

"Joe's" offered the extra benefit of being hidden from the prying eyes of wealthy students, so every afternoon at four o'clock Amory would head there with either a friend or a book to test his appetite. One March day, when he found all the tables taken, he slid into a seat across from a first-year student who was deeply absorbed in reading at the corner table. They exchanged quick nods. For twenty minutes Amory sat eating bacon rolls while reading "Mrs. Warren's Profession" (he had stumbled upon Shaw completely by chance while browsing through the library during midterm exams); meanwhile, the other first-year student, equally focused on his book, polished off three chocolate malted milks.

Soon Amory's eyes drifted with curiosity to his dining companion's book. He made out the name and title reading it upside down—"Marpessa," by Stephen Phillips. This title meant nothing to him, since his education in poetry had been limited to Sunday classics like "Come into the Garden, Maude," and whatever bits of Shakespeare and Milton had been recently imposed on him.

Feeling compelled to speak to the person sitting across from him, he pretended to be absorbed in his book for a moment, and then called out loudly as if he couldn't help himself:

"Ha! Great stuff!"

The other first-year student looked up and Amory noticed his fake embarrassment.

"Are you talking about your bacon rolls?" His weathered but gentle voice matched perfectly with his thick glasses and the sense of expansive sharpness he projected.

"No," Amory replied. "I was talking about Bernard Shaw." He turned the book around to show what he meant.

"I've never read any Shaw. I've always intended to." The young man paused and then went on: "Have you ever read Stephen Phillips, or do you enjoy poetry?"

"Yes, absolutely," Amory confirmed enthusiastically. "I haven't read much of Phillips, though." (He had never heard of any Phillips except the late David Graham.)

"It's pretty fair, I think. Of course he's a Victorian." They launched into a discussion of poetry, during which they introduced themselves, and Amory's companion turned out to be none other than "that terrible intellectual, Thomas Parke D'Invilliers," who wrote the passionate love poems in the Lit. He was probably nineteen, with hunched shoulders, pale blue eyes, and, as Amory could see from his overall appearance, little understanding of social rivalry and other such fascinating phenomena. Still, he loved books, and it felt like ages since Amory had met anyone who did; if only that St. Paul's group at the nearby table wouldn't mistake him for an intellectual snob as well, he would thoroughly enjoy this conversation. They didn't appear to be paying attention, so he relaxed completely, talking about dozens of books—books he had read, books he had only read about, books he had never even heard of, reeling off lists of titles with the skill of a bookstore employee. D'Invilliers was somewhat convinced and completely charmed. In his good-natured way, he had almost concluded that Princeton was half deadly anti-intellectuals and half deadly academic grinders, and discovering someone who could mention Keats without stumbling over the words, yet clearly maintained basic hygiene, was quite refreshing.

"Have you ever read anything by Oscar Wilde?" he asked.

"No. Who wrote it?"

"It's a man—don't you know?"

"Oh, absolutely." A distant memory stirred in Amory's mind. "Wasn't the comic opera, 'Patience,' written about him?"

"Yes, that's the guy. I just finished reading one of his books, 'The Picture of Dorian Gray,' and I really think you should read it. You'd enjoy it. You can borrow my copy if you'd like."

"Why, I'd really like that—thanks."

"Don't you want to come up to the room? I've got a few other books."

Amory paused, looked over at the St. Paul's group—one of whom was the impressive, refined Humbird—and thought about how decisive adding this friend would be. He never reached the point of making friends and then discarding them—he wasn't tough enough for that—so he weighed Thomas Parke D'Invilliers' clear appeal and worth against the threat of unfriendly eyes behind tortoiseshell glasses that he imagined were staring from the nearby table.

"Yes, I'll go."

So he discovered "Dorian Gray" and the "Mystic and Somber Dolores" and the "Belle Dame sans Merci"; for a month he was passionate about nothing else. The world became pale and fascinating, and he worked hard to view Princeton through the jaded eyes of Oscar Wilde and Swinburne—or "Fingal O'Flaherty" and "Algernon Charles," as he playfully called them in affected humor. He read voraciously every night—Shaw, Chesterton,

Barrie, Pinero, Yeats, Synge, Ernest Dowson, Arthur Symons, Keats, Sudermann, Robert Hugh Benson, the Savoy Operas—just a random assortment, for he suddenly realized that he had read nothing for years.

Tom D'Invilliers started out more as an acquaintance than a true friend. Amory would see him roughly once a week, and during these visits they would work together to gild the ceiling of Tom's room and decorate the walls with fake tapestry they'd purchased at an auction, along with tall candlesticks and patterned curtains. Amory appreciated him for being intelligent and well-read without being feminine or pretentious. Actually, Amory did most of the showing off and struggled painfully to turn every comment into a witty saying, which, if someone is satisfied with superficial wit, ranks among the easier accomplishments to master. Univee found this entertaining. Kerry had read "Dorian Gray" and began imitating Lord Henry, following Amory around, calling him "Dorian" and pretending to encourage sinful thoughts and a refined tendency toward boredom in him. When Kerry brought this act into the dining hall, much to the surprise of everyone else at their table, Amory became intensely embarrassed, and from then on only made clever remarks when he was alone with D'Invilliers or in front of a handy mirror.

One day Tom and Amory attempted to recite their own poetry along with Lord Dunsany's verses while Kerry's gramophone played music in the background.

"Chant!" cried Tom. "Don't recite! Chant!"

Amory, who was putting on a performance, appeared irritated and insisted that he required a record with fewer piano parts. Kerry immediately collapsed onto the floor, struggling to contain his laughter.

"Put on 'Hearts and Flowers'!" he yelled. "Oh, my God, I'm going to have a fit."

"Turn off that damn record player," Amory shouted, his face flushed red. "I'm not putting on a show."

In the meantime, Amory carefully tried to help D'Invilliers understand the social expectations around them, knowing that this poet was actually more traditional than himself and only needed slicked-back hair, a more limited range of topics to discuss, and a darker brown hat to fit in completely. But the rules about Livingstone collars and dark ties went unheard; in fact, D'Invilliers slightly resented these attempts to change him; so Amory limited himself to visiting once a week and occasionally brought him to 12 Univee. This led to quiet snickering among the other freshmen, who nicknamed them "Doctor Johnson and Boswell."

Alec Connage, who visited often, had a general fondness for him but felt intimidated by his intellectual nature. Kerry, however, could see past his poetic pretensions to the genuine, almost conventional character underneath, and found this tremendously entertaining. He would ask him to recite poetry for hours while he stretched out with his eyes closed on Amory's couch and listened:

"Asleep or awake, which is it? Her neck, kissed too intensely, still bears a purple mark where the troubled blood hesitates and fades away; tender and gently stung—made more beautiful by this small blemish..."

"That's good," Kerry would say quietly. "It makes the elder Holiday happy. That's a great poet, I suppose." Tom, thrilled to have listeners, would wander through the "Poems and Ballades" until Kerry and Amory were nearly as familiar with them as he was.

Amory began writing poetry during spring afternoons in the gardens of large estates near Princeton, where swans created a striking atmosphere in the man-made pools, and leisurely clouds drifted peacefully above the willow trees. May arrived too quickly, and suddenly finding himself unable to tolerate being indoors, he roamed the campus at every hour through starlight and rain.

A Damp Symbolic Interlude

The evening mist descended. It rolled down from the moon, gathering around the spires and towers before settling beneath them, leaving the dreaming peaks still reaching upward toward the heavens in noble aspiration. People who had moved about during the day like tiny ants now drifted along as ghostly shadows, weaving in and out of view. The Gothic halls and cloisters became infinitely more mysterious as they emerged suddenly from the darkness, each one outlined by countless dim squares of golden light. From somewhere in the distance, a bell tolled the quarter-hour, and Amory, stopping beside the sundial, stretched himself out at full length on the wet grass. The coolness soothed his eyes and seemed to slow the passage of time—time that had crept so quietly through the drowsy April afternoons and felt so elusive during the long spring evenings. Night after night, the senior singing had floated across the campus with melancholy beauty, and through the surface of his undergraduate awareness had emerged a deep and reverent love for the gray walls and Gothic spires and everything they represented as repositories of bygone eras.

The tower visible from his window stretched upward, transforming into a spire that reached ever higher until its peak nearly disappeared into the morning sky, giving him his first understanding of how temporary and insignificant the campus personalities were, except as carriers of scholarly tradition. He enjoyed learning that Gothic architecture, with its vertical emphasis, was especially fitting for universities, and this concept became meaningful to him personally. The peaceful expanses of lawn, the hushed corridors with an occasional lamp still glowing from late-night study sessions captured his imagination powerfully, and the purity of the spire became a representation of this insight.

"Damn it all," he whispered out loud, dampening his hands with moisture and running them through his hair. "Next year I'll work!" But he understood that where the atmosphere of spires and towers now made him dreamily compliant, it would then intimidate him. Where he currently recognized only his own insignificance, trying hard would make him conscious of his own powerlessness and inadequacy.

The college continued its dreaming—while awake. He experienced a nervous excitement that could have been the actual pulse of its slow-beating heart. It was like a stream where he would cast a stone whose weak ripple would be disappearing almost before it left his grasp. Up to this point he had contributed nothing, he had received nothing.

A late freshman, his waterproof jacket making loud scraping sounds, trudged through the muddy path. A voice from somewhere shouted the predictable phrase, "Stick out your head!" from beneath a hidden window. A hundred small sounds of the present moment flowing beneath the fog eventually broke through into his awareness.

"Oh, God!" he suddenly cried out, startled by the sound of his own voice breaking the silence. The rain continued to drip steadily. He remained motionless for another minute, his hands clenched tightly. Then he jumped to his feet and gave his clothes a quick, testing pat.

"I'm absolutely soaked!" he said aloud to the sundial.

Historical

The war started during the summer after his first year of college. Apart from a casual interest in Germany's rapid advance toward Paris, the entire conflict didn't manage to excite or captivate him. With the same attitude he might have toward an entertaining drama, he wished it would drag on and be violent. If it hadn't continued, he would have felt like an angry ticket-holder at a boxing match where the fighters wouldn't engage with each other.

That was his complete response.

"Ha-Ha Hortense!"

"All right, ponies!"

"Shake it up!"

"Hey, ponies—how about taking a break from that dice game and showing off some serious dancing?"

"Hey, ponies!"

The coach was furious but powerless to do anything about it, while the Triangle Club president, scowling with worry, alternated between angry outbursts of trying to take control and periods of moody exhaustion, during which he sat there feeling defeated and wondering how on earth the show would ever be ready to go on tour by Christmas.

"All right. We'll take the pirate song."

The dancers took final puffs of their cigarettes and slouched into position; the star performer hurried to the front of the stage, positioning his hands and feet with theatrical flair; and as the instructor clapped and stomped and thumped and called out rhythms, they worked through a dance routine.

The Triangle Club was like a massive, bustling anthill. Each year, it produced a musical comedy that toured throughout Christmas vacation, complete with cast, chorus, orchestra, and all the scenery. Both the play and the music were created by undergraduates, and the club had become the most powerful institution on campus, with over three hundred men competing for membership annually.

After winning easily in the first sophomore Princetonian competition, Amory stepped into a vacant role in the cast as Boiling Oil, a Pirate Lieutenant. For the past week, they had been rehearsing "Ha-Ha Hortense!" every night in the Casino, working from two in the afternoon until eight in the morning, kept going by strong, dark coffee and catching up on sleep during lectures in between. The Casino presented quite a sight. It was a large, barn-like auditorium filled with boys dressed as girls, boys playing pirates, and boys acting as babies; the stage sets were being assembled with great energy; the spotlight operator practiced by casting strange beams of light into irritated eyes; throughout it all, the orchestra constantly tuned their instruments or played the cheerful rhythmic beats of a Triangle song. The student who wrote the lyrics stood in the corner, chewing on a pencil, with only twenty minutes to come up with an encore; the business manager debated with the secretary about how much money could be spent on "those damn milkmaid costumes"; the elderly alumnus, who had been president in ninety-eight, sat on a box reminiscing about how much easier things had been in his time.

How a Triangle show ever managed to get produced remained a mystery, but it was an entertaining mystery nonetheless, regardless of whether someone had done enough work to earn the right to wear a small gold Triangle on their watch chain. "Ha-Ha Hortense!" had been rewritten more than six times and featured the names of nine different collaborators listed in the program. Every Triangle show began with the intention of being "something different—not just another typical musical comedy," but after the various writers, the president, the director, and the faculty committee had all finished making their changes, what remained was simply the same dependable Triangle show featuring the same dependable jokes and the leading comic actor who inevitably got kicked out or fell ill or encountered some other problem right before the tour, along with the dark-bearded performer in the chorus line who "absolutely refuses to shave twice a day, darn it!"

There was one brilliant moment in "Ha-Ha Hortense!" Princeton has a tradition that whenever a Yale graduate who belongs to the famous "Skull and Bones" society hears that sacred name spoken, he must exit the room. There's also a tradition that these members always achieve success later in life, accumulating wealth or political power or stock certificates or whatever they set their minds to accumulating. So, at every performance of "Ha-Ha Hortense!" six seats were held back from sale and filled by six of the most disreputable-looking drifters who could be found on the streets, with their appearance further enhanced by the Triangle makeup artist. At the point in the show where Firebrand, the Pirate Chief, gestured toward his black flag and declared, "I am a Yale graduate—observe my Skull and Bones!"—at that exact moment the six vagabonds were told to stand up dramatically and exit the theater wearing expressions of profound sadness and wounded pride. It was rumored, though never confirmed, that on one occasion the hired Yale men were joined by an actual member of the society.

They performed throughout their vacation in eight fashionable cities. Amory enjoyed Louisville and Memphis the most: these cities knew how to welcome visitors, provided exceptional drinks, and displayed an impressive collection of beautiful women. He appreciated Chicago for a certain energy that went beyond its harsh accent—though it was a Yale town, and since the Yale Glee Club was expected to arrive in a week, the Triangle only received partial attention. In Baltimore, Princeton felt at home, and everyone fell in love. There was plenty of drinking all along the tour; one performer always went on stage quite drunk, insisting that his specific interpretation of the role demanded it. There were three private train cars; however, no one slept except in the third car, which was nicknamed the "animal car," where the bespectacled musicians of the orchestra were crowded together. Everything moved so quickly that there was no time to get bored, but when they reached Philadelphia, with vacation almost finished, it was refreshing to escape the heavy atmosphere of flowers and stage makeup, and the chorus boys removed their corsets with stomach cramps and sighs of relief.

When the group disbanded, Amory hurried to Minneapolis because Sally Weatherby's cousin, Isabelle Borge, was coming to spend the winter there while her parents traveled overseas. He only remembered Isabelle as a young girl he had sometimes played with during his first visits to Minneapolis. She had moved to Baltimore to live, but since that time she had developed quite a reputation.

Amory was moving at full speed, feeling confident, anxious, and thrilled all at once. Rushing back to Minneapolis to visit a girl he had known since childhood felt like an exciting and romantic adventure, so he sent his mother a telegram without any guilt telling her not to wait for him... He settled into his train seat and spent thirty-six hours thinking about himself.

"Petting"

During the Triangle trip, Amory had repeatedly encountered that major American cultural phenomenon of the time, the "petting party."

None of the Victorian mothers—and most of the mothers were Victorian—had any clue how casually their daughters were used to being kissed. "Servant-girls behave that way," Mrs. Huston-Carmelite tells her popular daughter. "They get kissed first and receive marriage proposals later."

But the Popular Daughter gets engaged every six months between the ages of sixteen and twenty-two, until she finally settles on a match with young Hambell from Cambell & Hambell, who foolishly believes himself to be her first love, and between these engagements the P. D. (she gets chosen through the cut-in system at dances, which ensures only the most socially adept survive) shares other romantic final kisses in the moonlight, or by the firelight, or in the darkness outside.

Amory witnessed girls engaging in behaviors that would have been unthinkable even within his own recollection: dining on three o'clock post-dance meals in questionable establishments, discussing all aspects of life with an attitude that was part serious, part mocking, yet with a secretive thrill that Amory believed represented a genuine decline in moral standards. However, he didn't grasp how extensive this phenomenon was until he observed the cities stretching between New York and Chicago as one enormous network of youthful scheming.

Afternoon at the Plaza, with winter twilight lingering outside and soft drums echoing from downstairs... they parade and fidget in the lobby, having another cocktail, carefully dressed and waiting. Then the revolving doors spin and three bundles of fur step delicately inside. The theater comes next; then a table at the Midnight Frolic—naturally, mother will be there too, but she will only serve to make things more secretive and dazzling as she sits alone in dignified isolation at the empty table and thinks such entertainment as this isn't nearly as bad as people say, just rather tiresome. But the P. D. is in love again... it was strange, wasn't it?— that even though there was plenty of space left in the taxi, the P. D. and the boy from Williams were somehow squeezed out and had to take a different car. Strange! Didn't you see how red-faced the P. D. was when she showed up exactly seven minutes late? But the P. D. "gets away with it."

The "belle" had transformed into the "flirt," and the "flirt" had evolved into the "baby vamp." The "belle" would receive five or six suitors every afternoon. If the P. D., through some unusual circumstance, happens to have two visitors, the situation becomes quite awkward for the one who doesn't have an appointment with her. The "belle" was encircled by a dozen men during the breaks between dances. Try to locate the P. D. between dances, just attempt to find her.

The same girl... immersed in an environment filled with jazz music and the challenging of traditional values. Amory discovered it quite captivating to realize that any well-liked girl he encountered before eight o'clock he could very well end up kissing before midnight.

"Why on earth are we here?" he asked the girl with the green combs one night as they sat in someone's limousine, outside the Country Club in Louisville.

"I don't know. I'm just full of the devil."

"Let's be honest—we'll never see each other again. I wanted to come out here with you because I thought you were the most beautiful girl around. You really don't care whether you ever see me again, do you?"

"No—but do you use this approach with every girl? What did I do to earn this treatment?"

"And you didn't feel tired from dancing or want a cigarette or any of the things you mentioned? You just wanted to be—"

"Oh, let's go in," she interrupted, "if you want to analyze. Let's not talk about it."

When hand-knitted sleeveless sweaters became fashionable, Amory had a moment of creative inspiration and called them "petting shirts." The name spread across the entire country through the conversations of smooth-talking men and popular debutantes.

Descriptive

Amory had just turned eighteen, standing just shy of six feet tall with striking good looks that defied conventional standards. His face appeared youthful, though its innocent quality was disrupted by piercing green eyes surrounded by long, dark lashes. He somehow missed that raw animal magnetism that typically comes with physical beauty in both men and women; his charisma felt more intellectual in nature, and he couldn't control it like flipping a switch. Yet his face left a lasting impression on everyone he met.

———————

Isabelle

She stopped at the top of the stairs. The feelings that divers experience on diving boards, actresses feel on opening nights, and awkward, stocky young men have on the day of the championship game all rushed through her at once. She should have walked down to the sound of beating drums or a clashing mix of melodies from "Thais" and "Carmen." She had never been so interested in how she looked, and she had never felt so pleased with her appearance. She had been sixteen years old for half a year.

"Isabelle!" her cousin Sally called out from the doorway of the dressing room.

"I'm ready." She felt a small knot of anxiety catch in her throat.

"I had to send someone back to the house to get another pair of slippers. It'll only take a minute."

Isabelle headed toward the dressing room to take one final look in the mirror, but something made her decide to stop and look down the wide staircase of the Minnehaha Club instead. The stairs curved in an enticing way, and she could just make out two pairs of men's feet in the hallway below. Both wore identical black dress shoes, which revealed nothing about who they might be, but she found herself wondering excitedly whether one of those pairs belonged to Amory Blaine. Though she hadn't met this young man yet, he had already occupied much of her thoughts today—her first day since arriving. During the car ride from the train station, Sally had offered up information between a flurry of questions, comments, revelations, and embellishments:

"You remember Amory Blaine, don't you? Well, he's absolutely dying to see you again. He's extended his stay from college by a day, and he's coming over tonight. He's heard so much about you—he says he remembers your eyes."

This had delighted Isabelle. It placed them on the same level, even though she was perfectly capable of creating her own romantic adventures, whether she announced them beforehand or not. But after her joyful flutter of excitement, a dropping feeling came over her that made her wonder:

"What do you mean he's heard about me? What kind of things?"

Sally smiled. She felt somewhat like a showman displaying her more exotic cousin.

"He knows you're—you're considered beautiful and all that"—she paused—"and I suppose he knows you've been kissed."

At this, Isabelle's small fist clenched suddenly beneath the fur robe. She had grown used to being haunted by her desperate past, and it never failed to stir the same feeling of anger within her; however, in an unfamiliar town, such a reputation could work in her favor. So she was a "Speed," was she? Well, let them discover that for themselves.

Through the window, Isabelle watched the snow drift past in the crisp morning air. The temperature here was much colder than Baltimore; she hadn't recalled it being this harsh; ice covered the glass of the side door, and snow had gathered in the window corners. Her thoughts kept returning to the same topic. Did he dress like that young man walking confidently down the busy commercial street, wearing moccasins and winter festival clothing? How distinctly Western! Naturally he wouldn't dress that way: he attended Princeton, was a sophomore or something similar. She really had no clear picture of him. An old photograph she had kept in a vintage camera album had struck her because of the large eyes (which he had likely grown into by now). Nevertheless, during the past month, when her winter trip to visit Sally had been arranged, he had taken on the significance of a formidable opponent. Children, being the most cunning matchmakers, devise their strategies swiftly, and Sally had orchestrated a skillful exchange of letters that appealed to Isabelle's passionate nature. For quite some time, Isabelle had been prone to very intense, though very fleeting feelings....

They pulled up to a sprawling, white-stone building that sat back from the snow-covered street. Mrs. Weatherby welcomed her with warmth, and her various younger cousins emerged from the corners where they had been politely hiding. Isabelle handled meeting them with skill. When she was at her finest, she won over everyone she encountered—except for older girls and certain women. Every impression she created was deliberate. The handful of girls she reconnected with that morning were all quite impressed, as much by her straightforward personality as by her reputation. Amory Blaine became an open topic of conversation. Apparently somewhat fickle in love, neither well-liked nor disliked—every girl present seemed to have had some romantic involvement with him at one point or another, but nobody offered any truly helpful details. He was destined to fall for her.... Sally had shared this prediction with her circle of young friends, and they were reporting it back to Sally as quickly as they laid eyes on Isabelle. Isabelle privately decided that she would, if needed, make herself like him—she owed Sally that much. What if she ended up terribly let down? Sally had described him in such brilliant terms— he was attractive, "kind of distinguished, when he chooses to be," had charm, and was appropriately unfaithful. In essence, he embodied all the romance that her age and circumstances made her crave. She found herself wondering if those were his dancing shoes that moved tentatively in a fox-trot pattern across the plush carpet below.

All impressions and, in fact, all ideas shifted constantly like a kaleidoscope for Isabelle. She possessed that fascinating blend of social and artistic temperaments often found in two groups: society women and actresses. Her education, or more accurately, her worldly sophistication, had been gained from the young men who had competed for her attention; her social grace came naturally, and her potential for romantic entanglements was limited only by the number of interested suitors she could reach by telephone. Flirtation sparkled in her large dark brown eyes and radiated through her powerful physical charm.

So she waited at the top of the stairs that evening while slippers were brought to her. Just as she was becoming impatient, Sally emerged from the dressing room, glowing with her usual cheerfulness and energy, and together they went down to the floor below, while Isabelle's restless thoughts jumped between two ideas: she was pleased she had good color in her cheeks tonight, and she wondered whether he was a good dancer.

Downstairs, in the club's great room, she found herself momentarily surrounded by the girls she had encountered that afternoon, then she heard Sally's voice calling out a series of names, and discovered herself nodding politely to a group of six figures in black and white, terribly formal, vaguely recognizable faces. The name Blaine came up somewhere, but initially she couldn't place him. A very chaotic, very youthful moment of awkward stepping back and bumping into each other followed, and everyone ended up talking to the person they least wanted to speak with. Isabelle maneuvered herself and Froggy Parker, a freshman at Harvard with whom she had once played hopscotch, to a spot on the stairs. A playful reference to their shared past was all she required. The things Isabelle could accomplish socially with a single idea were extraordinary. First, she would repeat it with delight in an enthusiastic contralto voice with a hint of Southern accent; then she would hold it at arm's length and smile at it—her magnificent smile; then she would deliver it with variations and play a kind of mental game of catch with it, all of this presented as natural conversation. Froggy was captivated and completely unaware that this performance wasn't meant for him, but for the green eyes that sparkled beneath the gleaming, carefully styled hair, slightly to her left, because Isabelle had spotted Amory. Just as an actress, even at the height of her own deliberate charm, forms a clear impression of most people in the front row, so Isabelle evaluated her rival. First, he had reddish-brown hair, and from her sense of disappointment she realized that she had expected him to be dark-haired and possessing that slender build featured in advertisements for men's garters.... As for the rest, a slight blush and a straight, romantic profile; the overall effect enhanced by a well-tailored evening suit and a silk ruffled shirt of the type that women still loved to see men wear, but that men were just starting to grow weary of.

During this inspection, Amory was quietly observing.

"Don't you think so?" she said suddenly, turning to him with innocent eyes.

There was a commotion, and Sally headed toward their table. Amory made his way to Isabelle's side and whispered:

"You're my dinner partner, you know. We're all coached for each other."

Isabelle gasped—this was exactly what she had expected. Yet she truly felt as though a perfect line had been stolen from the leading actress and handed to someone playing a background role.... She absolutely couldn't afford to lose her commanding presence even slightly. The dinner table sparkled with laughter as everyone scrambled to find their seats, and then curious gazes turned toward her as she sat close to the head of the table. She was thoroughly enjoying every moment of this, and Froggy Parker became so captivated by the extra radiance of her flushed cheeks that he completely forgot to pull out Sally's chair and stumbled into bewildered embarrassment. Amory sat on her other side, brimming with self-assurance and pride, staring at her with undisguised admiration. He started talking immediately, and so did Froggy:

"I've heard a lot about you since you wore braids—"

"Wasn't it funny this afternoon—"

Both came to a halt. Isabelle turned toward Amory with a shy expression. Her face always provided a sufficient response for anyone, but she chose to say something anyway.

"How—from whom?"

"From everybody—for all the years since you've been away." She blushed as expected. On her right, Froggy was already out of the fight, though he hadn't quite realized it yet.

"I'll tell you what I remembered about you all these years," Amory went on. She tilted slightly in his direction and gazed demurely at the celery sitting in front of her. Froggy let out a sigh—he was familiar with Amory and the kinds of situations that Amory appeared destined to manage. He shifted his attention to Sally and inquired whether she would be leaving for school the following year. Amory launched her opening attack.

"I have an adjective that perfectly describes you." This was one of his go-to conversation starters—he rarely had a specific word in mind, but it sparked curiosity, and he could always come up with something flattering if he found himself in a difficult situation.

"Oh—what?" Isabelle's face showed complete fascination and eager curiosity.

Amory shook his head.

"I don't know you very well yet."

"Will you tell me—afterward?" she whispered softly.

He nodded.

"We'll sit this one out."

Isabelle nodded.

"Has anyone ever told you that you have sharp eyes?" she said.

Amory tried to make them appear even sharper. He thought, though he wasn't certain, that her foot had just brushed against his beneath the table. But it could have simply been the table leg. It was so difficult to know for sure. Nevertheless, it excited him. He wondered immediately if there would be any trouble getting the small room upstairs.

_____

Babes In the Woods

Isabelle and Amory were clearly not innocent, but they weren't particularly bold either. Furthermore, being inexperienced had very little worth in the game they were playing, a game that would likely be her main focus for years ahead. She had started just as he had, with attractive looks and an easily excited personality, and everything else came from reading popular romance novels and picking up tips from dressing-room chatter with a slightly older crowd. Isabelle had been walking with an affected manner since she was nine and a half, and her wide, bright eyes made her seem like the perfect innocent young woman. Amory wasn't fooled as easily. He waited for her act to slip, but at the same time he didn't challenge her right to put it on. She, for her part, wasn't impressed by his carefully practiced air of worldly indifference. She had lived in a bigger city and had a slight edge in experience. But she went along with his act—it was one of the many small pretenses that came with this type of romance. He understood that he was receiving this special attention now because she had been taught how to behave; he knew that he simply represented the best option available to her at the moment, and that he would need to make the most of his chance before he lost his edge. So they continued with an endless cunning that would have shocked her parents.

After dinner, the dance started... smoothly. Smoothly?—boys kept cutting in on Isabelle every few steps and then argued in the corners with comments like: "You could at least let me dance more than a few seconds!" and "She didn't enjoy it either—she said so when I cut in next time." It was accurate—she said this to everyone, and gave each hand a farewell squeeze that conveyed: "You understand that your dances are what's making my night special."

But time passed, two hours of it, and the less perceptive suitors had learned to direct their fake passionate looks elsewhere, for eleven o'clock found Isabelle and Amory sitting on the couch in the small den off the reading room upstairs. She was aware that they made an attractive couple, and seemed to belong naturally in this private space, while less important people fluttered and chattered downstairs.

Boys who walked past the door peered in with envy—girls who passed by simply laughed and scowled and became wiser in their own minds.

They had reached a clear turning point in their conversation. They had exchanged updates about what they'd been doing since their last meeting, and she had listened to much that she'd heard him say before. He was a second-year student, served on the Princetonian editorial board, and hoped to become editor-in-chief during his final year. He discovered that some of the young men she dated in Baltimore were "reckless party-goers" who showed up to dances under the influence of alcohol; most of them were around twenty years old and drove eye-catching red Stutz automobiles. A good portion of them seemed to have already been kicked out of various schools and universities, but some carried prestigious athletic reputations that made him regard her with admiration. In reality, Isabelle's intimate knowledge of college life was just beginning. She had casual friendships with many young men who considered her a "lovely girl—worth watching." But Isabelle wove these names together into an elaborate tale of excitement that would have impressed a European aristocrat. Such is the influence of young, rich female voices spoken from comfortable couches.

He asked her whether she thought he was conceited. She told him there was a distinction between conceit and self-confidence. She loved self-confidence in men.

"Is Froggy a good friend of yours?" she asked.

"Rather—why?"

"He's a terrible dancer."

Amory laughed.

"He dances as if the girl were on his back instead of in his arms."

She valued this.

"You're really good at reading people."

Amory painfully rejected this idea. Nevertheless, he evaluated several people on her behalf. Afterward, they discussed hands.

"You have really beautiful hands," she said. "They look like you play piano. Do you?"

I mentioned they had reached a very clear stage—actually, more than that, a very critical stage. Amory had extended his stay by a day to see her, and his train was scheduled to depart at twelve-eighteen that night. His trunk and suitcase were waiting for him at the station; his watch was starting to feel heavy in his pocket.

"Isabelle," he said suddenly, "I need to tell you something." They had been chatting casually about "that strange expression in her eyes," and Isabelle could tell from the shift in his demeanor what was about to happen—she had actually been wondering when it would finally come. Amory reached up above them and switched off the electric light, leaving them in darkness except for the red glow streaming through the doorway from the reading room lamps. Then he started:

"I'm not sure if you already know what I'm about to tell you. God, Isabelle—this probably sounds like I'm feeding you a line, but I'm not."

"I know," Isabelle said quietly.

"Maybe we'll never have another moment like this—I seem to have terrible luck sometimes." He had shifted away from her to the far end of the couch, but she could still see his eyes clearly in the darkness.

"You'll meet me again—silly." There was just the slightest emphasis on the last word—so that it became almost a term of endearment. He continued a bit huskily:

"I've been attracted to many people—girls—and I imagine you have too—boys, I mean, but honestly, you—" he stopped abruptly and leaned forward, resting his chin on his hands: "Oh, what's the point—you'll follow your path and I suppose I'll follow mine."

Silence fell for a moment. Isabelle felt quite moved; she twisted her handkerchief into a tight ball, and in the dim light that fell across her, she intentionally dropped it to the floor. Their hands brushed for just an instant, but neither said a word. These quiet moments were happening more often and becoming more wonderful. Outside, another wandering couple had arrived and was trying out the piano in the adjoining room. After the typical warm-up of "chopsticks," one of them began playing "Babes in the Woods" and a light tenor voice carried the lyrics into their room:

"Give me your hand
I'll understand
We're off to slumberland."

Isabelle hummed it quietly and shivered as she felt Amory's hand cover hers.

"Isabelle," he whispered. "You know I'm crazy about you. You do care about me."

"Yes."

"How much do you care—do you like anyone better?"

"No." He could barely hear her, even though he leaned so close that he could feel her breath on his cheek.

"Isabelle, I'm going back to college for six long months, and why shouldn't we—if I could just have one thing to remember you by—"

"Close the door...." Her voice had barely stirred, making him wonder if she had actually spoken. As he gently pulled the door shut, the music seemed to tremble just beyond it.

"Moonlight is bright,
Kiss me good night."

What a beautiful song, she thought—everything felt magical tonight, especially this romantic moment in the den, with their hands intertwined and the inevitable drawing wonderfully near. The future path of her life appeared to be an endless series of moments like this: beneath moonlight and soft starlight, and in the back seats of warm limousines and in sleek, comfortable convertibles parked under protective trees—only the boy might be different, and this one was so sweet. He took her hand gently. With a swift motion he turned it over and, bringing it to his lips, kissed her palm.

"Isabelle!" His whisper merged with the music, and they seemed to drift closer together. Her breathing quickened. "Can't I kiss you, Isabelle—Isabelle?" With lips slightly parted, she turned her face toward him in the darkness. Suddenly the chorus of voices and the sound of rushing footsteps swept toward them. Lightning-fast, Amory reached up and switched on the light, and when the door burst open and three boys—including the angry and dance-hungry Froggy—charged in, he was casually flipping through the magazines on the table, while she sat perfectly still, calm and unruffled, even greeting them with a warm smile. But her heart was pounding frantically, and she felt as though something had been taken from her.

It was clearly finished. There was a demand for a dance, there was a look that passed between them—on his part desperation, on hers sorrow, and then the evening continued, with the relieved suitors and the endless cutting in.

At eleven forty-five, Amory shook hands with her solemnly, surrounded by a small group of people who had gathered to wish him well on his journey. For a moment he lost his composure, and she felt somewhat unsettled when a mocking voice from some hidden joker called out:

"Take her outside, Amory!" When he took her hand, he squeezed it gently, and she squeezed back just as she had done with twenty other hands that evening—that was all.

At two o'clock, back at the Weatherbys' house, Sally asked her whether she and Amory had enjoyed themselves in the den. Isabelle turned to face her calmly. In her eyes shone the light of an idealist, the pure dreamer of Joan-like dreams.

"No," she replied. "I don't do that kind of thing anymore; he asked me to, but I told him no."

As she slipped into bed, she wondered what he would say in his special delivery tomorrow. He had such an attractive mouth—would she ever—?

"Fourteen angels were watching over them," Sally sang sleepily from the next room.

"Damn!" Isabelle muttered, hitting the pillow to fluff it into a comfortable shape and carefully feeling around the cold sheets. "Damn!"

Carnival

Amory had made his mark through the Princetonian and established his presence. The lesser social climbers, who served as precise gauges of success, began warming up to him as club selection time approached, and both he and Tom received visits from groups of upperclassmen who showed up uncomfortably, perched awkwardly on the edges of chairs and sofas while discussing every topic except the one that truly mattered to them. Amory found it entertaining to notice their focused stares directed at him, and whenever the visitors came from a club that didn't interest him, he took great delight in startling them with unconventional comments.

"Oh, let me think—" he said one evening to a stunned group of representatives, "which organization do you speak for?"

With visitors from Ivy and Cottage and Tiger Inn, he played the role of the "nice, unspoiled, innocent boy" who was completely comfortable and seemingly oblivious to the purpose of their visit.

When the fateful morning came in early March and the campus erupted into complete hysteria, he slipped effortlessly into Cottage alongside Alec Connage and observed his suddenly frantic classmates with great curiosity.

There were unpredictable groups that switched from one club to another; there were friends of just a few days who declared emotionally and frantically that they had to join the same club, that nothing could come between them; there were bitter revelations of long-concealed resentments as those who had suddenly risen to prominence recalled the slights they had endured during their freshman year. Obscure men gained significance when they received certain highly sought-after invitations; others who had been thought to be "guaranteed acceptance" discovered they had made unforeseen adversaries, found themselves isolated and abandoned, and spoke frantically about dropping out of college.

In his own social circle, Amory witnessed men being excluded for wearing green hats, for being "a damn tailor's dummy," for having "too much pull in heaven," for getting drunk one night "not like a gentleman, by God," or for mysterious secret reasons known only to those who cast the black balls.

This celebration of social gathering reached its peak with a massive party at the Nassau Inn, where punch was served from enormous bowls, and the entire downstairs area transformed into a wild, swirling, boisterous maze of faces and voices.

"Hi, Dibby—congratulations!"

"Good boy, Tom, you got a good group in Cap."

"Listen, Kerry—"

"Oh, Kerry—I heard you went to Tiger with all the bodybuilders!" "Well, I didn't go to Cottage—that's where all the smooth-talking guys hang out."

"They say Overton fainted when he received his Ivy invitation—Did he sign up on the first day?—oh, no. He rushed over to Murray-Dodge on a bicycle—worried it was all a mistake."

"How did you get into Cap—you old rogue?"

"'Gratulations!"

"'Congratulations to you too. I heard you got a good crowd."

When the bar closed, the party split into groups and flowed across the snow-covered campus, singing as they went, caught up in the strange illusion that pretentiousness and pressure had finally ended, and that they were free to do whatever they wanted for the next two years.

Years later, Amory would look back on his sophomore spring as the happiest period of his entire life. His thoughts aligned perfectly with the life he was living; all he wanted was to float along, daydream, and savor a dozen newly discovered friendships during those April afternoons.

Alec Connage entered his room one morning and roused him awake to the sunlight and distinctive splendor of Campbell Hall gleaming through the window.

"Wake up, Original Sin, and pull yourself together. Meet me in front of Renwick's in thirty minutes. Someone has a car." He picked up the bureau cover and carefully placed it on the bed along with all the small items it held.

"Where did you get the car?" Amory asked cynically.

"Sacred trust, but don't be a critical gopher or you can't go!"

"I think I'll sleep," Amory said calmly, adjusting his position and reaching next to the bed for a cigarette.

"Sleep!"

"Why not? I've got a class at eleven-thirty."

"You damned pessimist! Of course, if you don't want to go to the coast—"

With a sudden leap, Amory jumped out of bed, sending everything on the dresser cover crashing to the floor. The coast... he hadn't seen it in years, not since he and his mother had gone on their pilgrimage.

"Who's going?" he asked as he pulled on his underwear.

"Oh, Dick Humbird and Kerry Holiday and Jesse Ferrenby and—oh about five or six. Speed it up, kid!"

Within ten minutes, Amory was hungrily eating cornflakes at Renwick's, and by nine-thirty they were driving cheerfully out of town, heading toward the sandy shores of Deal Beach.

"You see," Kerry explained, "the car actually belongs down there. The truth is, it was stolen from Asbury Park by some unknown people, who abandoned it in Princeton and then headed west. Our heartless friend Humbird here managed to get permission from the city council to return it."

"Does anyone have any money?" Ferrenby asked, turning around from the front seat.

There was a strong chorus of "no" responses.

"That makes it interesting."

"Money—what's money? We can sell the car."

"Charge him salvage or something."

"How are we going to get food?" asked Amory.

"Honestly," Kerry replied, looking at him with disapproval, "do you question Kerry's ability to manage for just three short days? Some people have survived on absolutely nothing for years at a stretch. Just read the Boy Scout Monthly."

"Three days," Amory thought to himself, "and I have classes."

"One of the days is the Sabbath."

"Even so, I can only skip six more classes, and there's still more than a month and a half left in the semester."

"Throw him out!"

"It's a long walk back."

"Amory, you're dragging this out, if I may coin a new phrase."

"Shouldn't you learn more about yourself, Amory?"

Amory gave up with resignation and fell into quietly observing the landscape around him. Somehow, Swinburne seemed to belong in this moment.

"Oh, winter's rains and destruction have ended, and all the seasons of snow and wrongdoing are past; the days that separated lovers from one another, the light that fades, the darkness that triumphs; and memories of the past become forgotten sorrow, and frost is destroyed while flowers are born, and in the green undergrowth and shelter, bloom by bloom, spring begins.

"The flowing streams nourish themselves on the flower of—"

"What's wrong, Amory? Amory's thinking about poetry, about the beautiful birds and flowers. I can see it in his eyes."

"No, I'm not," he lied. "I'm thinking about the Princetonian. I should catch up tonight, but I guess I can call back."

"Oh," Kerry said with respect, "these important men—"

Amory's face reddened, and it appeared to him that Ferrenby, a beaten rival, flinched slightly. Naturally, Kerry was just joking around, but he really shouldn't bring up the Princetonian.

It was a peaceful, beautiful day, and as they approached the shore with salt breezes rushing past them, he started to imagine the ocean with its long, flat expanses of sand and red rooftops overlooking the blue sea. Then they rushed through the small town and everything suddenly struck his awareness like a powerful song of overwhelming emotion....

"Oh, good Lord! Look at it!" he cried.

"What?"

"Let me out, quick—I haven't seen it for eight years! Oh, gentlefolk, stop the car!"

"What a strange child!" Alec commented.

"I really think he's a little eccentric."

The car had conveniently stopped at the curb, and Amory rushed toward the boardwalk. At first, he noticed that the ocean was blue and that there was a vast expanse of it, and that it thundered and thundered—truly all the clichés about the sea that anyone could observe, but if someone had told him at that moment that these observations were clichés, he would have stared in amazement.

"Now we're going to get lunch," Kerry commanded, strolling over with the group. "Come on, Amory, pull yourself away from that and be practical."

"We'll start with the finest hotel," he continued, "and work our way from there."

They walked along the boardwalk to the most impressive hotel they could see, and after entering the dining room, they spread out around a table.

"Eight Bronxes," Alec ordered, "and a club sandwich with julienne fries. The food is for one person. Pass the drinks around to everyone else."

Amory barely touched his food, having grabbed a seat where he could gaze out at the ocean and sense its rhythmic motion. After lunch ended, they settled back and smoked in comfortable silence.

"What's the bill?"

Someone scanned it.

"Eight twenty-five."

"Ridiculous overcharge. We'll give them two dollars and one for the waiter. Kerry, collect the small change."

The waiter came over, and Kerry solemnly gave him a dollar, threw two dollars onto the bill, and walked away. They strolled casually toward the exit, followed shortly by the wary Ganymede.

"Some mistake, sir."

Kerry took the bill and looked it over carefully.

"Absolutely not!" he declared, shaking his head seriously, and after ripping it into four pieces, he gave the torn bits to the waiter, who was so stunned that he remained frozen and blank-faced as they left.

"Won't he come after us?"

"No," Kerry said; "for a moment he'll think we're the owner's sons or something; then he'll look at the check again and call the manager, and meanwhile—"

They left the car at Asbury and took the streetcar to Allenhurst, where they searched through the crowded pavilions looking for attractive people. At four o'clock they had refreshments in a lunch room, and this time they paid an even smaller percentage of the total bill; something about how the crowd looked and carried themselves made their scheme work, and no one came after them.

"You see, Amory, we're Marxist Socialists," Kerry explained. "We don't believe in private property and we're putting that belief to the ultimate test."

"Night will come," Amory suggested.

"Watch, and put your trust in Holiday."

They got cheerful around five-thirty and, hooking arms together, walked back and forth along the boardwalk in a line, singing a repetitive song about the melancholy ocean waves. Then Kerry spotted a face in the crowd that caught his attention and, hurrying away, came back moments later with one of the most unattractive girls Amory had ever laid eyes on. Her colorless mouth stretched from one ear to the other, her teeth stuck out in a thick block, and she had small, narrow eyes that looked out flirtatiously over the curved bridge of her nose. Kerry introduced them in a formal manner.

"Name of Kaluka, Hawaiian queen! Let me introduce Messrs. Connage, Sloane, Humbird, Ferrenby, and Blaine."

The girl curtsied to everyone around her. Poor thing; Amory figured she had probably never received any attention in her entire life—perhaps she was mentally slow. While she joined them for the meal (Kerry had asked her to come to supper), she didn't say anything that would contradict this assumption.

"She likes her traditional food better," Alec said seriously to the waiter, "but any simple meal will work."

Throughout dinner he spoke to her with the utmost courtesy, while Kerry flirted with her foolishly from the other side, causing her to laugh and smile constantly. Amory was happy to sit back and observe their interactions, admiring Kerry's skillful approach and his ability to turn even the smallest moment into something graceful and meaningful. Everyone seemed to possess this quality to some degree, and being around them felt refreshing. Amory typically enjoyed people's company one-on-one, but felt uncomfortable in groups unless he was at the center of attention. He found himself wondering what each person brought to the gathering, since there seemed to be some kind of emotional cost involved. Alec and Kerry brought energy and liveliness to the group, but they weren't really the focal point. Somehow it was the reserved Humbird and Sloane, with his restless air of superiority, who commanded the group's attention.

Dick Humbird had seemed like the perfect example of an aristocrat to Amory ever since their freshman year. He was lean yet well-built, with black curly hair, sharp features, and somewhat dark skin. Everything he said carried an indefinable sense of appropriateness. He had unlimited courage, a reasonably good intellect, and a sense of honor combined with a natural charm and aristocratic duty that distinguished it from mere self-righteousness. He could indulge in excess without falling apart, and even his most unconventional escapades never appeared to be "going too far." People copied his style of dress and attempted to speak the way he did.... Amory concluded that he probably held the world back, but he wouldn't have wanted to change him. ...

He was different from the typical healthy person who was fundamentally middle class—he never appeared to sweat. Some people couldn't be friendly with a driver without having that familiarity thrown back at them; Humbird could have eaten lunch at Sherry's with a Black man, yet people would have instinctively understood that it was perfectly acceptable. He wasn't a snob, even though he only knew half his social class. His friends came from all walks of life, from the highest to the lowest, but it was impossible to "win him over" through calculated effort. Servants adored him and treated him like a deity. He appeared to be the perfect example of what the upper class aspires to become.

"He looks like those photographs in the Illustrated London News showing English officers who died in battle," Amory had told Alec. "Well," Alec had replied, "if you want to hear the startling truth, his father worked as a grocery store clerk who struck it rich in Tacoma real estate and moved to New York a decade ago."

Amory had experienced a strange, unsettling feeling in his stomach.

This kind of party became possible because the entire class came together after the club elections—as though making one final desperate effort to understand itself, to stay united, and to resist the increasingly exclusive atmosphere of the clubs. It represented a departure from the formal standards they had all maintained so strictly.

After dinner they walked Kaluka to the boardwalk, then wandered back along the beach toward Asbury. The evening ocean was a completely new experience, since all its vibrant colors and gentle warmth had disappeared, and it now appeared to be the desolate emptiness that gave the Norse sagas their melancholy tone; Amory found himself thinking of Kipling's

"Beaches of Lukanon before the sealers came."

It was still music, though, infinitely sorrowful.

By ten o'clock, they were completely broke. They had enjoyed a lavish dinner with their final eleven cents and, singing cheerfully, wandered up through the casinos and illuminated archways along the boardwalk, pausing to listen with approval to every band performance. At one location, Kerry organized a collection for French War Orphans that raised a dollar and twenty cents, which they used to purchase some brandy in case they got cold during the night. They ended their day at a movie theater and burst into deliberate, systematic fits of laughter at an old comedy, much to the shocked irritation of the other moviegoers. Their entry was clearly planned, as each man pointed accusingly at the person directly behind him as he walked in. Sloane, who was last in line, denied any involvement or responsibility once the others had dispersed throughout the theater; then, when the angry ticket collector rushed inside, Sloane casually followed behind him.

They met up again later near the Casino and made plans for the night. Kerry managed to get permission from the security guard to sleep on the platform, and after gathering a large pile of blankets from the booths to use as mattresses and covers, they talked until midnight before falling into a deep, dreamless sleep, even though Amory tried his best to stay awake and watch that incredible moon sink down toward the ocean.

So they spent two wonderful days exploring, traveling up and down the coastline by streetcar or automobile, or walking on foot along the busy boardwalk; occasionally eating at upscale establishments, but more often dining cheaply at the expense of an unsuspecting restaurant owner. They had their pictures taken, eight different poses, at a quick-development photography shop. Kerry insisted on arranging them like a college football team, and then posing as a rough gang from the East Side, with their jackets turned inside out, while he sat in the center on a cardboard moon prop. The photographer likely still has those photos—at least, they never returned to pick them up. The weather was ideal, and once again they slept outdoors, and once again Amory reluctantly drifted off to sleep.

Sunday arrived dull and proper, and even the ocean seemed to grumble and protest, so they headed back to Princeton in the borrowed cars of temporary farmers, and parted ways with head colds, but otherwise no worse off from their adventure.

Even more than the previous year, Amory ignored his schoolwork, not on purpose but out of laziness and because he was distracted by countless other interests. Coordinate geometry and the depressing hexameters of Corneille and Racine offered little appeal, and even psychology, which he had looked forward to with excitement, turned out to be a boring subject filled with muscle responses and scientific terminology rather than the exploration of personality and human influence. That class met at noon, and it always made him drowsy. After discovering that "subjective and objective, sir," worked as an answer to most questions, he relied on this phrase every time, and it became a running joke in the class when, after a question was directed at him, Ferrenby or Sloane would nudge him awake so he could mumble out his standard response.

Mostly there were parties—trips to Orange or the Shore, and less frequently to New York and Philadelphia, though one evening they gathered fourteen waitresses from Childs' and took them for a ride down Fifth Avenue on top of a bus. They all skipped more classes than the rules permitted, which would require taking an extra course the next year, but spring was too precious to allow anything to get in the way of their vibrant adventures. In May Amory was chosen for the Sophomore Prom Committee, and after spending a long evening discussing it with Alec, they created a preliminary list of likely candidates from their class for the senior council, putting themselves among the most certain picks. The senior council supposedly consisted of the eighteen most representative seniors, and considering Alec's position as football manager and Amory's possibility of beating out Burne Holiday for Princetonian chairman, their assumption seemed quite reasonable. Surprisingly, they both included D'Invilliers among the potential candidates, a prediction that would have shocked the class a year earlier.

Throughout the spring, Amory had maintained an on-and-off correspondence with Isabelle Borge, marked by heated arguments and mainly brightened by his efforts to discover fresh expressions for love. He found Isabelle to be carefully and irritatingly unromantic in her letters, but he clung to the hope that she wouldn't turn out to be too unusual a flower to suit the open expanses of spring as she had suited the cozy room in the Minnehaha Club. During May he composed thirty-page letters almost every night, mailing them to her in thick envelopes marked on the outside as "Part I" and "Part II."

"Oh, Alec, I think I'm getting tired of college," he said sadly, as they walked together through the twilight.

"I think I am, too, in a way."

"All I want is a small house in the countryside, somewhere warm, a wife, and just enough work to keep me from wasting away."

"Me, too."

"I'd like to quit."

"What does your girl say?"

"Oh!" Amory gasped in horror. "She wouldn't think of marrying... that is, not now. I mean in the future, you know."

"My girlfriend would. I'm engaged."

"Are you really?"

"Yes. Please don't tell anyone, but I am. I might not return next year."

"But you're only twenty! Give up college?"

"Why, Amory, you were saying a minute ago—"

"Yes," Amory interrupted, "but I was just daydreaming. I

wouldn't consider dropping out of college. It's just that I feel so melancholy on these beautiful nights. I have this feeling they'll never come again, and I'm not truly making the most of them. I wish my girlfriend lived here. But getting married—that's not happening. Especially since my father says the money isn't flowing like it used to."

"What a waste these nights are!" Alec agreed.

But Amory sighed and spent his nights writing to her. He kept a photograph of Isabelle tucked inside an old pocket watch, and almost every evening at eight o'clock he would turn off all the lights except his desk lamp and sit by the open windows with her picture in front of him, composing passionate letters to her.

Oh, it's so difficult to write down what I truly feel when I think about you constantly; you've come to represent a dream that I can no longer capture in words. Your most recent letter arrived and it was amazing! I read it approximately six times, particularly the final section, but I do wish, at times, that you would be more honest and tell me what you genuinely think of me, though your latest letter was too wonderful to believe, and I can barely wait until June! Make sure you're able to attend the prom. It's going to be great, I believe, and I want to escort you at the conclusion of an incredible year. I frequently reflect on what you said that evening and wonder how much you truly meant it. If it were anyone other than you—but you see I thought you were unpredictable the first time I met you and you are so well-liked and everything that I cannot imagine you actually preferring me above all others.

Oh, Isabelle, darling—it's a beautiful night. Someone is performing "Love Moon" on a mandolin somewhere across the campus, and the melody seems to draw you through the window. Now he's performing "Good-by, Boys, I'm Through," and how perfectly it describes my situation. Because I am finished with everything. I have resolved never to drink a cocktail again, and I know I'll never fall in love again—I couldn't—you've become too integral to my days and nights to ever allow me to consider another girl. I encounter them constantly and they don't capture my interest. I'm not pretending to be indifferent, because that's not it. It's simply that I'm in love. Oh, dearest Isabelle (somehow I cannot call you simply Isabelle, and I'm worried I'll blurt out the "dearest" in front of your family this June), you must attend the prom, and then I'll visit your house for a day and everything will be perfect....

And so it continued in an endless, unchanging rhythm that felt infinitely charming and endlessly fresh to both of them.

———————

June arrived and the days became so hot and languid that they couldn't even worry about exams, instead spending dreamy evenings in the courtyard of Cottage, discussing profound topics until the stretch of countryside toward Stony Brook turned into a blue haze and the lilacs appeared white around the tennis courts, and conversation gave way to quiet cigarettes.... Then down empty Prospect and along McCosh with music all around them, up to the warm cheerfulness of Nassau Street.

Tom D'Invilliers and Amory stayed up late during those days. A gambling craze spread throughout the sophomore class, and they hunched over the dice until three in the morning on many sweltering nights. Following one gaming session, they emerged from Sloane's room to discover that dew had settled and the stars appeared ancient in the sky.

"Let's borrow some bikes and go for a ride," Amory suggested.

"All right. I'm not tired at all and this is practically the final night of the year, really, since the prom activities begin Monday."

They discovered two unlocked bicycles in Holder Court and rode out around three-thirty along the Lawrenceville Road.

"What are you going to do this summer, Amory?"

"Don't ask me—same old things, I suppose. A month or two in Lake Geneva—I'm counting on you to be there in July, you know—then there'll be Minneapolis, and that means hundreds of summer parties, socializing, getting bored—But oh, Tom," he added suddenly, "hasn't this year been amazing!"

"No," Tom declared firmly, a transformed Tom, dressed by Brooks, wearing shoes by Franks, "I've won this game, but I feel like I never want to play another one. You're fine—you're like a rubber ball, and somehow that works for you, but I'm tired of adjusting myself to the local snobbery of this part of the world. I want to go somewhere where people aren't excluded because of the color of their ties and the cut of their jackets."

"You can't, Tom," Amory argued as they drove through the dispersing night. "Wherever you go now, you'll always unconsciously apply these standards of 'having it' or 'not having it.' For better or worse, we've marked you—you're a Princeton type!"

"Well, then," Tom complained, his strained voice rising with frustration, "why do I need to go back at all? I've already absorbed everything Princeton can teach me. Spending two more years dealing with pointless academic formalities and lounging around some club isn't going to benefit me. It's only going to mess me up and turn me into a complete conformist. I'm already so weak-willed that I'm amazed I can even function."

"Oh, but you're missing the real point, Tom," Amory interrupted. "You've just had your eyes opened to how snobbish the world really is, and it happened pretty suddenly. Princeton always gives thoughtful people a better understanding of social dynamics."

"You think you're the one who taught me that, don't you?" he asked with a puzzled look, studying Amory in the dim light.

Amory laughed quietly.

"Didn't I?"

"Sometimes," he said slowly, "I think you're my bad angel. I might have been a pretty decent poet."

"Come on, that's pretty harsh. You decided to attend an Eastern college. Either you had your eyes opened to how people scramble and compete in petty ways, or you would have gone through it completely oblivious, and you'd hate to have done that—ended up like Marty Kaye."

"Yes," he agreed, "you're right. I wouldn't have liked it. Still, it's difficult to become cynical at twenty."

"I was born one," Amory whispered. "I'm a cynical idealist." He stopped and wondered if that actually meant anything.

They arrived at the quiet, sleeping campus of Lawrenceville School and turned around to head back.

"This ride is really good, isn't it?" Tom said after a moment.

"Yes; it's a perfect ending, it's a knockout; everything's wonderful tonight. Oh, for a hot, lazy summer and Isabelle!"

"Oh, you and your Isabelle! I'll bet she's a simple one... let's say some poetry."

So Amory recited "The Ode to a Nightingale" to the bushes they walked by.

"I'll never be a poet," Amory said when he was done. "I'm really not sensual enough for it. There are only a handful of clear things that strike me as fundamentally beautiful: women, spring nights, music in the darkness, the ocean. I don't pick up on the nuanced details like 'silver-snarling trumpets.' I might become an intellectual, but I'll never create anything beyond average poetry."

They drove into Princeton just as the sun painted colorful patterns across the sky behind the graduate school, and rushed to take a refreshing shower that would have to substitute for sleep. By midday, alumni dressed in vibrant costumes filled the streets with their bands and singing groups, and inside the tents there was a grand reunion beneath the orange-and-black banners that fluttered and pulled in the wind. Amory gazed for a long time at one house that displayed the sign "Sixty-nine." There, a small group of gray-haired men sat talking quietly while the graduating classes passed by in a sweeping display of life.

***

Under The Arc-Light

Then tragedy's emerald eyes suddenly stared at Amory over the edge of June. The night after his trip to Lawrenceville, a group headed to New York looking for adventure, and began the journey back to Princeton around midnight in two cars. It had been a lively party with everyone at different levels of intoxication. Amory was in the second car; they had taken the wrong route and gotten lost, so they were rushing to catch up with the others.

It was a clear night and the excitement of the open road filled Amory with energy. He could feel the beginnings of two verses of a poem taking shape in his thoughts.

The gray car slowly moved through the darkness toward the night, and no signs of life stirred as it passed by. Just as the calm ocean waters part before a shark in starlit and sparkling channels, rising to beautiful heights, the moonlit trees separated in pairs while night birds flapped their wings and called out across the air.

For a brief moment, the car paused by an inn glowing with lamps and shadows, a yellow inn beneath a yellow moon—then silence fell as the crescendo of laughter faded away. The car pulled out once more into the June winds, softening the shadows as the distance stretched ahead, then crushing the yellow shadows and turning them blue.

They came to an abrupt halt, and Amory looked up in surprise. A woman stood by the roadside, speaking to Alec who was behind the wheel. Later he would recall how her worn kimono made her look like a harpy, and the broken, hollow quality of her voice when she said:

"You Princeton boys?"

"Yes."

"Well, one of you has been killed here, and two others are nearly dead."

"My God!"

"Look!" She pointed and they stared in horror. Beneath the bright glow of a streetlight lay a body, face down in an expanding pool of blood.

They jumped out of the car. Amory couldn't stop thinking about the back of that head—that hair—that hair... and then they turned the body over.

"It's Dick—Dick Humbird!"

"Oh, Christ!"

"Feel his heart!"

Then the persistent voice of the old woman rang out in a kind of rasping victory:

"He's definitely dead. The car flipped over. Two of the men who weren't injured just brought the others inside, but there's nothing that can be done for this one."

Amory rushed into the house and the others followed, carrying a limp body that they placed on the sofa in the shabby little front parlor. Sloane, with his shoulder wounded, was lying on another couch. He was half delirious and kept mumbling something about a chemistry lecture at 8:10.

"I have no idea what happened," Ferrenby said, his voice tight with strain. "Dick was behind the wheel and refused to let anyone else drive; we kept telling him he'd had too much to drink—then we hit that terrible curve—oh, dear God!..." He collapsed face-first onto the floor and began sobbing uncontrollably.

The doctor had arrived, and Amory walked over to the couch, where someone handed him a sheet to cover the body. With sudden coldness, he lifted one of the hands and let it drop back limply. The forehead was cold, but the face still held some expression. He stared at the shoelaces—Dick had tied them that morning. He had tied them—and now he was this lifeless white form. All that was left of the charm and character of the Dick Humbird he had known—oh, it was all so terrible and undignified and earthly. All tragedy carries that element of the grotesque and ugly—so pointless, meaningless... the way animals die.... Amory was reminded of a cat that had lain horribly torn apart in some alley from his childhood.

"Someone go to Princeton with Ferrenby."

Amory walked through the door and felt a slight chill from the late night breeze—a wind that caused a damaged fender on the pile of twisted metal to make a mournful, metallic noise.

———————

Crescendo!

The next day, by a stroke of luck, flew by in a blur of activity. When Amory found himself alone, his thoughts inevitably drifted back to the image of that crimson mouth gaping strangely against the pale face, but with deliberate determination he layered current distractions over that memory and pushed it firmly out of his mind.

Isabelle and her mother drove into town at four o'clock, and they traveled up cheerful Prospect Avenue, through the lively crowd, to have tea at Cottage. The clubs were hosting their annual dinners that evening, so at seven he let a freshman escort her and made plans to meet her in the gymnasium at eleven, when the upperclassmen would be allowed into the freshman dance. She was everything he had hoped for, and he felt joyful and excited to make that night the focus of all his dreams. At nine o'clock the upper classes gathered in front of the clubs as the freshman torchlight parade moved wildly past, and Amory wondered if the formally dressed groups against the dark, dignified buildings and beneath the glow of the torches made the night as spectacular to the watching, cheering freshmen as it had been to him the previous year.

The following day brought another whirlwind of activity. They had lunch with a cheerful group of six in a private dining room at the club, while Isabelle and Amory gazed at each other lovingly over the fried chicken, knowing their love would last forever. They danced through the prom until five in the morning, and the unaccompanied men cut in on Isabelle with enthusiastic abandon that grew more spirited as the night wore on, their wine bottles hidden in overcoat pockets in the coat room helping old fatigue wait for another day. The line of unaccompanied men forms a remarkably uniform group. It practically moves as one entity. A dark-haired beauty dances past and there's a collective intake of breath as the wave pushes forward and someone smoother than the others darts out to cut in. But when the six-foot-tall girl (brought by Kaye from your class, whom he's been trying to introduce to you all evening) sweeps by, the line pulls back and the groups turn around to focus intently on distant corners of the hall, because Kaye, worried and sweating, appears pushing through the crowd looking for familiar faces.

"Listen, my friend, I have something really wonderful—"

"Sorry, Kaye, but I'm committed to this dance. I need to cut in on someone."

"Well, what's the next one?"

"What—ah—er—I swear I need to go cut in—find me when she has a dance free."

It thrilled Amory when Isabelle proposed they step away for a bit and take a drive in her car. For one wonderful hour that ended far too quickly, they cruised the quiet roads surrounding Princeton and shared their feelings with tentative excitement, speaking from just beneath the surface of their hearts. Amory felt unusually innocent and made no effort to kiss her.

The next day they traveled through the New Jersey countryside, had lunch in New York, and in the afternoon attended a problem play where Isabelle cried throughout the entire second act, which embarrassed Amory somewhat—though watching her filled him with affection. He felt the urge to lean over and kiss her tears away, and she quietly slipped her hand into his in the darkness so he could gently squeeze it.

Then at six they arrived at the Borges' summer house on Long Island, and Amory hurried upstairs to change into his dinner jacket. As he fastened his shirt studs, he realized he was enjoying life in a way he would probably never experience again. Everything felt sacred, touched by the glow of his youth. He had made it—he was among the best of his generation at Princeton. He was in love, and that love was returned. Turning on all the lights, he studied himself in the mirror, searching his reflection for the qualities that allowed him to see more clearly than most people, that gave him the ability to make firm decisions and follow his own will with confidence. There was little in his life now that he would have wanted to change. Oxford might have offered greater opportunities.

Quietly, he admired his reflection. How perfectly handsome he appeared, and how well the dinner jacket suited him. He walked into the hallway and paused at the top of the staircase, hearing footsteps approaching. It was Isabelle, and from the crown of her gleaming hair down to her small golden shoes, she had never looked so beautiful.

"Isabelle!" he shouted, almost without thinking, and stretched out his arms toward her. Just like in fairy tales, she rushed into his embrace, and in that brief moment when their lips first met, his pride reached its peak and his youthful self-centeredness hit its highest point.

Chapter 3. The Egotist Considers

"Ouch! Let me go!"

He let his arms fall to his sides.

"What's the matter?"

"Your shirt stud—it hurt me—look!" She gazed down at her neck, where a small blue mark about the size of a pea spoiled its pale smoothness.

"Oh, Isabelle," he scolded himself, "I'm an idiot. Really, I'm sorry—I shouldn't have held you so close."

She glanced up with irritation.

"Oh, Amory, of course you couldn't help it, and it didn't hurt much; but what are we going to do about it?"

"Do about it?" he asked. "Oh—that spot; it'll disappear in a moment."

"It's not," she said, after staring intently for a moment, "it's still there—and it looks like the Devil—oh, Amory, what are we going to do! It's exactly as tall as your shoulder."

"Massage it," he suggested, holding back the slightest urge to laugh.

She gently touched it with her fingertips, and then a tear formed in the corner of her eye and rolled down her cheek.

"Oh, Amory," she said despairingly, lifting up a deeply pitiful face, "I'll just make my entire neck turn bright red if I rub it. What am I going to do?"

A quote popped into his mind and he couldn't help but say it out loud.

"All the perfumes of Arabia will not whiten this little hand."

She looked up and the sparkle of the tear in her eye was like ice.

"You're not very sympathetic."

Amory misunderstood what she meant.

"Isabelle, darling, I think it'll—"

"Don't touch me!" she shouted. "Don't I have enough to worry about without you standing there laughing at me!"

Then he slipped again.

"Well, it is funny, Isabelle, and we were talking the other day about a sense of humor being—"

She was looking at him with something that wasn't quite a smile, but rather the faint, joyless shadow of a smile at the corners of her mouth.

"Oh, shut up!" she suddenly shouted, then ran down the hallway toward her room. Amory remained standing there, overwhelmed with regretful bewilderment.

"Damn!"

When Isabelle came back, she had draped a light shawl around her shoulders, and they walked down the stairs without speaking, a silence that continued throughout dinner.

"Isabelle," he said with clear irritation as they settled into the car, heading to a dance at the Greenwich Country Club, "you're upset, and I'm about to be as well. Let's kiss and make things right between us."

Isabelle thought about it with a heavy heart.

"I hate being laughed at," she said finally.

"I won't laugh anymore. I'm not laughing now, am I?"

"You did."

"Oh, don't be so overly emotional."

Her lips curved into a slight smile.

"I'll be anything I want."

Amory struggled to keep his composure. He realized he didn't have a shred of genuine affection for Isabelle, but her distant attitude irritated him. He felt an urge to kiss her, to kiss her thoroughly, because he knew that would allow him to leave the next morning without a second thought. If he didn't kiss her, however, it would gnaw at him.... It would somehow undermine his self-image as someone who always got what he wanted. There was nothing dignified about being defeated by a formidable opponent like Isabelle, especially while begging for her attention.

Perhaps she sensed this. In any case, Amory observed the night that was meant to be the fulfillment of romance slip away with large moths flying above and the rich scent of gardens along the road, but without those fragmented words, those soft sighs....

Afterward they had supper with ginger ale and devil's food cake in the pantry, and Amory announced a decision.

"I'm leaving early in the morning."

"Why?"

"Why not?" he shot back.

"There's no need."

"However, I'm going."

"Well, if you insist on being ridiculous—"

"Oh, don't say it like that," he protested.

"—just because I won't let you kiss me. Do you think—"

"Listen, Isabelle," he cut her off, "you know that's not what this is about—even if we pretend it is. We've gotten to the point where we should either kiss—or—or—do nothing at all. It's not like you're saying no because you think it's wrong."

She hesitated.

"I honestly don't know what to make of you," she started, making a weak, contradictory effort to make peace. "You're so strange."

"How?"

"Well, I thought you had plenty of self-confidence and everything; don't you remember telling me the other day that you could accomplish anything you set your mind to, or obtain whatever you desired?"

Amory's face reddened. He had shared many things with her. "Yes."

"Well, you didn't seem to feel so self-confident tonight. Maybe you're just plain conceited."

"No, I'm not," he hesitated. "At Princeton—"

"Oh, you and Princeton! You act like it's the center of the universe the way you go on about it! Sure, maybe you can write better than anyone else for your Princeton newspaper; maybe the first-year students do think you're some big shot—"

"You don't understand—"

"Yes, I do," she cut him off. "I do, because you're constantly talking about yourself and I used to enjoy it; now I don't."

"Have I tonight?"

"That's exactly what I mean," Isabelle insisted. "You got all worked up tonight. You just sat there staring at my eyes. And another thing—I have to think about every word when I'm talking to you because you're so judgmental."

"I make you think, don't I?" Amory said again with a hint of pride.

"You're a nervous strain"—this emphatically—"and when you analyze every little emotion and instinct I just don't have them."

"I know." Amory acknowledged her point and shook his head in defeat.

"Let's go." She stood up.

He stood up distractedly and they walked to the bottom of the stairs.

"What train can I take?"

"There's one around 9:11 if you absolutely have to leave."

"Yes, I've got to go, really. Good night."

"Good night."

They stood at the top of the staircase, and as Amory walked into his room he thought he glimpsed the slightest hint of dissatisfaction on her face. He remained awake in the dark and pondered how deeply he felt—how much of his sudden misery was wounded pride—whether he was, in the end, naturally unsuited for love.

When he woke up, it was with a joyful rush of awareness. The early morning breeze moved the floral curtains at the windows, and he found himself confused about why he wasn't in his Princeton dorm room with his high school football photo hanging above the dresser and the Triangle Club poster on the opposite wall. Then the grandfather clock in the hallway chimed eight times, and the memories of the previous night flooded back to him. He jumped out of bed and got dressed quickly, moving like the wind; he had to leave the house before he encountered Isabelle. What had felt like a tragic event the night before now seemed like a tedious letdown. He finished getting dressed by eight-thirty, so he sat down near the window and realized that his heart felt more twisted and damaged than he had initially believed. How bitterly ironic the morning appeared to be!—bright and cheerful, filled with the fragrance of the garden; when he heard Mrs. Borge's voice coming from the sunroom downstairs, he wondered where Isabelle might be.

There was a knock at the door.

"The car will arrive at ten minutes before nine, sir."

He turned his attention back to looking outside and started repeating a line from Browning over and over again, almost automatically—the same verse he had once included in a letter to Isabelle:

> "Every unfulfilled life, you see,
> Remains incomplete, fragmented and rough;
> We haven't breathed deeply, laughed freely,
> Gone hungry, celebrated, felt despair—or found happiness."

But his life wouldn't be empty or meaningless. He found a dark sense of satisfaction in the thought that maybe she had never been anything more than what he had imagined her to be; that this moment represented her peak, that no one else would ever challenge her mind or make her truly think. Still, that was exactly what she had criticized him for; and suddenly Amory was exhausted by all the thinking, the endless thinking!

"Damn her!" he said bitterly, "she's ruined my entire year!"

The Superman Grows Careless

On a dusty September day, Amory reached Princeton and became part of the sweating masses of students preparing for entrance exams who filled the streets. It felt like a foolish way to begin his final years of school, spending four hours each morning in the stifling classroom of a prep school, absorbing the endless tedium of geometric curves and mathematical formulas. Mr. Rooney, who catered to the intellectually uninspired, led the class and chain-smoked countless Pall Mall cigarettes while sketching diagrams and solving mathematical problems from six in the morning until the stroke of midnight.

"Now, Langueduc, if I used that formula, where would my A point be?"

Langueduc lazily adjusts his six-foot-three frame of athletic build and attempts to focus.

"Oh—ah—I have no idea, Mr. Rooney."

"Oh, why of course, of course you can't use that formula. That's what I wanted you to say."

"Why, sure, of course."

"Do you see why?"

"You bet—I suppose so."

"If you don't see, tell me. I'm here to show you."

"Well, Mr. Rooney, if you don't mind, I wish you'd go over that again."

"Gladly. Now here's 'A'..."

The room was a perfect example of stupidity—two enormous stands for paper, Mr. Rooney in his shirt-sleeves standing in front of them, and slumped around on chairs, a dozen men: Fred Sloane, the pitcher, who absolutely had to become eligible; "Slim" Langueduc, who would defeat Yale this fall, if only he could achieve a measly fifty percent; McDowell, cheerful young sophomore, who thought it was quite an exciting thing to be getting tutored here with all these well-known athletes.

"Those unfortunate students who don't have any money for tutoring and must study throughout the semester are the ones I feel sorry for," he declared to Amory one day, with a weak sense of fellowship evident in the way his cigarette drooped from his colorless lips. "I imagine it must be so tedious, considering there's so much else to do in New York during the semester. I suppose they don't realize what they're missing, anyway." There was such an attitude of "you and I" about Mr. McDowell that Amory nearly pushed him out of the open window when he made this comment. ... Next February his mother would wonder why he didn't join a club and would increase his allowance... simple little fool....

Through the smoke and the atmosphere of serious, heavy solemnity that filled the room would come the unavoidable helpless cry:

"I don't get it! Repeat that, Mr. Rooney!" Most of the students were either too stupid or too careless to admit when they didn't understand something, and Amory fell into the latter category. He found it impossible to study conic sections; something about their calm and maddening respectability that seemed to breathe defiantly through Mr. Rooney's stuffy classrooms twisted their equations into unsolvable puzzles. He made one final attempt the night before with the classic wet towel method, and then peacefully took the exam, wondering sadly why all the excitement and drive from the previous spring had disappeared. Somehow, after losing Isabelle, the idea of college success had lost its hold on his imagination, and he faced the possibility of failing to pass his probationary status with calm acceptance, even though it would automatically mean his removal from the Princetonian board and the destruction of his chances for the Senior Council.

There was always his luck.

He yawned, wrote his honor pledge on the cover, and strolled out of the room.

"If you don't pass it," said Alec, who had just arrived, as they sat on the window seat in Amory's room and thought about a plan for decorating the walls, "you're the world's biggest fool. Your reputation will plummet like a falling elevator at the club and around campus."

"Oh, hell, I know it. Why rub it in?"

"Because you deserve it. Anyone who would risk what you were about to receive should be disqualified from becoming Princetonian chairman."

"Oh, forget about it," Amory objected. "Just watch and wait and keep quiet. I don't want everyone at the club questioning me about it, like I'm some prize potato being prepared for a vegetable competition." One evening a week later, Amory paused beneath his own window while heading to Renwick's, and noticing a light was on, he called up:

"Oh, Tom, any mail?"

Alec's head appeared against the yellow square of light.

"Yes, your result is here."

His heart pounded violently.

"What is it, blue or pink?"

"I don't know. You'd better come up."

He entered the room and walked directly to the table, then suddenly realized that other people were present in the room.

"'Hey there, Kerry." He was extremely polite. "Ah, Princeton men." They appeared to be mostly friends, so he grabbed the envelope labeled "Registrar's Office," and held it nervously in his hands.

"We have here quite a slip of paper."

"Open it, Amory."

"Just to be dramatic, I'll let you know that if it's blue, my name is withdrawn from the editorial board of the Prince, and my short career is over."

He stopped speaking and noticed Ferrenby's eyes for the first time, which had a hungry expression and were watching him with intense interest. Amory stared back at him deliberately.

"Watch my face, gentlemen, for the primitive emotions."

He ripped it open and held the piece of paper up to the light.

"Well?"

"Pink or blue?"

"Say what it is."

"We're all ears, Amory."

"Smile or swear—or something."

There was a pause... a small group of seconds passed by... then he looked again and another group moved forward into time.

"Blue as the sky, gentlemen...."

Aftermath

What Amory did that year from early September until late spring was so aimless and disconnected that it hardly seems worth documenting. He was, naturally, immediately regretful about what he had lost. His philosophy of success had collapsed around him, and he searched for explanations.

"Your own laziness," Alec said later.

"No—something deeper than that. I've started to feel that I was supposed to lose this opportunity."

"The guys at the club are pretty disappointed in you, you know; every person who doesn't follow through just makes our group that much weaker."

"I hate that point of view."

"Of course, with a little effort you could still stage a comeback."

"No—I'm finished—when it comes to having any influence in college."

"But, Amory, honestly, what makes me angriest isn't that you won't become chairman of the Prince or serve on the Senior Council, but simply that you didn't buckle down and pass that exam."

"Not me," Amory said slowly. "I'm angry at the actual situation. My own laziness fit perfectly with my approach, but my luck ran out."

"Your system broke, you mean."

"Maybe."

"Well, what are you planning to do? Find a better one quickly, or just waste the next two years as someone whose best days are behind them?"

"I don't know yet..."

"Oh, Amory, cheer up!"

"Maybe."

Amory's perspective, while risky, came close to being accurate. If we could map out his responses to his surroundings, the diagram would have looked like this, starting from his childhood:

The fundamental Amory.

Amory plus Beatrice.

Amory plus Beatrice plus Minneapolis.

Then St. Regis had torn him apart and made him start over from the beginning:

4. Amory plus St. Regis'.

5. Amory plus St. Regis' plus Princeton.

That had been his closest brush with success through following the rules. The essential Amory—lazy, creative, defiant—had almost been buried completely. He had played by the rules, he had achieved what he set out to do, but since his imagination wasn't fulfilled or captured by his own achievements, he had carelessly, almost by accident, thrown it all away and returned to being:

6. The fundamental Amory.

Financial

His Father Passed Away Peacefully And Without Fanfare During Thanksgiving. The strange contrast between death and the beautiful scenery of Lake Geneva, as well as his mother's composed and reserved demeanor, struck him as oddly fascinating, and he observed the funeral with detached amusement. He concluded that burial was ultimately better than cremation, and he found himself smiling when he remembered his childhood preference for slow decay high up in a tree. The day following the ceremony, he entertained himself in the grand library by reclining on a sofa in elegant funeral poses, attempting to decide whether he would, when his time arrived, be discovered with his arms folded reverently across his chest (Monsignor Darcy had previously recommended this position as the most dignified), or with his hands clasped behind his head, a more unconventional and Byronic pose.

What fascinated him far more than his father's final departure from earthly matters was a three-way discussion between Beatrice, Mr. Barton from the law firm Barton and Krogman, and himself that occurred several days following the funeral. For the first time, he gained real understanding of the family's financial situation and grasped what a substantial fortune had previously been under his father's control. He picked up a ledger marked "1906" and examined it quite thoroughly. The total spending for that year had reached slightly more than one hundred and ten thousand dollars. Forty thousand of this amount had been Beatrice's personal income, and no effort had been made to track its use: everything appeared under the category "Drafts, checks, and letters of credit forwarded to Beatrice Blaine." The distribution of the remaining funds was documented in considerable detail: the taxes and renovations for the Lake Geneva property had totaled nearly nine thousand dollars; the general maintenance costs, including Beatrice's electric vehicle and a French automobile purchased that year, exceeded thirty-five thousand dollars. The remainder was completely accounted for, and there were consistently entries that didn't balance properly on the credit side of the ledger.

When Amory looked at the 1912 financial records, he was stunned to see how much their bond investments had declined and how dramatically their income had dropped. While Beatrice's personal funds hadn't suffered quite as severely, it was clear that his father had spent the previous year making several disastrous investments in oil ventures. Very little oil had actually been extracted, but Stephen Blaine had suffered significant financial losses. The following years continued to show similar declines, and for the first time, Beatrice had started dipping into her own money to maintain their household expenses. Even so, her medical bills alone for 1913 had exceeded nine thousand dollars.

Mr. Barton had only a vague and confused understanding of the exact state of affairs. There had been recent investments whose outcomes were currently uncertain, and he suspected there were additional speculations and transactions that had taken place without his knowledge or input.

It took several months before Beatrice finally wrote to Amory explaining the complete financial situation. All that remained of the Blaine and O'Hara family wealth was the property at Lake Geneva and roughly half a million dollars, which was currently invested in relatively safe securities earning six percent interest. Beatrice mentioned in her letter that she was moving the money into railroad and streetcar bonds as quickly as she could manage the transfers.

"I'm absolutely certain," she wrote to Amory, "that if there's one thing we can be sure of, it's that people won't stay in one place. This Ford fellow has definitely made the most of that concept. So I'm telling Mr. Barton to focus on things like Northern Pacific and these Rapid Transit Companies, as they call the streetcars. I'll never forgive myself for not buying Bethlehem Steel. I've heard the most incredible stories. You really should go into finance, Amory. I'm convinced you'd love it. You start as a messenger or a teller, I think, and from there you move up—practically without limit. I'm certain if I were a man I'd enjoy handling money; it's become quite an obsession with me in my old age. Before I continue, I want to talk about something. A Mrs. Bispam, an overly friendly little woman I met at a tea recently, told me that her son, who's at Yale, wrote her that all the boys there wear their summer underwear throughout the winter, and also walk around with wet hair and low shoes on the coldest days. Now, Amory, I don't know if that's a trend at Princeton as well, but I don't want you to be so foolish. It not only makes a young man susceptible to pneumonia and polio, but to all kinds of lung problems, which you're especially prone to. You can't take risks with your health. I've learned that lesson. I won't make myself look foolish like some mothers surely do by demanding that you wear galoshes, though I remember one Christmas when you wore them constantly without fastening a single buckle, making such a strange swishing noise, and you refused to buckle them because it wasn't the fashionable thing to do. The very next Christmas you wouldn't even wear rubber boots, despite my pleading. You're almost twenty years old now, dear, and I can't be there constantly to see whether you're doing the smart thing.

"This has been a very practical letter. I warned you in my last one that not having money to do what one wants makes a person quite dull and ordinary, but there's still enough for everything if we're not too wasteful. Take care of yourself, my dear boy, and please try to write at least once a week, because I imagine all kinds of terrible things when I don't hear from you. Affectionately, MOTHER."

First Appearance of The Term "Personage"

Monsignor Darcy invited Amory to spend a week at Christmas at the Stuart palace on the Hudson, where they engaged in lengthy conversations by the open fireplace. Monsignor had gained some weight and his character had grown along with his physical presence, and Amory found comfort and peace settling into a low, padded armchair and sharing the mature pleasure of smoking a cigar with him.

"I've felt like dropping out of college, Monsignor."

"Why?"

"My entire career has been destroyed; you probably think it's trivial and everything, but—"

"Not at all petty. I think it's most important. I want to hear the whole thing. Everything you've been doing since I saw you last."

Amory spoke at length; he explored thoroughly the dismantling of his self-centered ways of thinking, and within thirty minutes the lifeless tone had disappeared from his voice.

"What would you do if you left college?" asked Monsignor.

"I'm not sure. I'd love to travel, but obviously this exhausting war makes that impossible. Besides, mother would be devastated if I didn't graduate. I'm completely lost. Kerry Holiday wants me to come with him and join the Lafayette Esquadrille."

"You know you wouldn't like to go."

"Sometimes I would—tonight I'd go in a second."

"Well, you'd have to be much more tired of living than I believe you are. I know you."

"I'm afraid you do," Amory agreed reluctantly. "It just seemed like an easy way out of everything—when I think of another pointless, tedious year."

"Yes, I know; but to be honest with you, I'm not concerned about you; it seems to me that you're developing in a completely natural way."

"No," Amory protested. "I've lost half of who I am in just one year."

"Not at all!" Monsignor scoffed. "You've simply lost a great deal of vanity and nothing more."

"Good Lord! I feel like I've been through another year of high school at St. Regis all over again."

"No." Monsignor shook his head. "That was unfortunate; this has been beneficial. Whatever worthwhile comes your way won't be through the paths you were exploring last year."

"What could be more pointless than my current lack of energy?"

"Maybe by itself... but you're growing. This has given you time to reflect and you're letting go of much of your old baggage about success and the superman and everything. People like us can't embrace entire theories, as you did. If we can handle the next task, and have an hour each day to think, we can achieve wonders, but when it comes to any arrogant plan of blind control—we'd just make fools of ourselves."

"But, Monsignor, I can't do the next thing."

"Amory, just between us, I've only recently figured out how to do it myself. I can handle a hundred different tasks that come after the immediate one, but I trip up on that next step, just like you struggled with mathematics this semester."

"Why do we have to do the next thing? It never seems like the kind of thing I should be doing."

"We have to do it because we're not personalities, but personages."

"That's a good line—what do you mean?"

"A personality is what you believed you were, what these Kerry and Sloane individuals you mention clearly represent. Personality is almost entirely a physical phenomenon; it diminishes the people it influences—I've witnessed it disappear during prolonged illness. But while a personality remains active, it takes precedence over 'what comes next.' A personage, however, accumulates meaning. He is never considered separately from his accomplishments. He serves as a framework upon which countless achievements have been displayed—sometimes brilliant achievements, like ours; but he employs those achievements with a calculated mindset behind them."

"And several of my most brilliant possessions had abandoned me when I needed them most." Amory pursued the comparison with enthusiasm.

"Yes, that's exactly it; when you feel that your accumulated reputation and abilities and everything else are on display, you never need to worry about anyone; you can handle them easily."

"But on the flip side, if I don't have my possessions, I'm completely helpless!"

"Absolutely."

"That's certainly an idea."

"Now you have a fresh beginning—a start that Kerry or Sloane can never constitutionally achieve. You knocked down three or four decorations, and in a moment of anger, you swept away all the rest. What matters now is gathering some new ones, and the further ahead you plan for this collecting, the better off you'll be. But remember, focus on the next step!"

"How clearly you can explain things!"

So they talked, often about themselves, sometimes about philosophy and religion, and life as either a game or a mystery. The priest seemed to understand Amory's thoughts before they were even clear in his own mind, so closely aligned were their ways of thinking.

"Why do I make lists?" Amory asked him one night. "Lists of all kinds of things?"

"Because you're a medievalist," Monsignor answered. "We both are. It's the passion for classifying and finding a type."

"It's a desire to get something definite."

"It's the core of academic philosophy."

"I was starting to think I was becoming eccentric until I came up here. It was just an act, I suppose."

"Don't worry about that; for you, not posing might be the biggest pose of all. Pose—"

"Yes?"

"But do the next thing."

After Amory returned to college, he received several letters from Monsignor that provided him with more material to feed his ego.

I'm worried that I gave you too much confidence about your certain safety, and you need to remember that I did this because I believe in your capacity for hard work, not because I foolishly think you'll succeed without any struggle. There are certain aspects of your character that you'll need to accept about yourself, though you should be cautious about admitting them to other people. You're practical rather than sentimental, almost unable to show deep affection, clever without being sneaky, and conceited without being truly proud.

Don't allow yourself to feel worthless; many times throughout your life you'll actually be at your lowest point when you think most highly of yourself; and don't worry about losing your "personality," as you keep calling it; at fifteen you had the brightness of early morning, at twenty you'll start to have the sad brilliance of the moon, and when you reach my age you'll radiate, as I do, the warm golden glow of 4 P.M.

If you write letters to me, please make them genuine ones. Your most recent letter, that essay about architecture, was absolutely terrible—so pretentiously intellectual that I imagine you living in a mental and emotional void; and be careful not to try categorizing people too rigidly into types; you'll discover that throughout their youth they'll frustratingly keep moving from one category to another, and by slapping a condescending label on everyone you encounter you're simply creating a Jack-in-the-box that will pop up and mock you when you start having real conflicts with the world. Looking up to someone like Leonardo da Vinci would serve as a better guide for you right now.

You're destined to experience ups and downs, just as I did when I was young, but do maintain your mental clarity, and if foolish people or wise ones dare to judge you, don't be too hard on yourself.

You mention that social expectations are all that really keep you on the right path regarding this "woman proposition"; but it's more than that, Amory; it's the fear that once you start something you won't be able to stop; you would lose all control, and I know what I'm talking about; it's that almost miraculous sixth sense that helps you recognize evil, it's the partially understood fear of God in your heart.

Whatever your calling turns out to be—religion, architecture, literature—I'm convinced you'd be much safer connected to the Church, but I won't risk losing my influence over you by debating this point even though I'm privately certain that the "black chasm of Romanism" opens up beneath you. Please write to me soon.

With affectionate regards,

THAYER DARCY.

Even Amory's reading lost its appeal during this time; he explored deeper into the obscure corners of literature: Huysmans, Walter Pater, Theophile Gautier, and the more provocative passages of Rabelais, Boccaccio, Petronius, and Suetonius. During one week, driven by simple curiosity, he examined the personal book collections of his fellow students and discovered that Sloane's library was as representative as any other: complete sets of Kipling, O. Henry, John Fox, Jr., and Richard Harding Davis; "What Every Middle-Aged Woman Ought to Know," "The Spell of the Yukon"; a "gift" edition of James Whitcomb Riley, a collection of worn, marked-up textbooks, and, to his amazement, one of his own recent literary finds, the collected poems of Rupert

Brooke.

Together with Tom D'Invilliers, he searched among Princeton's brightest minds for someone who could establish the Great American Poetic Tradition.

The student body itself was much more fascinating that year than the completely conventional Princeton of two years earlier. Things had become surprisingly lively, though this came at the cost of much of the natural appeal of freshman year. In the old Princeton they never would have found Tanaduke Wylie. Tanaduke was a sophomore, with enormous ears and a habit of saying, "The earth swirls down through the ominous moons of preconsidered generations!" that made them somewhat wonder why it didn't sound entirely clear, but never doubt that it was the expression of a superior soul. At least that's how Tom and Amory saw him. They told him with complete sincerity that he had a mind like Shelley's, and showcased his extremely free verse and prose poetry in the Nassau Literary Magazine. But Tanaduke's brilliance absorbed the many influences of the era, and he embraced the Bohemian lifestyle, much to their disappointment. He spoke of Greenwich Village now instead of "noon-swirled moons," and encountered winter muses, non-academic, and sheltered by Forty-second Street and Broadway, instead of the Shelleyan dream-figures with whom he had entertained their eager appreciation. So they gave up Tanaduke to the futurists, deciding that he and his bright ties would fare better there. Tom offered him the final suggestion that he should stop writing for two years and read the complete works of Alexander Pope four times, but on Amory's observation that Pope for Tanaduke was like foot-ease for stomach trouble, they backed away with laughter, and called it a coin flip whether this genius was too great or too small for them.

Amory deliberately stayed away from the popular professors who handed out clever sayings and small portions of intellectual stimulation to their groups of followers each evening, looking down on this practice with some contempt. He also felt let down by the atmosphere of widespread doubt about every topic that appeared to be connected with overly academic personalities; his views formed into a small satirical piece titled "In a Lecture-Room," which he convinced Tom to publish in the Nassau Lit.

"Good morning, Fool...
Three times a week
You hold us captive while you speak,
Taunting our eager minds with the
Smooth 'yes' answers of your philosophy...
Well, here we are, your hundred followers,
Start up, play on, pour it out... we drift off...
You are a scholar, so they claim;
You pieced together the other day
A course outline, from what we understand
Of some long-forgotten manuscript;
You had sniffed through decades of mustiness,
Filling your nose with dust,
And then, getting up from your knees,
Published it all in one enormous sneeze...
But here's a classmate to my right,
An Eager Fool, thought to be smart;
Questioner extraordinaire.... How he'll stand there,
With serious expression and restless hand,
After this class, telling you
He stayed up all night and dug through
Your book.... Oh, you'll act modest and he
Will pretend to be brilliant,
And both being show-offs, you'll grin and smirk,
And sneer, and hurry back to work....

It was a week ago today, sir, that you returned
An essay of mine, from which I discovered
(Through various notes in the margins
Which you had written) that I violated
The most important rules of literary criticism
For cheap and thoughtless humor....
'Are you completely certain that this is accurate?'
And

'Shaw is not a reliable source!'
But Eager Fool, with what he's submitted,
Destroys your grading standards.

Still—still I encounter you here and there...
When Shakespeare's performed you occupy a seat,
And some dead, outdated actor
Captivates the intellectual snob you are...
A revolutionary speaker comes and disturbs
The non-believing establishment?
You're there representing Common Sense,
Mouth agape, in the crowd.
And, sometimes, even religious services attract
That self-aware tolerance of yours,
That generous and glowing view of truth
(Including Kant and General Booth...)
And so from surprise to surprise you exist,
A shallow, weak yes-man...

The hour's finished... and awakened from slumber
One hundred blessed students
Rob you of a word or two with feet
That pound down the loud hallways...
Forget on this narrow-minded world
The Great Boredom that created you."

In April, Kerry Holiday dropped out of college and sailed to France to join the Lafayette Esquadrille. Amory's jealousy and respect for this decision was overshadowed by his own experience, one he never managed to properly understand or appreciate, but which continued to trouble him for the next three years.

The Devil

They left Healy's at twelve and took a taxi to Bistolary's. The group included Axia Marlowe and Phoebe Column from the Summer Garden show, along with Fred Sloane and Amory. The night was still so early that they were buzzing with extra energy, and they burst into the cafe like wild party-goers celebrating with abandon.

"Table for four in the middle of the floor," shouted Phoebe. "Hurry up, sweetheart, tell them we're here!"

"Tell them to play 'Admiration'!" Sloane yelled. "You two go ahead and order; Phoebe and I are going to dance," and they disappeared into the chaotic crowd. Axia and Amory, who had only known each other for an hour, pushed behind a waiter to get a table with a good view; they sat down there and watched.

"There's Findle Margotson, from New Haven!" she shouted over the noise. "Hey, Findle! Whoo-ee!"

"Oh, Axia!" he called out in greeting. "Come on over to our table." "No!" Amory whispered.

"I can't do it, Findle; I'm with someone else! Call me tomorrow around one o'clock!"

Findle, an unremarkable regular at Bisty's, mumbled an unclear response and turned back to the stunning blonde he was trying to guide around the room.

"There's a natural damn fool," Amory remarked.

"Oh, he's fine. Here comes the old rickety waiter. If you're asking me, I'll have a double Daiquiri."

"Make it four."

The crowd swirled and shifted constantly. Most people were college students, mixed with some of Broadway's male outcasts and two types of women, the better of which were chorus girls. Overall, it was a typical crowd, and their group was just as typical as any other. About three-quarters of the entire scene was just for show and therefore harmless, ending at the cafe door in time to catch the five o'clock train back to Yale or Princeton; about one-quarter carried on into the darker hours and picked up strange experiences from unusual places. Their group was supposed to be one of the harmless ones. Fred Sloane and Phoebe Column were old friends; Axia and Amory were new ones. But strange events can unfold even in the dead of night, and the unexpected, which appears least likely in the cafe—that home of the ordinary and predictable—was about to ruin the fading romance of Broadway for him. What happened was so incredibly terrible, so unbelievable, that afterward he never considered it a real experience; instead, it was like a scene from a foggy tragedy, performed far behind a curtain, and he knew it held some definite meaning.

Around one o'clock they headed to Maxim's, and by two they found themselves at Deviniere's. Sloane had been drinking steadily and was in a wobbly state of excitement, but Amory remained frustratingly sober; they hadn't encountered any of those seasoned, wealthy champagne buyers who typically helped fund their New York celebrations. They had just finished dancing and were making their way back to their seats when Amory noticed that someone at a nearby table was staring at him. He turned and looked casually... it was a middle-aged man wearing a brown business suit, sitting somewhat isolated at his own table and watching their group with intense focus. When Amory looked his way, the man gave a slight smile. Amory turned to Fred, who was just taking his seat.

"Who's that pale fool watching us?" he complained indignantly.

"Where?" Sloane shouted. "We'll have him kicked out!" He stood up and wobbled back and forth, gripping his chair for support. "Where is he?"

Axia and Phoebe suddenly leaned toward each other and whispered across the table, and before Amory knew what was happening, they were all heading toward the door.

"Where to now?"

"Let's go up to the apartment," Phoebe suggested. "We have brandy and champagne—and everything's moving so slowly down here tonight."

Amory thought it over quickly. He hadn't been drinking, and he figured that if he didn't have any more, it would be reasonably appropriate for him to tag along with the group. Actually, it might be the right thing to do to keep watch over Sloane, who wasn't in any condition to think clearly for himself. So he took Axia's arm and, crowding together into a taxi, they drove out through the numbered streets and pulled up at a tall, white-stone apartment building. ... He would never forget that street.... It was a wide street, bordered on both sides with similar tall, white-stone buildings, spotted with dark windows; they extended as far as you could see, bathed in bright moonlight that gave them a chalky white appearance. He pictured each one having an elevator and a Black attendant and a rack for keys; each one being eight stories tall and filled with three and four room apartments. He felt quite relieved to step into the warmth of Phoebe's living room and settle onto a couch, while the women went searching for food.

"Phoebe's really great," Sloane whispered confidentially.

"I'm only staying for half an hour," Amory said firmly. He wondered if he sounded self-righteous.

"What the hell are you talking about," Sloane protested. "We're here now—let's not rush."

"I don't like this place," Amory said sulkily, "and I don't want any food."

Phoebe came back carrying sandwiches, a bottle of brandy, a siphon, and four glasses.

"Amory, pour them out," she said, "and we'll drink to Fred Sloane, who has a rare, distinguished edge."

"Yes," said Axia, walking into the room, "and Amory. I like Amory." She settled down next to him and rested her blonde head against his shoulder.

"I'll pour," said Sloane; "you use the siphon, Phoebe."

They filled the tray with glasses.

"Ready, here she goes!"

Amory paused, holding his glass.

126

There was a moment when temptation washed over him like warm wind, his imagination igniting into flames as he took the glass from Phoebe's hand. That was all it lasted; the instant his decision crystallized, he glanced up and spotted, ten yards away, the man who had been in the cafe, and with his startled jump the glass tumbled from his raised hand. There the man half sat, half reclined against a stack of pillows on the corner divan. His face appeared cast in the same yellow wax as it had in the cafe, not the dull, pasty shade of a corpse—rather a kind of masculine pallor— nor sickly, you would have said; but like a robust man who had labored in a mine or worked night shifts in a humid climate. Amory examined him thoroughly and later he could have sketched him somewhat accurately, down to the smallest details. His mouth was the type that people call honest, and he possessed steady gray eyes that shifted slowly from one member of their group to another, with just a hint of an inquiring expression. Amory observed his hands; they weren't delicate at all, but they possessed adaptability and a subtle strength... they were restless hands that rested lightly on the cushions and moved continuously with small jerky openings and closings. Then, abruptly, Amory noticed the feet, and with a surge of blood to his head he realized he was frightened. The feet were completely wrong... with a kind of wrongness that he sensed rather than understood.... It was like frailty in a virtuous woman, or blood on silk; one of those dreadful contradictions that disturb small things in the depths of the mind. He wore no shoes, but instead, a type of half moccasin, pointed, however, like the footwear they wore in the fourteenth century, and with the small ends curling upward. They were a dark brown and his toes appeared to fill them completely.... They were unspeakably horrible....

He must have said something, or his expression must have revealed something, because Axia's voice emerged from the darkness with an unusual kindness.

"Well, look at Amory! Poor old Amory's sick—old head spinning?"

"Look at that man!" Amory shouted, pointing toward the corner couch.

"You mean that purple zebra!" Axia screamed playfully. "Ooo-ee! Amory's got a purple zebra watching him!"

Sloane laughed vacantly.

"Did that old zebra get you, Amory?"

There was a silence.... The man looked at Amory with a puzzled expression.... Then he could faintly hear human voices:

"I thought you weren't drinking," Axia said with sarcasm, but hearing her voice was comforting; the entire couch where the man lay seemed to pulse with life, vibrant like heat shimmering above hot pavement, like squirming earthworms....

"Come back! Come back!" Axia's hand landed on his arm. "Amory, sweetheart, you're not leaving, are you, Amory!" He had already made it halfway to the door.

"Come on, Amory, stick with us!"

"Are you sick?"

"Sit down for a moment!"

"Take some water."

"Take a little brandy...."

The elevator was nearby, and the young Black man was half asleep, his skin pale to a sickly bronze color... Axia's pleading voice drifted down the elevator shaft. Those feet... those feet...

As they descended to the lower floor, their feet became visible in the pale electric light that illuminated the tiled hallway.

In The Alley

Down the long street, the moon appeared, and Amory turned away from it and began walking. Ten, fifteen steps behind him, footsteps echoed. They sounded like slow dripping, with just the faintest persistence in their rhythm. Amory's shadow stretched about ten feet in front of him, and the soft-soled shoes were likely that same distance behind. With a child's instinct, Amory pressed himself against the blue darkness beneath the white buildings, cutting through the moonlight for desperate moments, at one point breaking into an awkward, stumbling jog. Then he stopped abruptly; he had to maintain control, he told himself. His lips felt dry, so he moistened them with his tongue.

If he encountered anyone good—were there any good people left in the world, or did they all live in white apartment buildings now? Was everyone being followed in the moonlight? But if he met someone good who would understand what he meant and hear this terrible scuffling... then the scuffling suddenly grew closer, and a dark cloud drifted over the moon. When the pale light once again swept across the building edges, it was almost right beside him, and Amory thought he heard quiet breathing. Suddenly he realized that the footsteps weren't behind him, had never been behind him—they were ahead, and he wasn't escaping but following... following. He started to run blindly, his heart pounding heavily, his hands clenched into fists. Far ahead, a dark shape appeared, slowly taking the form of a human figure. But Amory was beyond caring about that now; he turned off the street and rushed into an alley that was narrow and dark and reeked of old decay. He twisted through a long, winding stretch of blackness, where the moonlight was blocked out except for tiny gleams and spots... then suddenly collapsed, gasping, into a corner by a fence, completely drained. The footsteps ahead came to a stop, and he could hear them shifting slightly with a steady rhythm, like waves lapping against a dock.

He buried his face in his hands and covered his eyes and ears as completely as possible. Throughout this entire experience, it never crossed his mind that he might be delirious or intoxicated. He possessed a sense of reality that physical objects could never provide him. His mind seemed to surrender willingly to this experience, and it aligned perfectly with everything that had ever happened in his life before. It didn't confuse him. It resembled a mathematical problem whose answer he could see written down, yet whose solution remained beyond his understanding. He had moved far past the point of horror. He had broken through that thin layer and now existed in a place where the sound of footsteps and the terror of white walls were actual, breathing entities that he had no choice but to accept. Only deep within his spirit did a small flame dance and cry out that something was dragging him downward, attempting to force him through a doorway and lock it shut behind him. Once that door closed, there would be nothing left except the sound of footsteps and white structures bathed in moonlight, and perhaps he would become one of those footsteps himself.

During the five or ten minutes he waited in the shadow of the fence, there was somehow this fire... that was as close as he could describe it later. He remembered calling out loud:

"I need someone stupid. Oh, send me someone stupid!" He directed this plea toward the black fence across from him, where footsteps shuffled back and forth in the shadows. He figured that "stupid" and "good" had somehow gotten mixed up in his mind through past experiences. When he called out like this, it wasn't a deliberate choice at all—his willpower had already made him turn away from the moving figure in the street. Instead, it was almost pure instinct that made him call out, just layers upon layers of inherited tradition or some desperate prayer drifting across the night. Then something rang out like a distant gong being struck, and in that moment a face flashed before his eyes above those two feet—a face that was pale and twisted with a kind of endless evil that warped it like a flame bending in the wind. But he recognized, in that brief instant while the gong echoed and vibrated, that it was the face of Dick Humbird.

Minutes later he jumped to his feet, vaguely realizing that the sounds had stopped and that he was by himself in the darkening alley. The air was cold, and he began running steadily toward the light that marked the street at the far end.

At The Window

It was late morning when he woke to find the telephone beside his hotel bed ringing frantically, and he recalled that he had requested an eleven o'clock wake-up call. Sloane was snoring loudly, his clothing scattered in a heap next to his bed. They got dressed and had breakfast without speaking, then wandered outside to get some fresh air. Amory's thoughts moved sluggishly as he tried to process what had occurred and extract the basic facts from the jumbled images crowding his memory. If the morning had been cold and overcast, he might have been able to grasp control of the past immediately, but this was one of those days that New York sometimes experiences in May, when the atmosphere on Fifth Avenue feels like delicate, light wine. How much or how little Sloane recalled, Amory had no desire to discover; Sloane clearly didn't share the nervous anxiety that was consuming Amory and driving his thoughts back and forth like a screaming saw.

Then Broadway opened up before them, and with the chaotic mix of sounds and the made-up faces, a sudden wave of nausea swept over Amory.

"For God's sake, let's go back! Let's get off of this—this place!"

Sloane stared at him in astonishment.

"What do you mean?"

"This street is awful! Come on! Let's get back to the Avenue!"

"Are you seriously telling me," Sloane said matter-of-factly, "that because you had some kind of stomach problem that made you act completely crazy last night, you're never going to perform on Broadway again?"

At the same time, Amory grouped him with the masses, and he no longer appeared to be Sloane with his charming wit and cheerful character, but simply one of the sinister faces that spun along in the murky current.

"Man!" he yelled so loudly that the people standing on the corner turned around and watched them with their eyes, "it's disgusting, and if you can't see that, you're disgusting too!"

"I can't help it," Sloane said stubbornly. "What's wrong with you? Is guilt catching up with you? You'd be in terrible shape if you had actually gone through with our plan."

"I'm leaving, Fred," Amory said quietly. His legs were trembling beneath him, and he realized that if he remained on this street for even another moment, he would collapse right where he stood. "I'll be at the Vanderbilt for lunch." He walked away quickly and headed toward Fifth Avenue. Once he returned to the hotel, he felt somewhat better, but when he entered the barber shop with the intention of getting a head massage, the scent of the powders and tonics reminded him of Axia's sideways, knowing smile, and he departed in haste. At the entrance to his room, a sudden darkness surrounded him like a river splitting in two.

When he regained consciousness, he realized that several hours had gone by. He collapsed onto the bed and turned face-down, gripped by a paralyzing fear that he was losing his mind. He craved human contact—people, anyone who was rational and ordinary and decent. He remained motionless for an unknown length of time. He could sense the small blood vessels on his forehead bulging, and his terror had solidified around him like hardened plaster. He felt himself rising once more through the fragile layer of nightmare, and only now could he make out the dim twilight he was emerging from. He must have drifted off to sleep again, because the next thing he remembered was settling the hotel bill and climbing into a taxi outside the entrance. Rain was pouring down in sheets.

On the train to Princeton, he didn't recognize anyone, just a crowd of exhausted-looking people from Philadelphia. The sight of a heavily made-up woman sitting across the aisle made him feel sick again, so he moved to a different car and tried to focus on an article in a popular magazine. He kept reading the same paragraphs repeatedly, so he gave up on that effort and leaned over tiredly, pressing his feverish forehead against the wet window. The car was designated for smokers and felt hot and stuffy, filled with the various odors from the state's diverse population; he opened a window and shivered as a cloud of fog drifted in around him. The two-hour journey felt like it lasted for days, and he almost cried out with relief when Princeton's towers appeared beside him and the golden rectangles of light shone through the blue rain.

Tom stood in the center of the room, thoughtfully relighting the stub of his cigar. Amory thought he seemed rather relieved when he saw him.

"I had one hell of a dream about you last night," came the raspy voice through the cigar smoke. "I got the feeling you were in some kind of trouble."

"Don't tell me about it!" Amory nearly screamed. "Don't say a word; I'm exhausted and completely drained."

Tom gave him a strange look and then settled into a chair and opened his Italian notebook. Amory tossed his coat and hat onto the floor, loosened his collar, and grabbed a Wells novel randomly from the shelf. "Wells is sensible," he thought, "and if he doesn't work I'll read Rupert Brooke."

Half an hour went by. Outside, the wind picked up, and Amory jumped as the wet branches moved and scraped against the window with their fingertips. Tom was absorbed in his work, and inside the room only the occasional strike of a match or the creak of leather as they moved in their chairs disturbed the silence. Then the change came like a flash of lightning in a jagged line. Amory sat straight up, ice-cold and motionless in his chair. Tom was staring at him with his mouth hanging open, his eyes locked in place.

"God help us!" Amory cried.

"Oh my God!" Tom yelled, "look behind you!" In an instant, Amory spun around. All he could see was the dark window glass. "It's not there anymore," Tom's voice came a moment later, still filled with fear. "Something was watching you."

Shaking uncontrollably, Amory collapsed back into his chair.

"I have to tell you," he said. "I've had an absolutely incredible experience. I think I've—I've encountered the devil or—something similar to him. What face did you just see?—or no," he added quickly, "don't tell me!"

And he told Tom the entire story. By the time he finished, it was midnight, and afterward, with every light blazing, two drowsy, trembling boys took turns reading aloud to each other from "The New Machiavelli," until dawn emerged from behind Witherspoon Hall, and the Princetonian newspaper slumped against the door, and the May birds welcomed the sun shining on the previous night's rain.

Chapter 4. Narcissus Off Duty

During Princeton's period of change—specifically during Amory's final two years there—while he watched the university transform and expand and live up to its Gothic splendor through better methods than nighttime parades, certain people arrived who stirred the institution to its very core. Some of these individuals had been first-year students alongside Amory, wild first-year students at that; others belonged to the class below his; and it was at the start of his final year, gathered around small tables at the Nassau Inn, that they began openly questioning the institutions that Amory and countless students before him had questioned privately for so long. Initially, and somewhat by chance, they discovered certain books—a specific type of biographical novel that Amory labeled "quest" books. In these "quest" books, the protagonist began life equipped with the finest tools and openly planned to use them as such tools are typically employed: to push their owners forward as selfishly and blindly as possible. However, the heroes of these "quest" books realized there might be a more noble purpose for these abilities. "None Other Gods," "Sinister Street," and "The Research Magnificent" served as examples of such literature; it was the last of these three that captivated Burne Holiday and made him question, at the beginning of his senior year, whether it was worthwhile to continue being a diplomatic ruler within his club on Prospect Avenue and enjoying the spotlight of class leadership. Burne discovered his path distinctly through aristocratic channels. Amory had maintained a casual, distant acquaintance with him through Kerry, but their friendship didn't truly begin until January of their senior year.

"Did you hear the news?" Tom said as he walked in late one rainy evening, wearing that victorious expression he always had after winning a good argument.

"No. Did someone fail out? Or did another ship go down?"

"Even worse than that. Roughly one-third of the junior class students are planning to quit their clubs."

"What!"

"Actual fact!"

"Why!"

"Spirit of reform and all that. Burne Holiday is behind it. The club presidents are holding a meeting tonight to see if they can find a way to work together to fight it."

"Well, what's the point of this whole thing?"

"Oh, clubs that harm Princeton's democratic values; they're expensive; they create social divisions, consume time; the usual complaints you sometimes hear from disappointed sophomores. Woodrow believed they should be eliminated and all that."

"But this is the real thing?"

"Absolutely. I think it'll go through."

"For Pete's sake, tell me more about it."

"Well," Tom started, "it appears that the concept emerged at the same time in multiple minds. I was speaking with Burne recently, and he maintains that it's a natural conclusion when an intelligent person reflects deeply enough on the social structure. They had a 'discussion group' and the idea of eliminating the clubs was raised by someone—everyone present jumped on it—it had been lurking in each person's thoughts, to some degree, and it simply required a catalyst to bring it to the surface."

"Fine! I swear I think it'll be most entertaining. How do they feel up at Cap and Gown?"

"Crazy, obviously. Everyone's been sitting around arguing and cursing and getting angry and getting emotional and getting vicious. It's the same at all the clubs; I've made the rounds. They corner one of the radicals and bombard him with questions."

"How do the radicals hold their ground?"

"Oh, pretty well. Burne's an excellent speaker, and he's so clearly genuine that you can't make any headway with him. It's so obvious that quitting his club matters far more to him than stopping him does to us that I felt useless when I tried to argue with him; I eventually took a stance that was cleverly neutral. Actually, I think Burne believed for a time that he'd won me over."

"And you're saying that almost a third of the junior class is going to resign?"

"Call it a fourth and be safe."

"Lord—who would have thought it was possible!"

There was a sharp knock at the door, and Burne himself walked in. "Hello, Amory—hello, Tom."

Amory stood up.

"Evening, Burne. Don't mind if I seem to rush; I'm going to Renwick's."

Burne turned to him quickly.

"You probably know what I want to discuss with Tom, and it's not private at all. I wish you would stay."

"I'd be happy to." Amory settled back into his seat, and while Burne positioned himself on a table and began debating with Tom, he studied this rebel more closely than he had ever done before. With his wide forehead and strong jaw, along with a refinement in those sincere gray eyes that reminded him of Kerry's, Burne was someone who immediately conveyed an impression of strength and reliability—clearly stubborn, but his obstinacy carried no trace of dullness, and after he had spoken for five minutes Amory realized that this sharp passion contained no hint of superficiality.

The powerful influence Amory later experienced from Burne Holiday was different from the admiration he had felt for Humbird. This time it started as purely an intellectual fascination. With other men he had considered to be exceptional, he had been drawn first to their personalities, and with Burne he lacked that instant appeal to which he typically pledged his loyalty. But that evening Amory was impressed by Burne's deep sincerity, a trait he was used to connecting only with terrible foolishness, and by the great passion that awakened silent feelings in his heart. Burne represented in some unclear way a destination Amory hoped he was moving toward—and it was nearly time for that destination to come into view. Tom and Amory and Alec had come to a standstill; they never seemed to share new experiences together, because Tom and Alec had been as thoughtlessly occupied with their committees and organizations as Amory had been thoughtlessly lounging around, and the topics they had to analyze—college, modern character and similar subjects—they had discussed and rediscussed through many a modest conversational gathering.

That night they talked about the clubs until midnight, and for the most part, they agreed with Burne. To the roommates, the topic didn't seem as important as it had during the previous two years, but Burne's reasoning against the social system aligned so perfectly with everything they had been thinking that they asked questions rather than argued, and they envied the clear thinking that allowed this man to take such a strong stand against all established traditions.

Then Amory explored further and discovered that Burne was deeply involved in other matters as well. Economics had captured his interest and he was becoming a socialist. Pacifism lingered in his thoughts, and he regularly read The Masses and Leo Tolstoy.

"What about religion?" Amory asked him.

"I don't know. I'm confused about many things—I've just realized that I have a mind, and I'm beginning to read."

"Read what?"

"Everything. I have to pick and choose, of course, but mostly things to make me think. I'm reading the four gospels now, and the 'Varieties of Religious Experience.'"

"What mainly got you started?"

"Wells, I suppose, and Tolstoy, and a man named Edward Carpenter. I've been reading for more than a year now—focusing on a few areas, on what I believe are the essential areas."

"Poetry?"

"Well, honestly, it's not what you'd consider poetry, or for the same reasons you do—you both write, naturally, and see things from a different perspective. Whitman is the one who appeals to me."

"Whitman?"

"Yes; he's a definite ethical force."

"Well, I'm embarrassed to admit that I don't know anything about Whitman. What about you, Tom?"

Tom nodded with embarrassment.

"Well," Burne went on, "you might come across a few poems that are boring, but I'm talking about the majority of his work. He's incredible—like Tolstoy. They both confront reality directly, and despite how different they are, they somehow represent similar values."

"You've got me completely puzzled, Burne," Amory confessed. "I've read 'Anna Karenina' and the 'Kreutzer Sonata,' naturally, but as far as I'm concerned, Tolstoy might as well be in the original Russian."

"He's the greatest man in hundreds of years," Burne exclaimed with enthusiasm. "Have you ever seen a picture of that wild, unkempt head of his?"

They talked until three in the morning, covering everything from biology to organized religion, and when Amory crawled shivering into bed, his mind was burning with new ideas and the shocking realization that someone else had found the path he might have taken. Burne Holiday was clearly growing and developing—and Amory had thought he was doing the same thing. He had fallen into deep cynicism about everything he had encountered, mapped out the flawed nature of humanity, and read enough Shaw and Chesterton to keep his thoughts from sliding into complete moral decay—but now suddenly all his thinking from the past year and a half seemed stale and pointless—a shallow version of his true self... and like a dark backdrop loomed that incident from the previous spring, which filled half his nights with grim terror and left him unable to pray. He wasn't even a Catholic, yet that was the only trace of a moral code he possessed, the flashy, ceremonial, contradictory Catholicism whose prophet was Chesterton, whose supporters were reformed literary libertines like Huysmans and Bourget, whose American champion was Ralph Adams Cram, with his worship of thirteenth-century cathedrals—a Catholicism that Amory found convenient and ready-made, requiring no priest or sacraments or sacrifice.

He couldn't sleep, so he switched on his reading lamp and pulled down the "Kreutzer Sonata," examining it closely for the source of Burne's passion. Being like Burne suddenly seemed so much more authentic than being intelligent. Still, he sighed... here were other potential weaknesses.

He reflected on the past two years, remembering Burne as a rushed, anxious freshman who was completely overshadowed by his brother's strong personality. Then he recalled an event from sophomore year where Burne was believed to have played the main part.

Dean Hollister had been overheard by a large crowd getting into an argument with a taxi driver who had given him a ride from the junction. During their heated exchange, the dean commented that he "might as well buy the taxicab." He paid his fare and walked away, but the following morning when he entered his private office, he discovered the actual taxicab sitting in the spot where his desk normally stood, complete with a sign that read "Property of Dean Hollister. Bought and Paid for."... It required two skilled mechanics half a day to take it apart piece by piece and haul it out, which only demonstrates the extraordinary determination of sophomore pranks when guided by capable leadership.

Then again, that very fall, Burne had created quite a stir. A certain Phyllis Styles, who made a habit of attending college social events, had failed to receive her usual yearly invitation to the Harvard-Princeton game.

Jesse Ferrenby had brought her to a smaller poker game a few weeks earlier, and had convinced Burne to join in—which completely destroyed Burne's hatred of women.

"Are you coming to the Harvard game?" Burne had asked carelessly, just to keep the conversation going.

"If you ask me," Phyllis said quickly.

"Of course I do," Burne replied weakly. He wasn't familiar with Phyllis's tactics and assumed this was just empty teasing. Within an hour, he realized he was truly trapped. Phyllis had cornered him completely, told him which train she'd be taking, and left him feeling utterly dejected. Beyond his dislike of Phyllis, he had especially wanted to attend that game alone and spend time with some friends from Harvard.

"She'll find out," he told the group that came to his room to tease him. "This will be the last game she ever convinces any naive young man to take her to!"

"But, Burne—why did you invite her if you didn't want her?"

"Burne, you know you're secretly crazy about her—that's the real problem."

"What can you do, Burne? What can you do against Phyllis?"

But Burne just shook his head and mumbled threats that were mostly made up of the phrase: "She'll see, she'll see!"

The cheerful Phyllis carried her twenty-five years lightly as she stepped off the train, but a horrifying sight greeted her on the platform. There stood Burne and Fred Sloane, dressed down to the smallest detail like the garish figures from college advertisements. They had purchased flashy suits with enormous balloon-style pants and massive padded shoulders. Their heads were topped with stylish college hats, turned up at the front and decorated with bright orange-and-black bands, while vivid orange ties bloomed from their stiff celluloid collars. They sported black armbands featuring orange "P's" and carried walking sticks adorned with Princeton banners, the look completed by socks and visible handkerchiefs in matching colors. On a rattling chain, they dragged along a large, furious tomcat that had been painted to look like a tiger.

A good half of the people at the station were already staring at them, caught between feeling horrified sympathy and wanting to burst out laughing, and as Phyllis approached with her slender jaw hanging open, the two young men bent forward and shouted out a college cheer in loud, carrying voices, thoughtfully including the name "Phyllis" at the end. She received a boisterous welcome and was enthusiastically escorted across the campus, followed by about fifty local kids—while hundreds of alumni and visitors watched with suppressed laughter, half of whom had no clue this was a prank, but assumed that Burne and Fred were two varsity athletes showing their girlfriend a good college time.

Phyllis's emotions as she was led past the Harvard and Princeton bleachers, where dozens of her former admirers were seated, are easy to picture. She attempted to walk slightly ahead, she attempted to walk slightly behind—but they remained close beside her, making sure there was no question about who she was accompanying, speaking loudly about their friends on the football team, until she could nearly hear her acquaintances murmuring:

"Phyllis Styles must be really desperate for money to have to come with those two."

That had been Burne—energetically funny yet deeply serious at his core. From that foundation had grown the drive he was now attempting to align with forward movement.

So the weeks went by and March arrived, but the weaknesses that Amory expected to see never showed up. Around a hundred juniors and seniors quit their clubs in one last burst of moral outrage, and the clubs, feeling powerless, turned their most effective weapon against Burne: mockery. Everyone who knew him personally liked him—but what he represented (and he was starting to represent more and more as time went on) became the target of harsh criticism from many people, enough to overwhelm someone less resilient than he was.

"Don't you mind losing prestige?" Amory asked one night. They had started calling each other several times a week.

"Of course I don't. What's prestige, at best?"

"Some people say that you're just a rather original politician."

He burst out laughing.

"That's what Fred Sloane told me today. I suppose I deserve it."

One afternoon they explored a topic that had fascinated Amory for quite some time—how physical characteristics influence a person's overall character and personality. Burne had delved into the biological aspects of this question, and then:

"Of course health matters—a healthy person has twice the opportunity to be good," he said.

"I don't agree with you—I don't believe in 'muscular Christianity.'"

"I do—I believe Christ had great physical vigor."

"Oh, no," Amory objected. "He pushed himself too hard for that to be true. I think that by the time he died, he was completely worn out—and the greatest saints have never been physically strong."

"Half of them have."

"Well, even if I accept that point, I don't believe health has any connection to moral goodness; certainly, it's beneficial for a great saint to endure tremendous pressures, but this trend of popular preachers standing on their tiptoes in fake displays of strength, shouting that physical exercise will save the world—no, Burne, I can't support that."

"Well, let's drop it—we're not going to get anywhere with this, and besides, I haven't completely decided what I think about it myself. Now, here's something I'm certain of—how someone looks plays a big part in it."

"Coloring?" Amory asked eagerly.

"Yes."

"That's what Tom and I figured," Amory agreed. "We went through the yearbooks from the past ten years and examined the photos of the senior council. I know you don't have much respect for that distinguished group, but it does represent success here in a broad sense. Well, I'd guess that only about thirty-five percent of each class here consists of blonds, people who are genuinely fair-haired—yet two-thirds of every senior council are fair-haired.

We studied photographs spanning ten years, keep in mind; that means out of every fifteen light-haired men in the senior class, one serves on the senior council, while for dark-haired men it's only one in fifty."

"That's true," Burne agreed. "Generally speaking, men with light hair represent a superior type. I once analyzed this with the Presidents of the United States and discovered that well over half of them had light hair—yet consider how many more brunettes there are in the population."

"People unconsciously acknowledge this," Amory said. "You'll see that blonde people are expected to be talkative. When a blonde woman doesn't speak much, we label her a 'doll'; when a fair-haired man stays quiet, he's thought to be stupid. Yet the world is filled with 'mysterious quiet men' and 'dreamy brunettes' who don't have much intelligence either, but somehow they're never blamed for lacking brains."

"And the large mouth and broad chin and rather big nose undoubtedly make the superior face."

"I'm not so sure." Amory was completely in favor of classical features.

"Oh, absolutely—I'll show you," and Burne reached into his desk and pulled out a photographic collection featuring heavily bearded, shaggy-haired celebrities—Tolstoy, Whitman, Carpenter, and others.

"Aren't they wonderful?"

Amory made a polite effort to appreciate them, but eventually gave up with a laugh.

"Burne, I think they're the ugliest-looking group I've ever encountered. They look like residents of a nursing home."

"Oh, Amory, look at Emerson's forehead; look at Tolstoy's eyes." His tone was reproachful.

Amory shook his head.

"No! Call them striking or whatever you like—but they're definitely ugly."

Unashamed, Burne ran his hand affectionately across the broad foreheads, and stacking up the photographs, he placed them back in his desk.

Walking at night was one of his favorite activities, and one evening he convinced Amory to come along with him.

"I hate the dark," Amory protested. "I never used to—except when my imagination was running wild, but now I really do—I'm completely ridiculous about it."

"That's useless, you know."

"Quite possibly."

"We'll head east," Burne suggested, "and take that series of roads that wind through the forest."

"That doesn't sound very appealing to me," Amory admitted reluctantly, "but let's go."

They started off at a good pace, and for an hour they moved along engaged in a lively argument until the lights of Princeton became glowing white spots behind them.

"Anyone with any imagination is bound to be afraid," Burne said earnestly. "And this very act of walking at night is one of the things I was afraid of. I'm going to tell you why I can walk anywhere now and not be afraid."

"Keep going," Amory said eagerly. They were walking quickly toward the woods, with Burne's anxious, passionate voice becoming more animated as he discussed his topic.

"I used to come out here by myself at night about three months ago, and I would always pause at that crossroads we just went by. The woods were towering up in front of me, exactly like they are now, with dogs howling and shadows everywhere, but no sounds from people. Naturally, I filled those woods with all kinds of terrifying things in my mind, just like you do; don't you?"

"I do," Amory admitted.

"Well, I started analyzing it—my imagination kept inserting terrifying things into the darkness—so I placed my imagination into the dark instead, and allowed it to look back at me—I let it become a stray dog or an escaped prisoner or a ghost, and then watched myself walking along the road. That solved the problem—just as it always solves everything to put yourself completely in someone else's position. I understood that if I were the dog or the prisoner or the ghost, I wouldn't pose a threat to Burne Holiday any more than he posed a threat to me. Then I remembered my watch. I should probably go back and leave it behind before attempting to enter the woods. No; I decided, it's better overall that I lose a watch than turn around and go back—and I did enter them—not only followed the road that went through them, but walked directly into them until I was no longer scared—kept doing it until one night I sat down and fell asleep in there; then I knew I had overcome my fear of the dark."

"Good Lord," Amory whispered. "I never could have done that. I would have come out halfway, and the moment a car drove by and made the darkness even deeper when its headlights vanished, I would have turned back inside."

"Well," Burne said suddenly, after a few moments of silence, "we're halfway through, so let's turn back."

On his way back, he started talking about willpower.

"It's everything," he declared. "It's the single boundary that separates good from evil. I've never encountered a person who lived a corrupt life and possessed strong willpower."

"What about major criminals?"

"They're usually mentally unstable. If they're not, then they're weak. There's no such thing as a strong, mentally sound criminal."

"Burne, I completely disagree with you; what about the superman?"

"Well?"

"He's evil, I think, yet he's strong and sane."

"I've never met him. I'll bet, though, that he's stupid or insane."

"I've encountered him repeatedly, and he's neither of those things. That's why I believe you're mistaken."

"I'm certain I'm not—and that's why I don't believe in imprisonment except for those who are mentally ill."

On this issue, Amory couldn't see eye to eye with him. It appeared to Amory that both life and history were filled with powerful criminals who were sharp-minded but frequently deceived themselves; you could find such people in politics and business, as well as among former statesmen, kings, and generals; however, Burne never shared this view, and their paths started to diverge on this matter.

Burne was withdrawing more and more from the world around him. He gave up his position as vice-president of the senior class and turned to reading and walking as nearly his only activities. He chose to attend graduate lectures in philosophy and biology, and sat through all of them with a somewhat sadly focused expression in his eyes, as though he was waiting for something the professor would never quite reach. Occasionally Amory would notice him shift restlessly in his chair; and his face would brighten; he was eager to argue a point.

He became increasingly lost in thought while walking the streets and some people even called him a snob, but Amory understood this wasn't the case at all, and one time when Burne walked right past him just four feet away, completely oblivious to his presence with his thoughts clearly somewhere far away, Amory nearly overwhelmed himself with the thrilling pleasure of observing him. Burne appeared to be reaching peaks that others could never hope to access.

"I'm telling you," Amory said to Tom, "he's the first person of our generation I've ever encountered who I'll acknowledge is smarter than me."

"It's a bad time to admit it—people are starting to think he's strange."

"He's way above their level—you know you think so yourself when you talk to him—Good Lord, Tom, you used to stand up against 'people.' Success has completely made you conventional."

Tom became quite irritated.

"What's he trying to do—be excessively holy?"

"No! He's not like anyone you've ever encountered. He never joins the Philadelphian Society. He has no faith in that nonsense. He doesn't believe that public swimming pools and a timely kind word will fix the world's problems; what's more, he takes a drink whenever he wants to."

"He's definitely making a mistake."

"Have you talked to him lately?"

"No."

"Then you don't have any understanding of him."

The argument reached no conclusion, but Amory observed more clearly than before how the attitude toward Burne had shifted throughout the campus.

"It's strange," Amory said to Tom one evening when they had become more friendly about the topic, "that the people who strongly oppose Burne's radical ideas are clearly the self-righteous types—I mean they're the most well-educated men at the college—the newspaper editors, like you and Ferrenby, the younger professors.... The uneducated athletes like Langueduc think he's becoming odd, but they simply say, 'Good old Burne has some weird ideas in his head,' and move on—the self-righteous types—Man! they mock him without mercy."

The next morning he encountered Burne rushing down McCosh walk after a class.

"Where are you going, Tsar?"

"Over to the Prince office to see Ferrenby," he said, waving a copy of the morning's Princetonian at Amory. "He wrote this editorial."

"Going to flay him alive?"

"No—but he's got me completely confused. Either I've been wrong about him this whole time, or he's suddenly turned into the most extreme radical you could imagine."

Burne rushed ahead, and several days passed before Amory learned what happened in the conversation that followed. Burne had walked into the editor's office, holding the newspaper with obvious satisfaction.

"Hello, Jesse."

"Hello there, Savonarola."

"I just read your editorial."

"Good boy—I didn't know you would sink that low."

"Jesse, you scared me."

"How so?"

"Aren't you worried that the faculty will come after you if you pull this irreligious stuff?"

"What?"

"Like this morning."

"What the hell—that editorial was about the coaching system."

"Yes, but that quotation—"

Jesse sat up.

"What quotation?"

"You know: 'He who is not with me is against me.'"

"Well—what about it?"

Jesse was confused but not worried.

"Well, you mention here—let me take a look." Burne unfolded the paper and read aloud: "'Anyone who isn't with me is against me, as that man said who was famously known for making only crude distinctions and childish generalizations.'"

"So what?" Ferrenby started to look worried. "Oliver Cromwell said it, didn't he? Or maybe it was Washington, or one of the saints? Good Lord, I can't remember."

Burne burst into laughter.

"Oh, Jesse, oh, good, kind Jesse."

"Who said it, for Pete's sake?"

"Well," said Burne, finding his voice again, "St. Matthew credits it to Christ."

"My God!" Jesse shouted, and fell backward into the trash can.

————————

Amory Writes a Poem

The weeks flew by rapidly. Amory sometimes traveled to New York hoping to discover a new gleaming green bus, thinking that its bright, candy-like appeal might lift his spirits. One afternoon he decided to attend a stock-company production of a play whose title seemed vaguely recognizable. The curtain went up—he observed with mild interest as a young woman walked onto the stage. Several lines echoed in his mind and stirred a distant memory. Where had he heard this before—? When had this happened—?

Then he seemed to hear a voice whispering beside him, a very soft, vibrant voice: "Oh, I'm such a poor little fool; do tell me when I do wrong."

The answer came to him suddenly, and he experienced a brief, joyful memory of Isabelle.

He found an empty space on his program and started writing quickly:

"Here in the shadowy darkness I watch once more,
There, with the curtain, the years roll away;
Two years of years—there was a carefree day
Of ours, when happy endings didn't bore
Our innocent souls; I could cherish
Your enthusiastic face beside me, bright-eyed, cheerful,
Displaying a range of expressions while the mediocre play
Reached me like a gentle wave reaches the shore.

"Yawning and pondering through an evening,
I watch alone... and chatter, naturally,
Ruins the one scene which, somehow, did possess charm;
You cried a little, and I became melancholy for you
Right here! Where Mr. X argues for divorce
And What's-Her-Name collapses unconscious in his arms."

Still Calm

"Ghosts are such stupid things," said Alec, "they're slow-witted. I can always outsmart a ghost."

"How?" asked Tom.

"Well, it depends on the location. Take a bedroom, for instance. If you exercise any caution, a ghost can never reach you in a bedroom."

"Come on, let's say you think there might be a ghost in your bedroom—what do you do when you get home at night?" Amory asked, intrigued.

"Get a stick," Alec replied with serious reverence, "one that's about as long as a broom handle. Now, the first thing you need to do is clear the room—to accomplish this, you rush into your study with your eyes shut and turn on the lights—then, as you approach the closet, carefully poke the stick through the door three or four times. After that, if nothing occurs, you can take a look inside. Always, always thrust the stick in aggressively first—never look first!"

"Of course, that's the ancient Celtic school," Tom said seriously.

"Yes—but they usually pray first. Anyway, you use this method to clear the closets and also for behind all doors—"

"And the bed," Amory suggested.

"Oh, Amory, don't!" Alec shouted in terror. "That's not how you should handle it—the bed needs a completely different approach—stay away from the bed if you want to keep your sanity—if there's a ghost in this room, which happens only about one-third of the time, it's almost always hiding underneath the bed."

"Well," Amory began.

Alec gestured for him to be quiet.

"Of course you never look. You stand in the middle of the floor and before he realizes what you're planning to do, make a sudden jump toward the bed—never walk close to the bed; to a ghost your ankle is your most vulnerable spot—once you're in bed, you're safe; he might lurk around under the bed all night, but you're as safe as can be. If you still have any doubts, pull the blanket over your head."

"All that's very interesting, Tom."

"Isn't it?" Alec smiled with pride. "All my own work, too—the Sir Oliver Lodge of the new world."

Amory was thoroughly enjoying college once more. The feeling of moving forward with clear purpose and determination had returned; his youthful spirit was awakening and displaying fresh vitality. He had even accumulated enough extra energy to experiment with adopting a new persona.

"What's with all this 'distracted' behavior, Amory?" Alec asked one day, and then as Amory pretended to be hunched over his book in a trance: "Oh, don't try to play Burne, the mystic, with me."

Amory looked up innocently.

"What?"

"What?" Alec mimicked. "Are you trying to read yourself into a frenzy with—let me see that book."

He grabbed it and looked at it with contempt.

"Well?" Amory said, his voice somewhat stiff.

"'The Life of St. Teresa,'" Alec read out loud. "Oh, my gosh!"

"Say, Alec."

"What?"

"Does it bother you?"

"Does what bother me?"

"My acting confused and everything?"

"Why, no—of course it doesn't bother me."

"Well, then, don't ruin it. If I enjoy going around telling people honestly that I think I'm a genius, let me do it."

"You're developing a reputation for being eccentric," Alec said with a laugh, "if that's what you're getting at."

Amory eventually won out, and Alec agreed to take him at face value when other people were around, as long as he could have breaks from the act when they were by themselves. So Amory went all out, inviting the most unusual characters to dinner—wild-eyed graduate students and instructors with bizarre ideas about God and politics—much to the cynical amusement of the snobbish Cottage Club members.

As February was brightened by sunshine and transitioned happily into March, Amory visited Monsignor several times for weekend stays; on one occasion he brought Burne along, which worked out wonderfully, since he felt equally proud and pleased to introduce them to one another. Monsignor brought him to visit Thornton Hancock on several occasions, and a couple of times to the home of a Mrs. Lawrence, one of those Americans who frequented Rome and whom Amory found appealing right away.

Then one day a letter arrived from Monsignor, which included an interesting P.S.:

"Do you know," the letter said, "that your third cousin, Clara Page, who became a widow six months ago and is very poor, is living in Philadelphia? I don't think you've ever met her, but I wish, as a favor to me, you'd go to see her. In my opinion, she's quite a remarkable woman, and just about your age."

Amory let out a sigh and made up his mind to go, as a favor....

———————

Clara

She had existed since time immemorial.... Amory wasn't worthy of Clara, Clara with her flowing golden hair, but then again, no man was. Her virtue transcended the mundane morality of women seeking husbands, standing apart from the tedious writings about feminine virtue.

Sadness rested gently upon her, and when Amory discovered her in Philadelphia, he believed her sharp blue eyes contained nothing but joy; an underlying resilience, a practical outlook, had been fully cultivated by the circumstances she was forced to confront. She stood alone in the world, caring for two young children, with limited funds, and, most challenging of all, countless friends. That winter in Philadelphia, he watched her host a house full of men for an entire evening, knowing full well she had no household staff except the young Black girl watching the babies upstairs. He witnessed one of the city's most notorious womanizers, a man who was regularly intoxicated and scandalous both locally and internationally, sitting across from her for the evening, talking about girls' boarding schools with an almost childlike enthusiasm. What an extraordinary mind Clara possessed! She could create captivating and nearly brilliant conversation from the most trivial topics that ever drifted through a living room.

The notion that the girl lived in poverty had captured Amory's imagination. He came to Philadelphia anticipating he would discover that 921 Ark Street sat in a wretched alley filled with shacks. He felt genuinely let down when it turned out to be completely different. The place was an old house that had belonged to her husband's family for generations. An aging aunt, who refused to allow its sale, had deposited ten years' worth of property taxes with an attorney and sailed off to Honolulu, leaving Clara to deal with the heating issues however she could manage. So no wild-haired woman carrying a starving infant and wearing a melancholy expression like Amelia welcomed him at the door. On the contrary, based on how she received him, Amory might have assumed she didn't have a single worry in her life.

A calm masculinity and a dreamy sense of humor, striking contrasts to her practical nature—she would sometimes slip into these moods as an escape. She could handle the most mundane tasks (though she was smart enough never to diminish herself with such "domestic skills" as knitting and embroidery), yet immediately afterward pick up a book and let her imagination wander like a shapeless cloud carried by the wind. The deepest aspect of her personality was the golden glow that she spread around her. Just as an open fire in a dark room casts romance and emotion onto the quiet faces at its edges, so she cast her light and shadows throughout the rooms that contained her, until she transformed her mundane old uncle into a man of charming and thoughtful appeal, changed the random telegraph boy into a Puck-like figure of wonderful originality. At first this quality of hers somehow annoyed Amory. He considered his own distinctiveness adequate, and it rather embarrassed him when she tried to discover new interests in him for the sake of whatever other admirers were around. He felt as if a courteous but persistent director were trying to make him give a fresh interpretation of a role he had studied for years.

But when Clara spoke, when Clara shared her delicate story about a hatpin, a drunk man, and herself... People later tried to retell her stories, but no matter how hard they tried, they couldn't make them sound like anything at all. They listened to her with a kind of pure attention and offered her the warmest smiles many of them had given in a long time; Clara rarely brought people to tears, but she made people smile with eyes full of emotion.

Very occasionally Amory would stay for brief half-hour periods after the rest of the court had left, and they would share bread and jam with tea late in the afternoon or what she referred to as "maple-sugar lunches" in the evening.

"You really are something special, aren't you!" Amory was getting predictable from his spot in the middle of the dining room table at six o'clock.

"Not at all," she replied. She was looking for napkins in the sideboard. "I'm actually quite ordinary and unremarkable. One of those people who aren't interested in anything except their children."

"Tell that to someone else," Amory scoffed. "You know you're absolutely radiant." He asked her the one thing that he knew might embarrass her. It was the remark that the first bore made to Adam.

"Tell me about yourself." And she gave the answer that Adam must have given.

"There's nothing to tell."

But eventually Adam probably shared with that tedious companion all the thoughts that occupied his mind during those nights when locusts chirped in the sandy grass, and he must have spoken condescendingly about how different he was from Eve, overlooking how different she was from him... in any case, Clara revealed much about herself to Amory that evening. She had lived a troubled life since turning sixteen, and her formal education had ended abruptly when her free time disappeared. While exploring her library, Amory discovered a worn gray book from which a yellowed piece of paper fell out, and he boldly opened it. It was a poem she had written during her school days about a gray convent wall on an overcast day, featuring a girl whose cloak was caught by the wind as she sat on top of it, contemplating the vibrant world around her. Typically, such sentimental writing would bore him, but this piece was crafted with such genuine simplicity and rich atmosphere that it conjured an image of Clara in his mind—Clara on just such a cool, gray day with her sharp blue eyes gazing outward, attempting to watch her sorrows march across the gardens beyond. He felt envious of that poem. How he wished he could have appeared and found her sitting on that wall, engaging her in playful conversation or romantic talk while she perched above him in the air. He started to feel intensely jealous of everything connected to Clara: her history, her children, the men and women who gathered around her to drink deeply from her refreshing kindness and find peace for their weary minds as if watching a captivating performance.

"Nobody seems to bore you," he protested.

"About half the world does," she acknowledged, "but I think that's a fairly good average, wouldn't you agree?" and she turned to search for something in Browning that related to the topic. She was the only person he had ever encountered who could look up passages and quotes to show him right in the middle of their conversation, and yet not be annoying beyond measure. She did this all the time, with such genuine enthusiasm that he became fond of watching her golden hair bent over a book, her forehead slightly creased as she hunted for her sentence.

Through early March he began making weekend trips to Philadelphia. Almost always there was someone else present, and she didn't seem eager to spend time with him alone, even though many opportunities arose when just a word from her could have given him another blissful half-hour of worship. But he gradually fell in love and started entertaining wild thoughts about marriage. Although this idea flowed through his mind and even to his lips, he realized later that the desire hadn't been deeply rooted. Once he dreamed that it had actually happened and woke up in a cold panic, because in his dream she had become a foolish, pale Clara, with the gold drained from her hair and empty platitudes falling dully from her transformed tongue. But she was the first refined woman he had ever known and one of the few good people who had ever captured his interest. She made her goodness such an advantage. Amory had concluded that most good people either dragged their virtue behind them like a burden, or else twisted it into artificial cheerfulness, and naturally there were always the self-righteous and hypocritical types—(but Amory never counted them among those worth saving).

St. Cecilia

> "Over her gray and velvet dress,
> Under her flowing, lustrous hair,
> Rose-colored blush in playful distress
> Appears and disappears and makes her beautiful;
> Fills the space between her and him
> With brightness and dreamy longing and soft sighs,
> So delicately that he barely realizes...
> Sparkling laughter, color of rose."

"Do you like me?"

"Of course I do," Clara said seriously.

"Why?"

"Well, we share some traits. Things that come naturally to both of us—or at least used to."

"Are you suggesting that I haven't made good use of myself?"

Clara hesitated.

"Well, I can't make that judgment. A man, naturally, has to endure much more, and I've been protected from hardship."

"Oh, don't delay, please, Clara," Amory interrupted; "but do talk about me a little, won't you?"

"Absolutely, I'd love to." She didn't smile.

"That's sweet of you. First answer some questions. Am I painfully conceited?"

"Well—no, you're incredibly vain, but it'll entertain the people who see how much of it you have."

"I see."

"You're truly modest deep down. You plunge into the deepest depths of despair when you believe someone has disrespected you. The truth is, you don't have much regard for yourself."

"Bull's-eye twice, Clara. How do you manage it? You never give me a chance to speak."

"Of course not—I can never judge a man while he's talking. But I'm not finished; the reason you have so little genuine self-confidence, even though you solemnly declare to the occasional uncultured person that you think you're a genius, is that you've assigned all kinds of terrible flaws to yourself and are attempting to live up to them. For example, you're constantly saying that you are a slave to cocktails."

"But I have the potential to be."

"And you say you're a weak person, that you have no willpower."

"Not a bit of will—I'm a slave to my emotions, to my preferences, to my hatred of boredom, to most of my desires—"

"You are not!" She slammed one small fist down onto the other. "You're a slave, a helpless prisoner to one thing in this world—your imagination."

"You definitely have my attention. If this isn't boring you, please continue."

"I notice that when you want to stay an extra day away from college, you have a reliable method. You never make the decision immediately while the pros and cons of leaving or staying are still clear in your mind. Instead, you let your imagination run wild in favor of what you want for a few hours, and then you make your choice. Naturally, your imagination, once given some freedom, comes up with countless reasons why you should stay, so when you finally decide, it isn't a genuine decision. It's prejudiced."

"Yes," Amory protested, "but isn't it a lack of willpower to let my imagination climb up the wrong side?"

"My dear boy, that's where you're completely wrong. This isn't about willpower at all—that's a ridiculous and meaningless concept anyway. What you're missing is good judgment—the ability to make quick decisions when you realize your imagination is going to deceive you if you give it even the slightest opportunity."

"Well, I'll be darned!" Amory exclaimed in surprise, "that's the last thing I expected."

Clara didn't gloat. She immediately changed the subject. But she had gotten him thinking, and he believed she was partially right. He felt like a factory owner who, after accusing a clerk of being dishonest, discovers that his own son in the office has been altering the books once a week. His poor, mistreated willpower that he had been holding up for himself and his friends to mock now stood before him innocent, while his judgment marched off to prison with the uncontrollable imp of imagination dancing beside him in mocking delight. Clara's was the only advice he ever sought without already knowing what answer he wanted to hear—except, perhaps, during his conversations with Monsignor Darcy.

How much he enjoyed doing anything at all with Clara! Going shopping with her was an extraordinary, luxurious fantasy. In every shop where she had ever made purchases, people would whisper about her as the gorgeous Mrs. Page.

"I'll bet she won't stay single long."

"Well, don't shout it out. She isn't looking for any advice."

"Isn't she beautiful!"

(A floor supervisor enters—everyone falls silent until he steps forward, wearing a smug grin.)

"She's a society person, isn't she?"

"Yeah, but poor now, I guess; so they say."

"Wow! Girls, isn't she something!"

Clara radiated warmth toward everyone she encountered. Amory was convinced that shopkeepers offered her discounts, sometimes openly and other times without her even realizing it. He understood that she dressed impeccably, consistently enjoyed the finest things their home had to offer, and without fail received personal attention from at least the head floor manager whenever she went shopping.

Sometimes they would attend church together on Sundays, and he would walk alongside her, delighting in how her cheeks glistened with moisture from the gentle mist in the fresh air. She had always been deeply religious, and only God knew what spiritual heights she reached and what power she drew to herself when she knelt and bowed her golden hair into the colored light streaming through the stained glass.

"St. Cecelia," he shouted out loud one day, completely without thinking, and people turned around to stare, and the priest stopped in the middle of his sermon while Clara and Amory's faces turned bright red.

That was their final Sunday together, because he ruined everything that evening. He couldn't stop himself.

They walked through the March twilight, where the air felt as warm as a June evening, and the happiness of being young filled his heart so completely that he knew he had to say something.

"I think," he said, his voice shaking, "that if I stopped believing in you, I'd stop believing in God."

She looked at him with such a surprised expression that he asked her what was wrong.

"Nothing," she said slowly, "only this: five men have told me that before, and it scares me."

"Oh, Clara, is that your fate!"

She didn't respond.

"I suppose love to you is—" he began.

She spun around instantly.

"I have never been in love."

They walked together, and gradually he began to understand the full weight of what she had revealed to him... she had never been in love.... In that moment, she appeared to him like a being made of pure light. He felt himself fall away from her elevated realm, and he yearned simply to brush against her clothing with something approaching the understanding that Joseph must have experienced when he grasped Mary's divine importance. Yet almost without thinking, he heard his own voice speaking:

"And I love you—whatever hidden potential I have is... oh, I can't put it into words, but Clara, if I return in two years with the means to marry you—"

She shook her head.

"No," she said; "I would never marry again. I have my two children and I want to dedicate myself to them. I like you—I like all intelligent men, you more than any—but you know me well enough to understand that I would never marry an intelligent man—" She stopped speaking abruptly.

"Amory."

"What?"

"You're not in love with me. You never wanted to marry me, did you?"

"It was the twilight," he said with wonder. "I didn't feel like I was speaking out loud. But I love you—or adore you—or worship you—"

"There you go—running through your catalogue of emotions in five seconds."

He smiled reluctantly.

"Don't make me seem like such a lightweight, Clara; you can be depressing sometimes."

"You're definitely not a lightweight," she said earnestly, taking his arm and opening her eyes wide—he could see their warmth in the fading twilight. "A lightweight is someone who always says no to everything."

"There's so much spring in the air—there's so much lazy sweetness in your heart."

She let go of his arm.

"You're all doing well now, and I feel amazing. Give me a cigarette. You've never seen me smoke, have you? Well, I do, about once a month."

And then that wonderful girl and Amory ran to the corner like two crazy children who had gone wild in the pale-blue twilight.

"I'm going to the countryside tomorrow," she announced, standing there breathless and safely beyond the glow of the corner streetlight. "These days are too beautiful to miss, though I might actually feel them more intensely here in the city."

"Oh, Clara!" Amory said. "What a devil you could have been if the Lord had just bent your soul a little the other way!"

"Maybe," she replied, "but I don't think so. I'm never truly wild and never have been. That small outburst was simply the effect of spring."

"And you are, too," he said.

They were walking together now.

"No—you're wrong again, how can someone who claims to be so smart be so consistently mistaken about me? I'm the complete opposite of everything spring represents. It's unfortunate that I happen to look like what appealed to some sentimental old Greek sculptor, but I promise you that if it weren't for my appearance I'd be a quiet nun in a convent without"—then she started running and her voice carried back to him as he chased after her—"my precious children, whom I must return to see."

She was the only girl he had ever known who made him understand how another man might be chosen over him. Amory often encountered wives he had known when they were debutantes, and when he looked closely at them, he imagined he could see something in their faces that seemed to say:

"Oh, if only I could have gotten you!" Oh, what incredible arrogance from that man!

But that night felt like a night filled with stars and singing, and Clara's radiant spirit still shone brightly on the paths they had walked together.

"Golden, golden is the air—" he sang to the small pools of water. ... "Golden is the air, golden notes from golden mandolins, golden frets of golden violins, beautiful, oh, wearily beautiful.... Threads from woven basket, humans may not grasp; oh, what young lavish God, who would know or question it?... who could give such gold..."

Amory Is Resentful

Slowly and inevitably, yet with a sudden surge at the end, while Amory talked and dreamed, war quickly rolled up the shore and swept over the sands where Princeton had played. Every night the gymnasium echoed as one platoon after another marched across the floor and erased the basketball court markings. When Amory traveled to Washington the following weekend, he absorbed some of the crisis atmosphere, which turned to disgust on the Pullman train ride back, since the sleeping berths across from him were filled with foul-smelling foreigners—Greeks, he assumed, or Russians. He reflected on how much simpler patriotism had been for a unified people, how much easier it would have been to fight as the Colonies had fought, or as the Confederacy had fought. He didn't sleep at all that night, instead listening to the foreigners laugh loudly and snore while they filled the train car with the thick smell of modern America.

In Princeton, everyone joked around in public while privately convincing themselves that their deaths would at least be heroic. The literature students read Rupert Brooke with intense passion; the social climbers fretted about whether the government would allow English-style uniforms for officers; some of the utterly lazy ones wrote letters to obscure departments within the War Department, hoping to secure an easy commission and a comfortable position.

After a week had passed, Amory encountered Burne and immediately realized that any debate would be pointless—Burne had declared himself a pacifist. The socialist publications, a considerable exposure to Tolstoy's writings, and his own deep yearning for a purpose that would draw out whatever inner strength he possessed, had ultimately led him to advocate for peace as a personal philosophy.

"When the German army entered Belgium," he began, "if the people had gone about their daily lives peacefully, the German army would have fallen into disarray in—"

"I know," Amory interrupted, "I've heard all of this before. But I'm not going to discuss propaganda with you. There's a possibility that you're right—but even if that's the case, we're still hundreds of years away from the time when non-resistance could actually affect us as a reality."

"But, Amory, listen—"

"Burne, we'd just argue—"

"Very well."

"Just one thing—I'm not asking you to think about your family or friends, because I know they don't matter at all to you compared to your sense of duty—but, Burne, how do you know that the magazines you read and the organizations you join and these idealists you meet aren't simply German?"

"Some of them are, of course."

"How do you know they aren't all pro-German—just a bunch of weak ones—with German-Jewish names."

"That's the risk, naturally," he said slowly. "I can't tell how much or how little my position is influenced by the propaganda I've been exposed to; of course I believe it comes from my deepest beliefs—right now it feels like a clear path laid out in front of me."

Amory's heart sank.

"But consider how easy it really is—nobody's actually going to make you a martyr for being a pacifist—it's just going to lump you in with the worst people—"

"I doubt it," he interrupted.

"Well, it all smells of Bohemian New York to me."

"I understand what you're saying, and that's exactly why I'm not certain I'll cause any trouble."

"You're just one person, Burne—going to talk to people who won't listen—with everything God has given you."

"That's what Stephen must have thought many years ago. But he delivered his sermon and they killed him. He probably thought as he was dying what a waste it all was. But you see, I've always believed that Stephen's death was the event that came to Paul on the road to Damascus, and sent him to preach the word of Christ all over the world."

"Go on."

"That's it—this is what I have to do. Even if right now I'm nothing more than a pawn being sacrificed. God! Amory—you don't think I actually like the Germans!"

"Well, I can't say anything else—I reach the conclusion of all the reasoning about non-resistance, and there, like an excluded middle, looms the enormous ghost of humanity as it exists and always will exist. And this ghost stands right next to Tolstoy's one logical necessity, and Nietzsche's other logical necessity—" Amory stopped abruptly. "When are you leaving?"

"I'm going next week."

"I'll see you, of course."

As he walked away, it seemed to Amory that the expression on his face looked remarkably similar to Kerry's when he had said goodbye under Blair Arch two years earlier. Amory wondered sadly why he could never approach anything with the fundamental honesty that those two possessed.

"Burne's a fanatic," he told Tom, "and he's completely wrong and, I'm starting to think, just an unwitting tool being used by anarchist publishers and German-funded troublemakers—but he gets to me—just abandoning everything worthwhile—"

Burne departed a week later in a subdued yet theatrical fashion. He sold everything he owned and came to the room to say farewell, carrying a worn old bicycle that he planned to ride all the way to his home in Pennsylvania.

"Peter the Hermit saying goodbye to Cardinal Richelieu," Alec suggested, relaxing in the window seat while Burne and Amory shook hands.

But Amory wasn't in the right frame of mind for that, and as he watched Burne's long legs push his absurd bicycle out of view past Alexander Hall, he realized he was in for a difficult week. It wasn't that he questioned the war—Germany represented everything he found disgusting; it stood for materialism and the channeling of enormous immoral power; it was simply that Burne's expression lingered in his thoughts and he was growing tired of the hysteria he was starting to hear.

"What's the point of suddenly attacking Goethe," he said to Alec and Tom. "Why write books trying to prove he caused the war—or that Schiller, who's stupid and overrated, is actually a demon in disguise?"

"Have you ever read any of their work?" Tom asked cleverly.

"No," Amory admitted.

"I haven't either," he said with a laugh.

"People will complain," Alec said quietly, "but Goethe's still sitting on his usual shelf in the library—ready to bore anyone who wants to read him!"

Amory settled down, and they stopped talking about it.

"What are you going to do, Amory?"

"Infantry or aviation, I can't decide—I hate working with mechanics, but then again aviation is definitely the right choice for me—"

"I agree with Amory," Tom said. "Infantry or aviation— aviation certainly sounds like the glamorous part of the war—the way cavalry used to be, you know; but like Amory, I can't tell the difference between horsepower and a piston rod."

Somehow Amory's frustration with his own lack of passion reached a breaking point when he tried to blame the entire war on the previous generations... all those people who had celebrated Germany's victory in 1870.... All the rampant materialists, all those who worshipped German science and efficiency. So one day he sat in an English literature class and heard "Locksley Hall" being quoted, which sent him into deep thought filled with disdain for Tennyson and everything he represented—because Amory saw him as the embodiment of the Victorian era.

> Victorians, Victorians, who never learned to cry
> Who planted the bitter seeds that your children now must harvest—

Amory jotted this down in his notebook. The professor was discussing Tennyson's substantial literary foundation while fifty students leaned forward to capture his words in their notes. Amory flipped to a clean page and started writing again.

> "They trembled with shock when they discovered what Mr. Darwin was doing,
> They trembled with shock when the waltz arrived and Newman quickly left"

But the waltz had arrived much earlier; he crossed that out.

"And entitled A Song in the Time of Order," the professor's voice droned from what seemed like a great distance. "Time of Order"—Good God! Everything stuffed into the box with the Victorians perched on top, smiling peacefully.... Meanwhile Browning in his Italian villa proclaimed boldly: "All's for the best." Amory wrote again.

> "You knelt in the temple and he leaned down to listen to your prayer,
> You thanked him for your 'magnificent victories'—while blaming him for 'China.'"

Why could he never manage more than two lines at a time? Now he needed something to rhyme with:

> "You would try to correct Him with science, even though He had made mistakes before..."

Well, anyway....

"You met your children in your home—'I've fixed it up!' you cried,

Took your fifty years of Europe, and then virtuously—died."

"That was largely Tennyson's concept," the lecturer said. "Swinburne's Song in the Time of Order could easily have been Tennyson's own title. He romanticized order in opposition to chaos, in opposition to waste."

Finally, Amory figured it out. He flipped to another page and wrote frantically for the remaining twenty minutes of the class period. When time was up, he walked to the front desk and handed in a page he had ripped from his notebook.

"Here's a poem for the Victorians, sir," he said coldly.

The professor picked it up with curiosity while Amory quickly backed out through the door.

Here is what he had written:

"Songs in the time of order
You left for us to sing,
Proofs with excluded middles,
Answers to life in rhyme,
Keys of the prison warder
And ancient bells to ring,
Time was the end of riddles,
We were the end of time...

Here were domestic oceans
And a sky that we might reach,
Guns and a guarded border,
Gantlets—but not to fling,
Thousands of old emotions
And a platitude for each,
Songs in the time of order—
And tongues, that we might sing."

———

The End of Many Things

Early April drifted past in a blur—a blur of lengthy evenings spent on the club's veranda while the phonograph played "Poor Butterfly" indoors... because "Poor Butterfly" had become the anthem of that final year. The war barely seemed to affect them, and it could have been any of the previous senior springs, aside from the military drills held every other afternoon, though Amory understood with sharp clarity that this was the final spring of the old order.

"This is the great protest against the superman," said Amory.

"I suppose so," Alec agreed.

"He's completely incompatible with any perfect society. As long as he exists, there will be problems and all the hidden evil that makes a crowd lean in and move when he speaks."

"And naturally, all he really is amounts to a talented person who lacks any moral compass."

"That's it. I believe the most troubling thing to consider is this—everything has occurred before, so how quickly will it occur again? Fifty years after Waterloo, Napoleon had become as much of a hero to English schoolchildren as Wellington. How can we be certain our grandchildren won't worship Von Hindenburg in the same manner?"

"What causes it?"

"Time, damn it, and the historian. If we could only learn to see evil for what it truly is, regardless of whether it appears wrapped in squalor, tedium, or splendor."

"God! Haven't we thoroughly examined and criticized the universe for four years?"

Then came the night that would be their last together. Tom and Amory, who were heading to different training camps in the morning, walked along the shadowy paths as they always did and could still picture the faces of the men they knew all around them.

"The grass is full of ghosts tonight."

"The entire campus is buzzing with them."

They stopped near Little and watched the moon rise, turning the slate roof of Dodd silver and making the rustling trees appear blue.

"You know," Tom whispered, "what we're experiencing right now is the feeling of all the beautiful young people who have lived wildly here over the past two hundred years."

A final wave of singing poured out from Blair Arch—voices cracking with emotion for some lengthy farewell.

"And what we're leaving behind here is more than just this class; it's the entire legacy of our youth. We're simply one generation—we're severing all the connections that appeared to tie us to those earlier generations with their tall boots and high stockings. We've strolled side by side with Burr and Light-Horse Harry Lee through many of these deep-blue nights."

"That's exactly what they are," Tom said, veering off on a tangent, "deep blue—any touch of color would ruin them, make them seem foreign. Spires rising against a sky that promises dawn, with blue light reflecting off the slate roofs—it's almost painful to look at—"

"Goodbye, Aaron Burr," Amory called toward the empty Nassau Hall, "you and I experienced unusual aspects of life."

His voice echoed in the silence.

"The torches have gone out," Tom whispered. "Ah, Messalina, the long shadows are creating minarets across the stadium—"

For a moment the voices of their first year of college rushed around them, and then they gazed at each other with slight tears forming in their eyes.

"Damn!"

"Damn!"

The final light slowly disappears and moves across the countryside—the flat, expansive countryside, the bright land filled with church towers; the spirits of twilight adjust their harps once more and roam while singing in a melancholy group through the lengthy pathways lined with trees; dim flames reflect the darkness from one tower peak to another: Oh, slumber that creates visions, and visions that never grow weary, extract from the petals of the lotus blossom some portion of this to preserve, the essential nature of a single moment.

No longer will I wait for the moon's twilight in this hidden valley of stars and towers, because one eternal morning of longing gives way to time and earthly afternoon. Here, Heraclitus, did you discover in fire and changing things the prophecy you cast down through the dead years; this midnight my desire will witness, shadowed among the glowing coals, wrapped in flame, the magnificence and sorrow of the world.

Interlude

May, 1917-February, 1919

A letter dated January 1918, written by Monsignor Darcy to Amory, who is a second lieutenant in the 171st Infantry, Port of Embarkation, Camp Mills, Long Island.

My Dear Boy:

All you need to tell me about yourself is that you're still alive; for everything else, I simply look back through my restless memory, like a thermometer that only measures fevers, and compare you to who I was when I was your age. But people will keep talking, and you and I will continue shouting our meaningless words at each other across life's stage until that final ridiculous curtain drops right on our nodding heads. But you're beginning life's flickering slideshow with pretty much the same collection of images that I had, so I feel compelled to write to you if only to point out the enormous foolishness of people....

This marks the end of one chapter: whether for good or bad, you'll never again be exactly the same Amory Blaine that I once knew, and we'll never meet again the way we used to, because your generation is becoming tough, much tougher than mine ever became, having been raised on the harsh realities of the nineties.

Amory, I recently reread Aeschylus and discovered in the divine irony of the "Agamemnon" the only response to our harsh times—the entire world has collapsed around us, and the closest comparison lies in ages past with that same hopeless acceptance. Sometimes I think of the soldiers out there as Roman legionaries, far from their decadent city, holding back the masses... masses that are, after all, somewhat more threatening than the corrupt city itself... yet another senseless attack on humanity, like the furies we celebrated with cheers years ago, over whose dead bodies we proclaimed victory throughout the entire Victorian era....

And then came a completely materialistic world—along with the Catholic Church. I wonder where you'll find your place in all of this. One thing I know for certain—you'll live as a Celt and die as a Celt; so if you don't use heaven as a constant vote of confidence for your beliefs, you'll discover that earth keeps pulling you back to your dreams and goals.

Amory, I've suddenly realized that I'm an old man. Like all old men, I sometimes have dreams, and I'm going to share them with you. I've enjoyed imagining that you were my son, that perhaps when I was young I fell into a coma and fathered you, and when I regained consciousness, I had no memory of it... it's the paternal instinct, Amory—celibacy runs deeper than physical desire....

Sometimes I believe that the reason for our striking similarity lies in a shared ancestor, and I've discovered that the only bloodline connecting the Darcys and the O'Haras is that of the O'Donahues... I believe his name was Stephen....

When lightning strikes one of us, it strikes both: you had barely reached the departure port when I received my orders to head for

Rome, and I'm waiting at any moment to be told where to board my ship. Before you even receive this letter, I'll already be at sea; then it will be your turn. You went to war as a gentleman should, just as you attended school and university, because it was the proper thing to do. It's better to leave the boastful displays and showy heroics to the middle classes; they handle it so much better.

Do you remember that weekend last March when you brought Burne Holiday from Princeton to visit me? What an incredible young man he is! It shocked me terribly afterward when you wrote that he thought I was splendid; how could he be so mistaken? Splendid is the one thing that neither you nor I could ever be called. We are many other things—we're remarkable, we're intelligent, we could be described, I suppose, as brilliant. We can draw people to us, we can create an atmosphere, we can nearly lose our Celtic souls in Celtic complexities, we can almost always get our way; but splendid—absolutely not!

I am heading to Rome with an excellent collection of documents and letters of introduction that will open doors in every major city across Europe, and there will be quite a commotion when I arrive. How I wish you could come with me! This comes across as a rather cynical statement, certainly not the kind of thing a middle-aged minister should be writing to a young person who is about to leave for war; the only justification is that the middle-aged minister is really speaking to himself. There are profound elements within us and you understand what they are just as well as I do. We possess great faith, although yours is currently unformed; we have a fierce honesty that all our clever reasoning cannot undermine and, most importantly, a childlike innocence that prevents us from ever being truly spiteful.

I have written a lament for you which follows. I am sorry your cheeks are not up to the description I have written of them, but you will smoke and read all night—

At any rate, here it is:

A Lament for a Foster Son, as He Goes to War Against the Foreign King.

"Ochone
He is gone from me, the son of my heart
And he in his golden youth like Angus Og
Angus of the bright birds
And his mind strong and keen like the mind of Cuchulainn on
Muirthemne.

Awirra sthrue
His brow is as white as the milk of Maeve's cattle
And his cheeks like the cherries of the tree
As it bends down to Mary while she feeds the Son of God.

Aveelia Vrone
His hair is like the golden torcs of the Kings at Tara
And his eyes like the four gray seas of Ireland.
And they are swept with the mists of rain.

Mavrone go Gudyo
For him to be in the joyful and crimson battle
Among the chieftains as they perform great acts of courage
Should his life leave him
The very strings of my soul would come undone.

A Vich Deelish
My heart lies within the heart of my son
And my life rests in his life truly
A man can be young twice over
Only through the lives of his sons.

Jia du Vaha Alanav
May the Son of God be above him and below him, before him and
behind him
May the King of the elements cast a veil over the eyes of the
Foreign King,
May the Queen of Graces take him by the hand so he can
pass through the middle of his enemies without them seeing him

May Patrick of the Gaels and Columba of the Churches and the five
thousand Saints of Ireland be better than a shield to him

175

When he enters the battle.
Och Ochone."

Amory—Amory—I have this feeling, somehow, that this is the end; one or both of us won't survive this war.... I've been attempting to explain to you how much this rebirth of myself in you has meant over these past few years... we're strangely similar... strangely different. Farewell, dear boy, and may God be with you.

Thayer Darcy.

Setting Sail at Night

Amory walked across the deck until he spotted a stool positioned beneath an electric light. He reached into his pocket to find his notebook and pencil, then started writing with slow, careful effort:

"We leave tonight...
Silent, we filled the still, deserted street,
A column of dim gray,
And ghosts rose startled at the muffled beat
Along the moonless way;
The shadowy shipyards echoed to the feet
That turned from night and day.

And so we linger on the windless decks,
See on the spectre shore
Shades of a thousand days, poor gray-ribbed wrecks...
Oh, shall we then deplore
Those futile years!
See how the sea is white!
The clouds have broken and the heavens burn
To hollow highways, paved with graveled light
The churning of the waves about the stern
Rises to one voluminous nocturne,
... We leave tonight."

A letter from Amory, headed "Brest, March 11th, 1919," to Lieutenant T. P. D'Invilliers, Camp Gordon, Ga.

Dear Baudelaire:—

We're meeting in Manhattan on the 30th of this month; then we'll get a really nice apartment together, you and I and Alec, who's right here beside me as I'm writing this. I'm not sure what I'm going to do, but I have this vague idea about getting into politics. Why is it that the best young men from Oxford and Cambridge go into politics, while here in the United States we leave it to the lowlifes?—people raised in political wards, educated in local assemblies, and sent to Congress as fat, corrupt politicians who lack "both ideas and ideals," as the debaters used to put it. Even forty years ago we had decent people in politics, but nowadays we're brought up to make a million dollars and "prove what we're made of." Sometimes I wish I had been born English; American life is so incredibly dull and stupid and wholesome.

Since poor Beatrice passed away, I'll probably have a little money, but very little indeed. I can forgive mother for almost everything except the fact that in a sudden burst of religious fervor near the end, she left half of what remained to be spent on stained-glass windows and seminary donations. Mr. Barton, my lawyer, tells me that my thousands are mostly invested in street railways and that these Street R.R.s are losing money because of the five-cent fares. Can you imagine a payroll that gives $350 a month to a man who can't read and write!—yet I believe in it, even though I've witnessed what was once a considerable fortune disappear between speculation, extravagance, the democratic administration, and the income tax—modern, that describes me perfectly, Mabel.

At any rate, we'll have really amazing rooms—you can get a job at some fashion magazine, and Alec can join the Zinc Company or whatever business his family owns—he's looking over my shoulder and says it's a brass company, but I don't think it makes much difference, do you? There's probably just as much corruption in money made from zinc as there is in money made from brass. As for the well-known Amory, he would write timeless literature if he felt confident enough about something to take the risk of sharing it with others. There's no more dangerous legacy to leave future generations than a handful of cleverly crafted clichés.

Tom, why don't you convert to Catholicism? Naturally, to be a devout Catholic you'd need to abandon those aggressive schemes you used to describe to me, but your poetry would improve if you connected yourself to towering golden candles and lengthy, rhythmic hymns, and even though the American clergy might be somewhat middle-class, as Beatrice always mentioned, you could simply attend the fashionable parishes, and I'll arrange for you to meet Monsignor Darcy who truly is remarkable.

Kerry's death hit hard, and Jesse's did too, though perhaps not quite as much. I'm incredibly curious about what strange corner of the world has swallowed up Burne. Do you think he might be locked up in prison using a fake name? I have to admit that the war, rather than making me more traditional in my beliefs, which would be the expected response, has turned me into a fervent agnostic. The Catholic Church has been weakened so many times recently that its role has become timidly insignificant, and they don't have any talented writers anymore. I'm tired of Chesterton.

I've only found one soldier who went through the heavily promoted spiritual crisis, like this person, Donald Hankey, and the one I knew was already preparing for the ministry, so he was ready for it. I genuinely believe that's all mostly nonsense, though it appeared to provide sentimental comfort to those back home; and might make fathers and mothers value their children more. This crisis-driven religion is quite worthless and temporary at best. I believe four men have found Paris for every one that found God.

But us—you and me and Alec—oh, we'll hire a Japanese butler and dress up for dinner and have wine on the table and live a thoughtful, detached life until we decide to use machine guns against the property owners—or throw bombs with the Bolshevik God! Tom, I hope something exciting happens. I'm restless as hell and terrified of getting fat or falling in love and becoming domesticated.

The place at Lake Geneva is now available for rent, but when I arrive, I'm heading west to meet with Mr. Barton and gather some information. Send your letters to me at the Blackstone in Chicago.

S'ever, dear Boswell,

Samuel Johnson.

Book Two:
The Education Of A Personage

Chapter 1. The Debutante

The time is February. The place is a large, elegant bedroom in the Connage house on Sixty-eighth Street, New York. A girl's room: pink walls and curtains with a pink bedspread on a cream-colored bed. Pink and cream are the room's main colors, but the only piece of furniture completely visible is an elegant dressing table with a glass top and a three-sided mirror. On the walls hangs an expensive print of "Cherry Ripe," several refined dogs by Landseer, and "The King of the Black Isles" by Maxfield Parrish.

Great chaos made up of the following items: seven or eight empty cardboard boxes with tissue-paper strips hanging limply from their openings like panting tongues; a mixture of daytime dresses tangled with their evening counterparts, all spread across the table, all clearly brand new; a roll of tulle that has lost all composure and twisted itself wildly around everything within reach, and on the two small chairs, a collection of undergarments that defies description. Anyone would be curious to see the bill for all this finery on display, and one can't help wanting to catch a glimpse of the princess for whom all this was purchased—Wait! There's someone! What a letdown! It's just a maid searching for something—she picks up a pile from one chair—Not there; she tries another pile, then the dressing table, then the dresser drawers. She uncovers several beautiful slips and an incredible set of pajamas, but this doesn't seem to be what she's looking for—she leaves the room.

An unclear murmur came from the adjacent room.

Now, things are heating up. This is Alec's mother, Mrs. Connage, full-figured, stately, with rouge applied to the point of looking like a dowager and completely exhausted. Her lips move meaningfully as she searches for IT. Her hunt is less comprehensive than the maid's, but there's a hint of rage in it that more than compensates for how superficial it is. She trips on the tulle and her "damn" can be clearly heard. She leaves without finding anything.

More chatter outside and a girl's voice, a very spoiled voice, says: "Of all the stupid people—"

After a brief pause, a third person enters the room—not the woman with the damaged voice, but a younger version of her. This is Cecelia Connage, sixteen years old, attractive, clever, and naturally cheerful. She's dressed for the evening in a gown whose deliberate simplicity likely bores her. She walks to the closest pile of clothes, picks up a small pink item, and holds it up to examine it critically.

CECELIA: Pink?

ROSALIND: (Outside) Yes!

CECELIA: Very snappy?

ROSALIND: Yes!

CECELIA: I've got it!

(She catches sight of herself in the dressing table mirror and begins to dance enthusiastically.)

ROSALIND: (Outside) What are you doing—trying it on?

CECELIA stops speaking and exits, carrying the garment over her right shoulder.

From the other door, ALEC CONNAGE enters. He glances around quickly and shouts in a booming voice: Mama! A chorus of protest erupts from the next room, and feeling encouraged, he begins moving toward it, but another chorus drives him back.

ALEC: So that's where you all are! Amory Blaine is here.

CECELIA: (Quickly) Take him downstairs.

ALEC: Oh, he is downstairs.

MRS. CONNAGE: Well, you can show him where his room is. Tell him I'm sorry that I can't meet him now.

ALEC: He's heard a lot about all of you. I wish you would hurry up. Father is telling him everything about the war and he's getting restless. He's somewhat temperamental.

(This final action is enough to bring CECELIA into the room.)

CECELIA: (Sitting down on top of the lingerie) What do you mean by temperamental? You always used to describe him that way in your letters.

ALEC: Oh, he writes stuff.

CECELIA: Does he play the piano?

ALEC: I don't think so.

CECELIA: (Thoughtfully) Something to drink?

ALEC: Yes—nothing strange about him.

CECELIA: Money?

ALEC: Good God—ask him, he used to have plenty of money, and he's got some income now.

(MRS. CONNAGE appears.)

MRS. CONNAGE: Alec, naturally we're happy to welcome any friend of yours—

ALEC: You really should meet Amory.

MRS. CONNAGE: Naturally, I do. But I find it quite immature of you to abandon a perfectly fine home just to go live with two other young men in some awful apartment. I hope this isn't so you can all drink however much you please. (She stops speaking.) He's going to be somewhat overlooked tonight. This happens to be Rosalind's week, you understand. When a young woman makes her debut, she requires all the focus.

ROSALIND: (Outside) Well, then, prove it by coming here and hooking me.

(MRS. CONNAGE leaves.)

ALEC: Rosalind hasn't changed a bit.

CECELIA: (In a lower tone) She's terribly spoiled.

ALEC: She'll meet her match tonight.

CECELIA: Who—Mr. Amory Blaine?

(ALEC nods.)

CECELIA: Well, Rosalind hasn't yet encountered a man she can't outmaneuver. Honestly, Alec, she treats men horribly. She mistreats them and dismisses them and cancels plans with them and shows complete boredom right to their faces—and they keep coming back for more.

ALEC: They love it.

CECELIA: They hate it. She's a—she's some kind of vampire, I think—and she can usually make girls do whatever she wants—except she hates girls.

ALEC: Personality runs in our family.

CECELIA: (Resignedly) I suppose it ran out before it reached me.

ALEC: Does Rosalind behave herself?

CECELIA: Not particularly well. Oh, she's average—smokes sometimes, drinks punch, frequently kissed—Oh, yes—common knowledge—one of the effects of the war, you know.

(MRS. CONNAGE enters.)

MRS. CONNAGE: Rosalind is almost done, so I can go downstairs and meet your friend.

(ALEC and his mother go out.)

ROSALIND: (Outside) Oh, mother—

CECELIA: Mother's gone down.

(And now ROSALIND enters. ROSALIND is—completely ROSALIND. She's one of those women who never has to try even a little bit to make men fall in love with her. Two kinds of men rarely do: boring men are typically intimidated by her intelligence, and intellectual men are typically intimidated by her beauty. All the rest belong to her by natural right.

If Rosalind could be spoiled, the process would have been finished by now, and truthfully, her temperament isn't everything it ought to be; she desires what she desires when she desires it and she tends to make everyone around her quite unhappy when she doesn't receive it—but in the genuine sense she isn't spoiled. Her vibrant enthusiasm, her desire to develop and discover, her boundless belief in the limitless nature of romance, her bravery and essential honesty—these qualities remain unspoiled.

There are extended stretches when she genuinely despises her entire family. She lacks moral principles entirely; her approach to life is to seize the day for herself while letting others do as they please. She delights in scandalous tales: she possesses that crude element that typically accompanies personalities that are both refined and expansive. She desires people's approval, but their rejection neither troubles her nor alters her behavior. She is far from being an exemplary person.

The education of every beautiful woman involves understanding men. ROSALIND had experienced disappointment with one man after another as individuals, yet she maintained strong faith in men as a gender. She despised women. They embodied traits that she recognized and loathed within herself—emerging pettiness, vanity, cowardice, and minor dishonesty. She once declared to a room filled with her mother's friends that women's sole justification was serving as a disruptive force among men. She was an exceptional dancer, sketched skillfully though quickly, and possessed a remarkable talent with language, which she reserved exclusively for writing love letters.

But every critique of Rosalind ultimately comes back to her stunning appearance. She had that magnificent shade of golden hair that the hair dye industry thrives on people trying to recreate. Her mouth was eternally kissable—small, subtly sensual, and completely captivating. She possessed gray eyes and flawless skin with just two hints of fading color. Her figure was slim and athletic without being underdeveloped, and watching her was pure pleasure whether she was moving around a room, walking down a street, swinging a golf club, or doing a cartwheel.

A final distinction—her vibrant, immediate presence lacked that deliberate, performative quality that Amory had discovered in Isabelle. Monsignor Darcy would have been completely puzzled about whether to classify her as a personality or a personage. She was perhaps the delightful, indefinable, once-in-a-century combination.

On the night of her debut, despite all her unusual, wandering wisdom, she's very much like a delighted little girl. Her mother's maid has just finished styling her hair, but she has impatiently decided that she can do it better herself. She's too anxious right now to remain in one spot. That's why we find her here in this cluttered room. She's about to speak. ISABELLE'S deep tones had resembled a violin, but if you could listen to ROSALIND, you would describe her voice as melodious as a waterfall.

ROSALIND: Honestly, there are only two outfits in the world that I really love wearing—(Brushing her hair at the vanity.) One's a hoop skirt with pantaloons; the other's a one-piece swimsuit. I look absolutely charming in both of them.

CECELIA: Are you happy you're coming out?

ROSALIND: Yes; aren't you?

CECELIA: (Cynically) You're happy because now you can get married and settle down on Long Island with that wild crowd of young married couples. You want your life to be nothing but one flirtation after another, with a different man at every turn.

ROSALIND: Want it to be one! You mean I've found it one.

CECELIA: Ha!

ROSALIND: Cecelia, darling, you have no idea what a burden it is to be like me. I have to keep my expression completely stoic on the street to prevent men from winking at me. When I laugh loudly from a front-row seat at the theater, the comedian performs for me for the entire rest of the show. If I lower my voice, glance down, or drop my handkerchief at a dance, my partner calls me on the phone every single day for a week.

CECELIA: It must be an awful strain.

ROSALIND: The unfortunate part is that the only men who interest me at all are the totally ineligible ones. Now—if I were poor I'd go on the stage.

CECELIA: Yes, you might as well get paid for all the acting you do.

ROSALIND: Sometimes when I've felt especially beautiful I've thought, why should this be wasted on just one man?

CECELIA: When you get especially moody, I often wonder why it should all be wasted on just one family. (Getting up.) I think I'll go downstairs and meet Mr. Amory Blaine. I like men with strong personalities.

ROSALIND: There aren't any. Men don't know how to be truly angry or truly happy—and those who do fall apart completely.

CECELIA: Well, I'm glad I don't have all your worries. I'm engaged.

ROSALIND: (With a scornful smile) Engaged? Why, you little lunatic! If mother heard you talking like that she'd send you off to boarding school, where you belong.

CECELIA: You won't tell her, though, because I know things I could tell—and you're too selfish!

ROSALIND: (A little annoyed) Run along, little girl! Who are you engaged to, the iceman? the man that keeps the candy-store?

CECELIA: Cheap wit—goodbye, darling, I'll see you later.

ROSALIND: Oh, be sure and do that—you're such a help.

(Exit CECELIA. ROSALIND finishes her hair and stands up, humming. She walks over to the mirror and begins to dance in front of it on the plush carpet. She doesn't watch her feet, but focuses on her eyes—never carelessly but always with intense concentration, even when she smiles. The door suddenly bursts open and then slams shut behind AMORY, who appears as cool and handsome as always. He immediately becomes flustered and confused.)

HE: Oh, I'm sorry. I thought—

SHE: (Smiling radiantly) Oh, you're Amory Blaine, aren't you?

HE: (Looking at her intently) And you're Rosalind?

SHE: I'm going to call you Amory—oh, come in—it's all right—mother will be right in—(under her breath) unfortunately.

HE: (Looking around) This is kind of a new experience for me.

SHE: This is No Man's Land.

HE: This is where you—you—(pause)

SHE: Yes—all those things. (She walks over to the dresser.) Look, here's my makeup—eyeliner pencils.

HE: I didn't know you were that way.

SHE: What did you expect?

HE: I thought you'd be kind of—kind of—without sexuality, you know, just swim and play golf.

SHE: Oh, I do—but not during business hours.

HE: Business?

SHE: Six to two—no exceptions.

HE: I'd like to have some stock in the corporation.

SHE: Oh, it's not a corporation—it's just "Rosalind, Unlimited." Fifty-one shares, name, goodwill, and everything goes for $25,000 a year.

HE: (Disapprovingly) That's a pretty cold suggestion.

SHE: Well, Amory, you don't mind—do you? When I meet a man who doesn't bore me to death after two weeks, maybe things will be different.

HE: Strange, you have the exact same perspective on men that I have on women.

SHE: I'm not really feminine, you know—in my mind.

HE: (Interested) Go on.

SHE: No, you—continue—you've gotten me to talk about

myself. That's against the rules.

HE: Rules?

SHE: My own rules—but you—Oh, Amory, I hear you're brilliant. The family expects so much of you.

HE: How encouraging!

SHE: Alec said you'd taught him to think. Did you? I didn't believe anyone could.

HE: No. I'm really quite dull.

(He clearly doesn't mean for this to be taken seriously.)

SHE: Liar.

HE: I'm—I'm religious—I'm literary. I've—I've even written poems.

SHE: Free verse—wonderful! (She recites dramatically.)

"The trees are green,
The birds are singing in the trees,
The girl sips her poison
The bird flies away the girl dies."

HE: (Laughing) No, not that kind.

SHE: (Suddenly) I like you.

HE: Don't.

SHE: Modest too—

HE: I'm scared of you. I'm always scared of girls—until I kiss them.

SHE: (Emphatically) My dear boy, the war is over.

HE: So I'll always be afraid of you.

SHE: (Rather sadly) I suppose you will.

(A brief pause from both of them.)

HE: (After careful thought) Listen. This is a terrible thing to ask.

SHE: (Knowing what's coming) After five minutes.

HE: But will you—kiss me? Or are you afraid?

SHE: I'm never afraid—but your reasons are so weak.

HE: Rosalind, I really want to kiss you.

SHE: So do I.

(They kiss—definitely and thoroughly.)

HE: (After a moment of breathless silence) Well, have I satisfied your curiosity?

SHE: Is yours?

HE: No, it's only aroused.

(He looks it.)

SHE: (Dreamily) I've kissed dozens of men. I suppose I'll kiss dozens more.

HE: (Distracted) Yes, I guess you could—in that way.

SHE: Most people enjoy the way I kiss.

HE: (Coming back to himself) Good God, yes. Kiss me one more time, Rosalind.

SHE: No—my curiosity is usually satisfied after just one.

HE: (Discouraged) Is that a rule?

SHE: I create rules that match each specific situation.

HE: You and I are quite similar—except that I have years more experience under my belt.

SHE: How old are you?

HE: Almost twenty-three. You?

SHE: Nineteen—just.

HE: I suppose you're the product of a fashionable school.

SHE: No—I'm pretty unrefined. I got kicked out of Spence—I can't remember why.

HE: What's your overall direction?

SHE: Oh, I'm intelligent, pretty self-centered, emotional when I get worked up, and I love being admired—

HE: (Suddenly) I don't want to fall in love with you—

SHE: (Raising her eyebrows) Nobody asked you to.

HE: (Continuing coldly) But I probably will. I love your mouth.

SHE: Quiet! Please don't fall for my lips—my hair, eyes, shoulders, slippers—but not my lips. Everyone falls for my lips.

HE: It's quite beautiful.

SHE: It's too small.

HE: No it isn't—let's see.

(He kisses her again with the same thoroughness.)

SHE: (Rather moved) Say something sweet.

HE: (Frightened) Lord help me.

SHE: (Pulling back) Well, don't—if it's so difficult.

HE: Should we start pretending? This quickly?

SHE: We don't have the same sense of time as other people.

HE: It's already become about other people.

SHE: Let's pretend.

HE: No—I can't—it's sentiment.

SHE: You're not sentimental?

HE: No, I'm romantic—a sentimental person believes things will endure—a romantic person hopes desperately that they won't. Sentiment is emotional.

SHE: And you're not? (With her eyes half-closed.) You probably tell yourself that's a superior attitude.

HE: Well—Rosalind, Rosalind, don't argue—kiss me again.

SHE: (Quite cold now) No—I don't want to kiss you.

HE: (Clearly surprised) You wanted to kiss me just a moment ago.

SHE: This is now.

HE: I should probably leave.

SHE: I suppose so.

(He walks toward the door.)

SHE: Oh!

(He turns.)

SHE: (Laughing) Score—Home Team: One hundred—Opponents: Zero.

(He jerks back.)

SHE: (Quickly) Rain—no game.

(He goes out.)

(She quietly walks to the chiffonier, takes out a cigarette case and conceals it in the side drawer of a desk. Her mother enters, holding a notebook.)

MRS. CONNAGE: Good—I've been wanting to speak to you alone before we go downstairs.

ROSALIND: Good heavens! You're scaring me!

MRS. CONNAGE: Rosalind, you've been a very expensive proposition.

ROSALIND: (Resignedly) Yes.

MRS. CONNAGE: And you know your father doesn't have what he once had.

ROSALIND: (Making a wry face) Oh, please don't talk about money.

MRS. CONNAGE: You can't accomplish anything without it. This is our final year in this house—and unless circumstances improve, Cecelia won't have the opportunities you've enjoyed.

ROSALIND: (Impatiently) Well—what is it?

MRS. CONNAGE: So I'm asking you to please follow several guidelines I've written down in my notebook. First: don't vanish with young men. There might come a time when that's worthwhile, but right now I want you on the dance floor where I can locate you. There are specific men I want you to meet, and I don't want to find you tucked away in some corner of the conservatory trading foolish talk with just anyone—or listening to such nonsense.

ROSALIND: (Sarcastically) Yes, listening to it is better.

MRS. CONNAGE: And don't spend too much time with the college crowd—those young men who are nineteen and twenty years old. I don't object to a prom or a football game, but skipping beneficial social gatherings to dine at small downtown restaurants with just anyone—

ROSALIND: (Presenting her own set of values, which are, in their own way, just as noble as her mother's) Mother, it's finished—you can't control everything now the way you did in the early nineties.

MRS. CONNAGE: (Paying no attention) There are several bachelor friends of your father's that I want you to meet tonight—young men.

ROSALIND: (Nodding wisely) About forty-five?

MRS. CONNAGE: (Sharply) Why not?

ROSALIND: Oh, that's perfectly fine—they understand life and look so charmingly exhausted (shakes her head)—but they'll still dance.

MRS. CONNAGE: I haven't met Mr. Blaine—but I don't think you'll like him. He doesn't seem like someone who can make money.

ROSALIND: Mother, I never think about money.

MRS. CONNAGE: You never hold onto it long enough to actually think about it.

ROSALIND: (Sighs) Yes, I suppose someday I'll marry a lot of it—out of pure boredom.

MRS. CONNAGE: (Looking at her notebook) I received a telegram from Hartford. Dawson Ryder is coming to visit. Now there's a young man I really like, and he's incredibly wealthy. It seems to me that since you appear to be losing interest in Howard Gillespie, you might want to show Mr. Ryder some encouragement. This is the third time he's made the trip up here in a month.

ROSALIND: How did you know I was tired of Howard Gillespie?

MRS. CONNAGE: That poor boy looks so miserable every time he visits.

ROSALIND: That was one of those romantic, pre-battle affairs. They're all wrong.

MRS. CONNAGE: (Her voice filled with emotion) At any rate, make us proud of you tonight.

ROSALIND: Don't you think I'm beautiful?

MRS. CONNAGE: You know you are.

(From downstairs comes the sound of a violin being tuned and the roll of a drum. MRS. CONNAGE quickly turns to her daughter.)

MRS. CONNAGE: Come!

ROSALIND: One minute!

Her mother leaves. Rosalind walks over to the mirror where she admires herself with obvious pleasure. She kisses her hand and presses it against her reflection's lips. Then she turns off the lights and exits the room. The space falls silent for a moment. A few piano notes, the subtle beat of quiet drums, and the whisper of fresh silk all merge together on the staircase outside and float in through the partially open door. Shadowy figures move past in the illuminated hallway. The laughter from downstairs grows louder and more abundant. Then someone enters, shuts the door, and flips on the lights. It is Cecelia. She walks to the dresser, searches through the drawers, pauses uncertainly—then moves to the desk where she picks up the cigarette case and takes one out. She lights it and then, smoking and exhaling, walks toward the mirror.

CECELIA: (Speaking with an extremely refined accent) Oh, absolutely, making your debut in society is such a joke these days, you know. You really experience so much before you turn seventeen that it's actually a letdown. (Shaking hands with an imaginary middle-aged nobleman.) Yes, your grace—I believe I've heard my sister mention you. Have a cigarette—they're excellent. They're—they're Coronas. You don't smoke? What a shame! The king doesn't permit it, I imagine. Yes, I'll dance.

(So she dances around the room to music coming from downstairs, her arms stretched out toward an imaginary partner, the cigarette moving in her hand.)

———————

Several Hours Later

The corner of a basement den, furnished with a very comfortable leather sofa. Small lights are positioned on each side above, and in the center, hanging over the couch is a painting of a very elderly, very distinguished gentleman from around 1860. Outside, music can be heard playing a fox-trot.

ROSALIND sits on the couch with HOWARD GILLESPIE on her left, a shallow young man around twenty-four years old. He's clearly very miserable, while she appears completely bored.

GILLESPIE: (Weakly) What do you mean I've changed. I feel the same way about you.

ROSALIND: But you don't look the same to me.

GILLESPIE: Three weeks ago you used to tell me that you liked me because I was so jaded, so detached—I still am.

ROSALIND: But not about me. I used to like you because you had brown eyes and thin legs.

GILLESPIE: (Helplessly) They're still thin and brown. You're a vampire, that's all.

ROSALIND: The only thing I understand about seducing men is what I read in sheet music. What throws men off is that I'm completely genuine. I used to believe you never felt jealous. Now you watch me with your eyes no matter where I move.

GILLESPIE: I love you.

ROSALIND: (Coldly) I know it.

GILLESPIE: And you haven't kissed me for two weeks. I thought that once a girl was kissed she was—was—won over.

ROSALIND: Those days are over. I have to be won all over again every time you see me.

GILLESPIE: Are you serious?

ROSALIND: Pretty much the same as always. There used to be two types of kisses: First, when girls were kissed and then abandoned; second, when they got engaged. Now there's a third type, where the man gets kissed and then abandoned. If Mr. Jones from the 1890s boasted that he'd kissed a girl, everyone knew he was done with her. If Mr. Jones from 1919 makes the same boast, everyone knows it's because he can't kiss her anymore. Give any girl a fair chance and she can outdo a man these days.

GILLESPIE: Then why do you play with men?

ROSALIND: (Leaning forward confidentially) For that first moment, when he's interested. There is a moment—Oh, just before the first kiss, a whispered word—something that makes it worthwhile.

GILLESPIE: And then?

ROSALIND: After that, get him to talk about himself. Before long, he'll think of nothing except being alone with you—he becomes moody, refuses to fight, loses interest in games—Victory!

(Enter DAWSON RYDER, twenty-six, handsome, wealthy, faithful to his own, a bore perhaps, but steady and sure of success.)

RYDER: I believe this is my dance, Rosalind.

ROSALIND: Well, Dawson, so you do recognize me. Now I know I'm not wearing too much makeup. Mr. Ryder, this is Mr. Gillespie.

(They shake hands and GILLESPIE leaves, feeling deeply dejected.)

RYDER: Your party is definitely a success.

ROSALIND: Is it—I haven't seen it lately. I'm tired—Do you mind if we sit this one out?

RYDER: Listen—I'm thrilled. You know how much I hate this whole "rushing" concept. Meet a girl yesterday, today, tomorrow.

ROSALIND: Dawson!

RYDER: What?

ROSALIND: I wonder if you know you love me.

RYDER: (Startled) What—Oh—you know you're incredible!

ROSALIND: Because you know I'm a terrible choice. Anyone who marries me will have their hands full. I'm difficult—really difficult.

RYDER: Oh, I wouldn't say that.

ROSALIND: Oh, yes, I am—especially to the people closest to me. (She stands up.) Come on, let's go. I've changed my mind and I want to dance. Mother is probably having a fit.

(They exit. ALEC and CECELIA enter.)

CECELIA: Just my luck to end up with my own brother during intermission.

ALEC: (Gloomily) I'll leave if that's what you want.

CECELIA: Good heavens, no—who would I start the next dance with? (Sighs.) Dancing hasn't been the same since the French officers left.

ALEC: (Thoughtfully) I don't want Amory to fall in love with Rosalind.

CECELIA: Well, I thought that was exactly what you wanted.

ALEC: I did, but ever since I saw those girls—I'm not sure anymore. I'm really fond of Amory. He's a sensitive person and I don't want him to get his heart broken by someone who doesn't care about him.

CECELIA: He's very good looking.

ALEC: (Still thoughtfully) She won't marry him, but a woman doesn't need to marry a man to break his heart.

CECELIA: What causes it? I wish I understood the secret.

ALEC: Well, you heartless little cat. It's fortunate for some people that God gave you a flat nose.

(Enter MRS. CONNAGE.)

MRS. CONNAGE: Where on earth is Rosalind?

ALEC: (Brilliantly) Of course you've come to the right people to find out. She would naturally be with us.

MRS. CONNAGE: Her father has arranged for eight unmarried millionaires to meet her.

ALEC: You could put together a team and walk through the hallways.

MRS. CONNAGE: I'm completely serious—for all I know she might be at the Cocoanut Grove with some football player on the night of her debut. You look to the left and I'll—

ALEC: (Casually) Wouldn't it be better to send the butler through the cellar?

MRS. CONNAGE: (Completely serious) Oh, you don't think she would be there?

CECELIA: He's only joking, mother.

ALEC: Mother had a photograph of herself tapping a beer keg with some high hurdler.

MRS. CONNAGE: Let's take a look right now.

(They exit. ROSALIND enters with GILLESPIE.)

GILLESPIE: Rosalind—I'm asking you one more time. Don't you care about me at all?

(AMORY walks in briskly.)

AMORY: My dance.

ROSALIND: Mr. Gillespie, this is Mr. Blaine.

GILLESPIE: I've met Mr. Blaine. You're from Lake Geneva, aren't you?

AMORY: Yes.

GILLESPIE: (Desperately) I've been there. It's in the Middle West, isn't it?

AMORY: (With spirit) More or less. But I've always believed I'd rather be a small-town firecracker than bland, flavorless broth.

GILLESPIE: What!

AMORY: Oh, no offense.

(GILLESPIE bows and leaves.)

ROSALIND: He's too much people.

AMORY: I was in love with a people once.

ROSALIND: So?

AMORY: Oh, yes—her name was Isabelle—there was nothing to her at all except what I imagined her to be.

ROSALIND: What happened?

AMORY: I finally managed to convince her that she was more intelligent than I was—and then she dumped me. She said I was too critical and impractical, you know.

ROSALIND: What do you mean impractical?

AMORY: Oh—drive a car, but can't change a tire.

ROSALIND: What are you going to do?

AMORY: Can't say—run for President, write—

ROSALIND: Greenwich Village?

AMORY: Good heavens, no—I said write—not drink.

ROSALIND: I'm attracted to businessmen. Smart men are typically so unattractive.

AMORY: I feel like I've known you forever.

ROSALIND: Oh, are you going to start the "pyramid" story?

AMORY: No—I was going to make it French. I was Louis XIV and you were one of my—my—(Changing his tone.) Suppose—we fell in love.

ROSALIND: I've suggested pretending.

AMORY: If we did it would be very big.

ROSALIND: Why?

AMORY: Because selfish people are in a way terribly capable of great loves.

ROSALIND: (Turning her lips up) Pretend.

(Very deliberately they kiss.)

AMORY: I can't say sweet things. But you are beautiful.

ROSALIND: Not that.

AMORY: What then?

ROSALIND: (Sadly) Oh, nothing—I just want genuine emotion, real feeling—and I never find it.

AMORY: I never find anything else in the world—and I hate it.

ROSALIND: It's so difficult to find a man who can satisfy one's artistic preferences.

(Someone has opened a door and the music of a waltz flows into the room. ROSALIND rises.)

ROSALIND: Listen! They're playing "Kiss Me Again."

(He looks at her.)

AMORY: Well?

ROSALIND: Well?

AMORY: (Quietly—defeated) I love you.

ROSALIND: I love you—now.

(They kiss.)

AMORY: Oh, God, what have I done?

ROSALIND: Nothing. Oh, don't talk. Kiss me again.

AMORY: I don't know why or how, but I love you—from the moment I saw you.

ROSALIND: Me too—I—I—oh, tonight's tonight.

(Her brother walks in, stops suddenly, and then says loudly: "Oh, excuse me," before leaving.)

ROSALIND: (Her lips barely moving) Don't let me go—I don't care who finds out what I do.

AMORY: Say it!

ROSALIND: I love you—right now. (They separate.) Oh— I'm so young, thank God—and quite beautiful, thank God—and happy, thank God, thank God—(She stops and then, in a strange moment of foresight, adds) Poor Amory!

(He kisses her again.)

———

Fate

Within two weeks, Amory and Rosalind had fallen deeply and passionately in love. The critical tendencies that had ruined a dozen previous relationships for each of them were overwhelmed by the powerful surge of emotion that swept through them both.

"It might be a crazy love affair," she told her worried mother, "but it's not meaningless."

The wave carried Amory into an advertising agency in early March, where he switched back and forth between remarkable bursts of truly outstanding work and wild fantasies of getting rich quickly and traveling through Italy with Rosalind.

They spent all their time together—sharing lunch, dinner, and almost every evening—always wrapped in a kind of breathless silence, as though they worried that at any moment the magic might shatter and cast them out of this heaven of passion and romance. Yet the enchantment deepened into something more profound, growing stronger with each passing day; they started discussing marriage in July—then moved it up to June. Everything in life became defined by their love, every experience, every longing, every dream was erased—their sense of humor retreated into hiding; their past relationships now seemed mildly amusing and barely worth remembering as youthful mistakes.

For the second time in his life, Amory had experienced a complete upheaval and was rushing to align himself with his generation.

A Little Interlude

Amory walked slowly up the avenue and felt that the night belonged to him—the spectacle and celebration of rich twilight and shadowy streets... it felt as though he had finally closed the book of fading melodies and entered the passionate, vibrant pathways of life. All around him were these countless lights, this promise of a night filled with streets and singing—he moved through the crowd in a dreamlike state as if he expected to see Rosalind rushing toward him with eager steps from every corner.... How the unforgettable faces of dusk would merge into her, the countless footsteps, a thousand musical beginnings, would merge into her footsteps; and there would be more intoxication than wine in the tenderness of her eyes meeting his. Even his dreams now were soft violins floating like summer sounds through the

200

summer air.

The room was dark except for the dim light from Tom's cigarette as he relaxed by the open window. When the door closed behind him, Amory paused for a moment with his back pressed against it.

"Hello, Benvenuto Blaine. How did the advertising business go today?"

Amory stretched out on a couch.

"I hated it as always!" The brief glimpse of the busy office was quickly replaced by another image.

"My God! She's wonderful!"

Tom sighed.

"I can't explain to you," Amory said again, "exactly how amazing she is. I don't want you to understand. I don't want anyone to understand."

Another sigh drifted from the window—a completely resigned sigh.

"She's life and hope and happiness, my whole world now."

He felt a tear trembling on his eyelid.

"Oh, wow, Tom!"

Bitter Sweet

"Sit like we do," she whispered.

He settled into the large chair and extended his arms so she could curl up within his embrace.

"I knew you would come tonight," she said softly, "like summer, just when I needed you most... darling... darling..."

His lips moved slowly across her face.

"You taste so good," he sighed.

"What do you mean, lover?"

"Oh, just sweet, just sweet..." he held her closer.

"Amory," she whispered, "when you're ready for me I'll marry you."

"We won't have much at first."

"Don't!" she cried. "It hurts when you blame yourself for what you can't give me. I have your precious self—and that's enough for me."

"Tell me..."

"You know, don't you? Oh, you know."

"Yes, but I want to hear you say it."

"I love you, Amory, with all my heart."

"Always, will you?"

"All my life—Oh, Amory—"

"What?"

"I want to belong to you. I want your people to be my people. I want to have your babies."

"But I don't have any people."

"Don't laugh at me, Amory. Just kiss me."

"I'll do what you want," he said.

"No, I'll do what you want. We're you—not me. Oh, you're so much a part, so much all of me..."

He closed his eyes.

"I'm so happy that I'm scared. Wouldn't it be terrible if this was—was the best it gets?..."

She gazed at him with a dreamy expression.

"Beauty and love fade away, I understand.... Oh, there's sorrow in that as well. I think all profound joy carries a touch of sadness. Beauty represents the fragrance of roses and then the inevitable death of those roses—"

"Beauty means the agony of sacrifice and the end of agony...."

"And, Amory, we're beautiful, I know. I'm sure God loves us—"

"He loves you. You're his most precious possession."

"I'm not his, I'm yours. Amory, I belong to you. For the first time I regret all the other kisses; now I know how much a kiss can mean."

Then they would smoke together, and he would share stories about his day at work and discuss where they might make their home. On occasions when he became especially talkative, she would drift off to sleep in his embrace, but he cherished that Rosalind—every version of Rosalind—more deeply than he had ever loved anyone else in his life. These were moments that slipped away like shadows, impossible to hold onto or fully recall.

Aquatic Incident

One day, when Amory and Howard Gillespie happened to run into each other downtown, they decided to have lunch together, and Amory heard a story that absolutely delighted him. After having several cocktails, Gillespie was feeling chatty and started by telling Amory that he was convinced Rosalind was a bit eccentric.

He had joined her for a swimming party in Westchester County, and someone mentioned that Annette Kellerman had visited there one day and had dove from the top of a shaky, thirty-foot summer house. Right away, Rosalind demanded that Howard climb up with her to see what it looked like.

A minute later, as he sat with his feet hanging over the edge, a figure rushed past him; Rosalind, with her arms stretched out in a graceful swan dive, had glided through the air into the crystal-clear water.

"Of course I had to go after that—and I almost killed myself. I thought I was doing pretty well to even attempt it. Nobody else in the group tried it. Well, afterwards Rosalind had the audacity to ask me why I bent over when I dove. 'It didn't make it any easier,' she said, 'it just took all the bravery out of it.' I ask you, what can a person do with a girl like that? Pointless, I call it."

Gillespie couldn't figure out why Amory kept grinning with such pleasure throughout their entire lunch. He suspected that Amory might be one of those superficial optimists.

Five Weeks Later

Again the library of the Connage house. ROSALIND sits alone on the couch, staring moodily and unhappily at nothing. She has changed noticeably—she's somewhat thinner, for one thing; the brightness in her eyes has dimmed; she looks easily a year older.

Her mother enters, wrapped in an opera cloak. She looks at Rosalind with a nervous glance.

MRS. CONNAGE: Who is coming tonight?

(ROSALIND doesn't hear her, or at least doesn't acknowledge it.)

MRS. CONNAGE: Alec is coming up to take me to this Barrie play, "Et tu, Brutus." (She realizes that she is talking to herself.) Rosalind! I asked you who is coming tonight?

ROSALIND: (Startled) Oh—what—oh—Amory—

MRS. CONNAGE: (Sarcastically) You have so many admirers these days that I couldn't possibly guess which one you mean. (ROSALIND doesn't respond.) Dawson Ryder has shown more patience than I expected he would. You haven't spent a single evening with him this week.

ROSALIND: (With a very weary expression that is quite new to her face.) Mother—please—

MRS. CONNAGE: Oh, I won't get involved. You've already thrown away more than two months on some supposed genius who doesn't have a dime to his name, but go right ahead, throw your life away on him. I won't get involved.

ROSALIND: (As if repeating a tiresome lesson) You know he has a little income—and you know he's earning thirty-five dollars a week in advertising—

MRS. CONNAGE: And it wouldn't pay for your clothes. (She pauses but ROSALIND doesn't respond.) I'm looking out for you when I tell you not to make a decision you'll regret for the rest of your life. It's not like your father could support you. He's been struggling financially recently and he's getting old. You'd be completely dependent on someone who lives in fantasies, a pleasant, well-bred young man, but still a dreamer—just clever. (She suggests that this trait itself is somewhat troubling.)

ROSALIND: For heaven's sake, mother—

(A maid appears and announces Mr. Blaine, who enters right behind her. For the past ten days, AMORY'S friends have been telling him that he "looks like the wrath of God," and they're absolutely right. The truth is, he hasn't been able to eat a single bite in the last thirty-six hours.)

AMORY: Good evening, Mrs. Connage.

MRS. CONNAGE: (Not unkindly) Good evening, Amory.

(AMORY and ROSALIND look at each other—and ALEC enters. ALEC has maintained a neutral stance throughout. Deep down, he believes that the marriage would turn AMORY into someone ordinary and make ROSALIND unhappy, but he feels deeply sorry for both of them.)

ALEC: Hi, Amory!

AMORY: Hi, Alec! Tom said he'd meet you at the theatre.

ALEC: Yeah, I just saw him. How's the advertising going today? Did you write some brilliant copy?

AMORY: Oh, it's about the same. I got a raise—(Everyone looks at him rather eagerly)—of two dollars a week. (General collapse.)

MRS. CONNAGE: Come on, Alec, I can hear the car.

(A good night, though somewhat chilly in places. After MRS. CONNAGE and ALEC leave, there is a moment of silence. ROSALIND continues to gaze pensively at the fireplace. AMORY walks over to her and wraps his arm around her.)

AMORY: Darling girl.

(They kiss. Another pause and then she grabs his hand, covers it with kisses and presses it to her chest.)

ROSALIND: (Sadly) I love your hands more than anything else. I picture them so often when you're not with me—looking so weary; I know every single line on them. My dear hands!

(Their eyes meet for a moment and then she starts to cry—a tearless sobbing.)

AMORY: Rosalind!

ROSALIND: Oh, we're so terribly pitiful!

AMORY: Rosalind!

ROSALIND: Oh, I want to die!

AMORY: Rosalind, I can't take another night like this—I'm falling apart. You've been acting this way for four days straight. You need to give me some hope, or I won't be able to work, eat, or sleep. (He glances around desperately, as though searching for fresh words to express a tired, overused sentiment.) We have to make a beginning. I want us to start fresh together. (His strained optimism disappears when he sees she remains distant.) What's wrong? (He suddenly stands up and begins walking back and forth across the room.) It's Dawson Ryder—that's what this is about. He's been getting under your skin. You've spent every afternoon with him this past week. People keep coming to me, telling me they've spotted you two together, and I have to smile and nod and act like it doesn't mean anything to me. And you refuse to tell me what's happening between you.

ROSALIND: Amory, if you don't sit down I'll scream.

AMORY: (Suddenly sitting down beside her) Oh, Lord.

ROSALIND: (Taking his hand gently) You know I love you, don't you?

AMORY: Yes.

ROSALIND: You know I'll always love you—

AMORY: Don't speak like that; you're scaring me. It sounds like we're not going to be together anymore. (She starts crying softly and gets up from the couch to move to the armchair.) I've had this feeling all afternoon that everything was falling apart. I almost lost it completely at the office—I couldn't write a single word. Tell me what's happening.

ROSALIND: There's nothing to tell, I say. I'm just nervous.

AMORY: Rosalind, you're considering the possibility of marrying Dawson Ryder.

ROSALIND: (After a pause) He's been asking me to all day.

AMORY: Well, he's got his nerve!

ROSALIND: (After another pause) I like him.

AMORY: Don't say that. It hurts me.

ROSALIND: Don't be ridiculous. You know you're the only man I've ever loved, and ever will love.

AMORY: (Quickly) Rosalind, let's get married—next week.

ROSALIND: We can't.

AMORY: Why not?

ROSALIND: Oh, we can't. I'd be your wife—in some awful place.

AMORY: We'll have two hundred and seventy-five dollars a month in total.

ROSALIND: Darling, I don't even do my own hair, usually.

AMORY: I'll do it for you.

ROSALIND: (Between a laugh and a sob) Thanks.

AMORY: Rosalind, you can't be thinking of marrying someone else. Tell me! You leave me in the dark. I can help you fight it out if you'll only tell me.

ROSALIND: It's just—us. We're pathetic, that's all. The exact qualities I love about you are the same ones that will forever make you unsuccessful.

AMORY: (Grimly) Go on.

ROSALIND: Oh—it's Dawson Ryder. He's so dependable, I almost feel like he would be just—just part of the scenery.

AMORY: You don't love him.

ROSALIND: I know, but I respect him, and he's a good man and a strong one.

AMORY: (Reluctantly) Yes—he's that.

ROSALIND: Well—here's one small thing. There was a little poor boy we encountered in Rye on Tuesday afternoon—and Dawson picked him up and put him on his lap and spoke with him and promised him an Indian costume—and the following day he remembered and purchased it—and it was so touching and I couldn't stop thinking about how wonderful he'd be with—with our children—looking after them—and I wouldn't need to worry.

AMORY: (In despair) Rosalind! Rosalind!

ROSALIND: (With a faint roguishness) Don't look like you're deliberately trying to appear miserable.

AMORY: What incredible power we possess to hurt one another!

ROSALIND: (Starting to cry again) It's been so perfect—you and I. So much like a dream that I had always wanted and never thought I would find. The first real unselfishness I have ever felt in my life. And I can't watch it fade away in a dull, lifeless atmosphere!

AMORY: It won't—it won't!

ROSALIND: I'd rather keep it as a beautiful memory—tucked away in my heart.

AMORY: Yes, women can handle that—but men can't. I would always remember not the beauty of it while it was happening, but only the pain, the endless pain.

ROSALIND: Don't!

AMORY: All these years of never seeing you, never being able to kiss you, with just a closed and locked gate between us—you don't have the courage to become my wife.

ROSALIND: No—no—I'm choosing the most difficult path, the toughest route. Marrying you would mean defeat and I never accept defeat—if you don't quit pacing back and forth I'll scream!

(Once again, he collapses onto the couch in despair.)

AMORY: Come over here and kiss me.

ROSALIND: No.

AMORY: Don't you want to kiss me?

ROSALIND: Tonight I want you to love me calmly and coolly.

AMORY: The beginning of the end.

ROSALIND: (With a sudden realization) Amory, we're both young. People forgive us right now for our pretenses and self-absorption, for treating people like servants while still managing to escape consequences. They're willing to overlook it now. But you're going to face a lot of hard lessons ahead—

AMORY: And you're afraid to take them with me.

ROSALIND: No, not that. There was a poem I read somewhere—you'll say Ella Wheeler Wilcox and laugh—but listen:

"For this is wisdom—to love and live,
To take what fate or the gods may give,
To ask no question, to make no prayer,
To kiss the lips and caress the hair,
Speed passion's ebb as we greet its flow,
To have and to hold, and, in time—let go."

AMORY: But we haven't had.

ROSALIND: Amory, I belong to you—you know that. There have been moments this past month when I would have given myself to you completely if you had asked. But I can't marry you and destroy both our lives.

AMORY: We have to take our chance for happiness.

ROSALIND: Dawson says I'd learn to love him.

(AMORY sits with his head buried in his hands, completely still. All the life appears to have suddenly drained from him.)

ROSALIND: Lover! Lover! I can't stand being with you, and I can't imagine life without you.

AMORY: Rosalind, we're getting on each other's nerves. It's just that we're both high-strung, and this week—

(His voice sounds strangely aged. She walks over to him and, cupping his face in her hands, kisses him.)

ROSALIND: I can't, Amory. I can't be cut off from the trees

and flowers, trapped in a small apartment, waiting for you. You'd end up hating me in such a confining environment. I'd cause you to hate me.

(Once again, sudden uncontrolled tears blur her vision.)

AMORY: Rosalind—

ROSALIND: Oh, darling, go—Don't make it harder! I can't stand it—

AMORY: (His face tense, his voice tight) Do you understand what you're telling me? Are you saying this is permanent?

(There is somehow a difference in the quality of their suffering.)

ROSALIND: Can't you see—

AMORY: I'm afraid I can't if you love me. You're scared of going through two years of hardship with me.

ROSALIND: I wouldn't be the Rosalind you love.

AMORY: (A little hysterically) I can't give you up! I can't, that's all! I've got to have you!

ROSALIND: (A hard note in her voice) You're acting like a child now.

AMORY: (Wildly) I don't care! You're spoiling our lives!

ROSALIND: I'm doing the wise thing, the only thing.

AMORY: Are you going to marry Dawson Ryder?

ROSALIND: Oh, please don't ask me that. You know I'm mature in some ways, but in others I'm still just a young girl. I love bright, sunny days and beautiful things and happiness, and I'm terrified of having responsibilities. I don't want to think about cooking pots and kitchens and cleaning. I want to worry about whether my legs will get smooth and tan when I go swimming in the summer.

AMORY: And you love me.

ROSALIND: That's exactly why this has to end. Drifting apart causes too much pain. We can't go through any more situations like this one.

(She pulls his ring off her finger and gives it to him. Their eyes fill with tears once more, blurring their vision.)

AMORY: (His lips against her wet cheek) Don't! Keep it, please—oh, don't break my heart!

(She gently presses the ring into his hand.)

ROSALIND: (Brokenly) You'd better go.

AMORY: Goodbye—

(She looks at him once more, with endless longing, endless sadness.)

ROSALIND: Don't ever forget me, Amory—

AMORY: Goodbye—

(He walks to the door, searches for the handle, locates it—she watches him tilt his head back—and then he's gone. Gone—she begins to rise from the lounge but then collapses forward, burying her face in the pillows.)

ROSALIND: Oh, God, I want to die! (After a moment she gets up and with her eyes shut feels her way to the door. Then she turns around and looks at the room one more time. This was where they had sat together and dreamed: that tray she had filled with matches for him so many times; that shade they had carefully lowered one long Sunday afternoon. With tears blurring her vision she stands there remembering; she speaks out loud.) Oh, Amory, what have I done to you?

(And beneath the profound, aching sadness that will eventually fade with time, Rosalind senses that she has lost something, though she cannot say what it is or understand why.)

Chapter 2. Experiments In Convalescence

The Knickerbocker Bar, watched over by Maxfield Parrish's cheerful, vibrant "Old King Cole," was packed with people. Amory paused at the entrance and checked his wrist-watch; he felt a strong need to know the exact time, because something in his mind that organized and categorized everything wanted to mark this moment precisely. Later, it would give him a strange sense of satisfaction to be able to think "that whole thing ended at exactly twenty minutes past eight on Thursday, June 10, 1919." This timing included the walk from her house—a walk that he would later have absolutely no memory of whatsoever.

He was in a rather disturbing state: two days of anxiety and tension, sleepless nights, meals left untouched, all leading up to the emotional breakdown and Rosalind's sudden decision—the stress of it all had numbed his conscious mind into a blessed stupor. As he awkwardly handled the olives at the complimentary lunch counter, a man came over and addressed him, causing the olives to fall from his trembling fingers.

"Well, Amory..."

It was someone he had known at Princeton; he had no idea what the name was.

"Hello, old friend—" he heard himself saying.

"My name is Jim Wilson—you've forgotten."

"Absolutely, Jim. I remember."

"Going to the reunion?"

"You know!" At the same moment, he realized that he wasn't going to the reunion.

"Get overseas?"

Amory nodded, his eyes staring strangely. Moving back to allow someone to pass, he knocked the bowl of olives, sending it crashing to the floor.

"Too bad," he muttered. "Want a drink?"

Wilson, using his heavy-handed diplomatic approach, reached over and slapped him on the back.

"You've had enough, old friend."

Amory stared at him speechlessly until Wilson became uncomfortable under his intense gaze.

"Plenty, hell!" Amory finally said. "I haven't had a drink today."

Wilson looked disbelieving.

"Want a drink or not?" Amory called out harshly.

Together they looked for the bar.

"Rye high."

"I'll just have a Bronx."

Wilson had another drink; Amory had several more. They decided to sit down. At ten o'clock Wilson was replaced by Carling, class of '15. Amory, his head spinning wonderfully, with wave after wave of gentle contentment washing over the wounded parts of his soul, was talking enthusiastically about the war.

"'It's a mental waste," he insisted with owl-like wisdom. "Two years of my life spent in intellectual vacuity. Lost idealism, got to be physical animal," he shook his fist expressively at Old King Cole, "got to be Prussian about everything, women especially. Used to be straight about women in college. Now don't give a damn." He expressed his lack of principle by sweeping a seltzer bottle with a broad gesture to noisy extinction on the floor, but this did not interrupt his speech. "Seek pleasure where you find it for tomorrow we die. That's philosophy for me now on."

Carling yawned, but Amory, growing more animated, kept talking:

"I used to wonder about things—people being satisfied with compromise, that fifty-fifty attitude toward life. Now I don't wonder, I don't wonder—" He became so emphatic in impressing on Carling the fact that he didn't wonder that he lost the thread of his discourse and concluded by announcing to the bar at large that he was a "physical animal."

"What are you celebrating, Amory?"

Amory leaned forward in a confidential manner.

"Celebrating blow my life. Great moment blow my life. Can't tell you about it—"

He heard Carling making a comment to the bartender:

"Give him a bromo-seltzer."

Amory shook his head with indignation.

"Forget about that nonsense!"

"But listen, Amory, you're making yourself sick. You're as white as a ghost."

Amory thought about the question. He attempted to see himself in the mirror, but even when he squinted with one eye, he could only make out the line of bottles sitting behind the bar.

"Like something solid. We're going to get some—some salad."

He adjusted his coat, trying to appear casual, but releasing his grip on the bar proved too difficult for him, and he collapsed against a chair.

"Let's head over to Shanley's," Carling suggested, extending his arm.

With this help, Amory was able to get his legs moving enough to carry him across Forty-second Street.

Shanley's restaurant was quite dark. He realized he was speaking loudly, very clearly and persuasively, he believed, about wanting to crush people beneath his foot. He ate three club sandwiches, wolfing down each one as if it were nothing more than a small piece of candy. Then Rosalind started appearing in his thoughts again, and he noticed his lips silently repeating her name repeatedly. Soon he felt drowsy, and he had a foggy, sluggish awareness of people in formal suits, likely waiters, gathering around his table....

He found himself in a room where Carling was talking about a tangle in his shoelace.

"No one," he managed to say drowsily. "Sleep in them...."

Still Alcoholic

He woke up laughing, his eyes slowly scanning the room around him—clearly a bedroom and bathroom in a nice hotel. His head was spinning and image after image kept forming, blurring, and dissolving before his eyes, but aside from wanting to laugh, he had no fully conscious response. He reached for the phone next to his bed.

"Hello—what hotel is this—?"

"Knickerbocker? All right, send up two rye high-balls—"

He lay there for a moment, casually wondering whether they would send up a full bottle or just a couple of those small glass containers. Then, with some effort, he forced himself out of bed and walked slowly into the bathroom.

When he came out, slowly drying himself with a towel, he discovered the bartender waiting with the drinks and felt a sudden urge to tease him. After thinking about it, he realized this would be beneath his dignity, so he dismissed him with a wave.

As the fresh alcohol poured into his stomach and warmed him from within, the scattered images slowly began to connect into a continuous film of the previous day. Once more he saw Rosalind curled up crying among the pillows, once more he felt her tears wet against his cheek. Her words started echoing in his ears: "Don't ever forget me, Amory—don't ever forget me—"

"Hell!" he stammered out loud, and then he gasped and fell onto the bed in a trembling fit of sorrow. After a moment he opened his eyes and stared at the ceiling.

"What an idiot!" he burst out in frustration, and with a heavy sigh got up and walked over to the bottle. After pouring himself another drink, he let himself sink into the indulgence of crying. He deliberately brought to mind small moments from the spring that had passed, putting his feelings into words that would make him feel the sadness even more deeply.

"We were so happy," he said with dramatic emphasis, "so very happy." Then he broke down again and dropped to his knees beside the bed, burying half his face in the pillow.

"My own girl—my own—Oh—"

He clenched his teeth so tightly that tears poured from his eyes in a torrent.

"Oh... my baby girl, you were everything I had, everything I ever wanted!... Oh, my girl, please come back, come back! I need you so much... I need you... we're so pathetic... all we brought each other was misery.... She's going to be kept away from me.... I won't be able to see her; I won't be able to be her friend. That's how it has to be—that's how it has to be—"

And then again:

"We've been so happy, so very happy...."

He stood up and threw himself onto the bed in a rush of overwhelming emotion, then lay there drained as he slowly came to understand that he had been extremely drunk the previous night, and that his head was spinning wildly once more. He laughed, got up, and walked back over to Lethe....

At noon he encountered a crowd in the Biltmore bar, and the chaos started all over again. He had a hazy memory later of talking about French poetry with a British officer who was presented to him as "Captain Corn, of his Majesty's Foot," and he recalled trying to recite "Clair de Lune" during lunch; then he dozed in a large, comfortable chair until nearly five o'clock when another group discovered and roused him; what followed was an alcohol-fueled preparation of various personalities for the challenge of dinner. They chose theater tickets at Tyson's for a show that had a four-drink program—a production with two droning voices, with murky, somber scenes, and lighting effects that were difficult to track when his eyes acted so strangely. He thought later that it must have been "The Jest."...

Then the Coconut Grove, where Amory slept again on a small balcony outside. Out at Shanley's in Yonkers, he became almost rational, and by carefully controlling how many highballs he consumed, he grew quite clear-headed and talkative. He discovered that the group consisted of five men, two of whom he knew casually; he became insistent about paying his portion of the bill and demanded in a loud voice to settle everything right then and there, much to the entertainment of the surrounding tables.

Someone mentioned that a famous cabaret star was sitting at the nearby table, so Amory stood up and, walking over with confidence, introduced himself... this got him into an argument, first with her companion and then with the headwaiter—Amory's behavior showing an overly formal and exaggerated politeness... he agreed, after being presented with undeniable reasoning, to be escorted back to his own table.

"I've decided to kill myself," he announced suddenly.

"When? Next year?"

"Right now. Tomorrow morning. I'm going to get a room at the Commodore, take a hot bath, and cut my wrists."

"He's becoming obsessed with death and darkness!"

"You need another rye, old boy!"

"We'll all discuss it tomorrow."

But Amory wasn't going to be talked out of arguing, at the very least.

"Did you ever feel that way?" he asked confidentially.

"Sure!"

"Often?"

"My ongoing condition."

This sparked a conversation. One person mentioned that he became so deeply depressed at times that he genuinely thought about it. Another person agreed that life seemed to offer nothing worth living for. "Captain Corn," who had somehow managed to rejoin their group, shared his belief that these feelings were strongest when someone's health was poor. Amory proposed that they should all order a Bronx cocktail, mix broken glass into it, and drink it down. To his relief, nobody supported this idea, so after finishing his highball, he rested his chin in his hand with his elbow propped on the table—what he convinced himself was an extremely subtle, barely noticeable sleeping position—and fell into a deep stupor....

He woke up to find a woman holding onto him tightly, an attractive woman with messy brown hair and deep blue eyes.

"Take me home!" she cried.

"Hello!" said Amory, blinking.

"I like you," she said softly.

"I like you too."

He saw that there was a loud man in the background and that one of his companions was arguing with him.

"The guy I was with is a complete idiot," the blue-eyed woman confided. "I can't stand him. I want to go home with you."

"Are you drunk?" Amory asked with profound insight.

She nodded shyly.

"Go home with him," he said seriously. "He brought you."

At this point the loud man in the background broke free from those holding him back and came forward.

"Hey!" he said angrily. "I brought this girl out here and you're interfering!"

Amory looked at him with cold indifference, while the girl held onto him more tightly.

"Let go of that girl!" shouted the loud man.

Amory attempted to make his eyes look menacing.

"Go to hell!" he snapped at last, then turned his attention to the girl.

"Love at first sight," he suggested.

"I love you," she whispered softly and snuggled up against him. Her eyes truly were beautiful.

Someone leaned over and spoke in Amory's ear.

"That's just Margaret Diamond. She's drunk and this guy brought her here. We should probably let her leave."

"Let him take care of her, then!" Amory shouted angrily. "I'm not a Y.W.C.A. worker, am I?—am I?"

"Let her go!"

"She's the one holding on, damn it! Let her hold on!"

The crowd around the table grew denser. For a moment a fight seemed about to break out, but a smooth-talking waiter bent Margaret Diamond's fingers backward until she let go of Amory, at which point she angrily slapped the waiter across the face and threw her arms around her furious original companion.

"Oh, Lord!" cried Amory.

"Let's go!"

"Come on, the taxis are getting scarce!"

"Check, waiter."

"Come on, Amory. Your romance is over."

Amory laughed.

"You have no idea how right you are. No clue at all. That's the entire problem."

Amory On the Labor Question

Two mornings later, he knocked on the president's door at Bascome and Barlow's advertising agency.

"Come in!"

Amory walked in with unsteady steps.

"'Morning, Mr. Barlow."

Mr. Barlow lifted his glasses to examine more closely and opened his mouth slightly so he could hear better.

"Well, Mr. Blaine. We haven't seen you for several days."

"No," said Amory. "I'm quitting."

"Well—well—this is—"

"I don't like it here."

"I'm sorry. I thought our relationship had been quite—ah—pleasant. You seemed to be a hard worker—maybe a little inclined to write fancy copy—"

"I just got tired of it," Amory interrupted rudely. "It didn't matter one bit to me whether Harebell's flour was any better than anyone else's. In fact, I never even tried it. So I got tired of telling people about it—oh, I know I've been drinking—"

Mr. Barlow's face hardened with layers of stern expression.

"You asked for a position—"

Amory gestured for him to be quiet.

"And I believe I was terribly underpaid. Thirty-five dollars a week—less than what a skilled carpenter makes."

"You had just started. You'd never worked before," Mr. Barlow said calmly.

"But it cost around ten thousand dollars to educate me so I could write your damn material for you. Besides, when it comes to how long someone has worked here, you have stenographers that you've been paying fifteen dollars a week for five years."

"I'm not going to argue with you, sir," said Mr. Barlow as he stood up.

"I'm not either. I just wanted to let you know that I'm quitting."

They stood there for a moment, looking at each other without showing any emotion, and then Amory turned around and walked out of the office.

A Brief Pause

Four days later, he finally came back to the apartment. Tom was working on a book review for The New Democracy, where he had a job on the staff. They looked at each other for a moment without saying anything.

"Well?"

"Well?"

"Good Lord, Amory, where did you get that black eye—and what happened to your jaw?"

Amory laughed.

"That's absolutely nothing."

He took off his coat and exposed his shoulders.

"Look here!"

Tom let out a quiet whistle.

"What hit you?"

Amory laughed again.

"Oh, many people. I was beaten up. That's the truth." He slowly put his shirt back on. "It was inevitable that it would happen eventually, and I wouldn't have wanted to miss it for the world."

"Who was it?"

"Well, there were some waiters and a couple of sailors and a few random people walking by, I think. It's the weirdest feeling. You should get beaten up just to experience what it's like. You eventually fall down and everyone kind of takes swipes at you before you hit the ground—then they start kicking you."

Tom lit a cigarette.

"I spent an entire day trying to track you down all over the city, Amory. But you managed to stay just out of reach the whole time. I'd guess you've been out partying."

Amory collapsed into a chair and asked for a cigarette.

"Are you sober now?" Tom asked with a puzzled look.

"Pretty sober. Why?"

"Well, Alec has left. His family had been pressuring him to come home and live with them, so he—"

A sharp wave of pain shot through Amory.

"Too bad."

"Yes, it's unfortunate. We'll need to find someone else if we're going to remain here. The rent is increasing."

"Sure. Get anybody. I'll leave it to you, Tom."

Amory entered his bedroom. The first thing that caught his eye was a photograph of Rosalind that he had planned to frame, leaning against a mirror on his dresser. He stared at it without emotion. Compared to the vivid mental images of her that filled his mind these days, the photograph seemed strangely artificial. He returned to the study.

"Do you have a cardboard box?"

"No," Tom replied, confused. "Why would I have one? Oh, wait—there might be one in Alec's room."

Eventually Amory discovered what he had been searching for and, walking back to his dresser, pulled open a drawer filled with letters, notes, part of a chain, two small handkerchiefs, and some photographs. While he carefully moved them into the box, his thoughts drifted to a scene from a book where the main character, after keeping a bar of soap that belonged to his lost love for an entire year, finally used it to wash his hands. He chuckled and started humming "After you've gone" ... then stopped suddenly...

The string snapped twice, but then he succeeded in fastening it, let the package fall to the bottom of his trunk, and after slamming the lid shut, he went back to the study.

"Going out?" Tom's voice carried a hint of worry.

"Uh-huh."

"Where?"

"I couldn't tell you, old friend."

"Let's have dinner together."

"Sorry. I told Sukey Brett I'd have dinner with him."

"Oh."

"By-by."

Amory crossed the street and ordered a highball; then he walked to Washington Square and found a seat on the top of a bus. He got off at Forty-third Street and strolled to the Biltmore bar.

"Hi, Amory!"

"What would you like?"

"Hey! Waiter!"

Temperature Normal

The start of prohibition during the "thirsty-first" brought an abrupt end to Amory's attempts to drown his sorrows, and when he woke up one morning to discover that the old days of going

222

from bar to bar were finished, he felt neither guilt about the past three weeks nor sadness that he couldn't repeat them. He had chosen the most extreme, though perhaps the weakest, way to protect himself from the sharp pangs of memory, and while it wasn't an approach he would have recommended to others, he realized in the end that it had accomplished its purpose: he had gotten through the initial wave of pain.

Don't get the wrong idea! Amory had loved Rosalind in a way he would never love another person again. She had captured the prime of his youth and brought out from his hidden depths a tenderness that had amazed him, along with a gentleness and selflessness that he had never shown to anyone else. He had romantic relationships afterward, but they were completely different: in those later relationships he returned to what was probably a more typical mindset, where the woman simply reflected his own emotions back to him. Rosalind had brought out something far deeper than intense attraction; he felt a profound, lasting love for Rosalind.

But toward the end, there had been so much intense drama and tragedy, reaching its peak in the twisted nightmare of his three-week drinking binge, that he felt completely drained emotionally. The people and places he recalled as being calm or elegantly refined seemed to offer him a safe haven. He composed a bitter story that centered on his father's funeral and sent it off to a magazine, getting back a sixty-dollar check and a request for more work in the same style. This flattered his ego, but it didn't motivate him to make any additional effort.

He read voraciously. "A Portrait of the Artist as a Young Man" left him confused and disheartened; "Joan and Peter" and "The Undying Fire" captivated him completely, and he was quite amazed by his discovery, through a critic named Mencken, of several outstanding American novels: "Vandover and the Brute," "The Damnation of Theron Ware," and "Jennie Gerhardt."

Writers like Mackenzie, Chesterton, Galsworthy, and Bennett had fallen in his estimation from wise, deeply experienced masters to simply entertaining writers of his time. Only Shaw's detached precision and brilliant logic, along with H. G. Wells's magnificently passionate attempts to make romantic idealism unlock the mysterious secrets of reality, could hold his complete fascination.

He wanted to see Monsignor Darcy, whom he had contacted when he arrived, but hadn't received a response; moreover, he realized that visiting Monsignor would require telling the story of Rosalind, and the idea of going through it again filled him with dread.

In his search for cool people, he remembered Mrs. Lawrence, a highly intelligent and very dignified woman who had converted to the church and was one of Monsignor's most devoted followers.

He called her on the phone one day. Yes, she remembered him perfectly; no, Monsignor wasn't in town, was in Boston she thought; he'd promised to come to dinner when he returned. Couldn't Amory have lunch with her?

"I thought I'd better catch up, Mrs. Lawrence," he said rather ambiguously when he arrived.

"Monsignor was here just last week," Mrs. Lawrence said with regret. "He really wanted to see you, but he had left your address at home."

"Did he think I'd thrown myself into Bolshevism?" asked Amory, intrigued.

"Oh, he's having a terrible time."

"Why?"

"About the Irish Republic. He thinks it lacks dignity."

"So?"

"He traveled to Boston when the Irish President came to visit, and he felt deeply troubled because the members of the welcoming committee would put their arms around the President when they rode together in a car."

"I don't blame him."

"Well, what struck you most during your time in the military? You look much older now."

"That's from a different, more devastating battle," he replied, managing a smile despite everything. "But regarding the army— let me think—well, I learned that physical bravery largely depends on a man's physical condition. I realized that I was just as courageous as anyone else—that used to concern me before."

"What else?"

"Well, the idea that people can endure anything if they become accustomed to it, and the fact that I received a high score on the psychological examination."

Mrs. Lawrence laughed. Amory found it incredibly refreshing to be in this cool house on Riverside Drive, away from the more crowded parts of New York and the feeling of people breathing heavily in cramped spaces. Mrs. Lawrence reminded him somewhat of Beatrice, not in personality, but in her flawless grace and dignity. The house, its decorations, and the way dinner was served stood in stark contrast to what he had experienced in the grand estates on Long Island, where the servants were so intrusive that you literally had to push past them, or even in the homes of more traditional "Union Club" families. He wondered whether this atmosphere of balanced restraint, this elegance, which struck him as European, came from Mrs. Lawrence's New England heritage or was developed during her extended time living in Italy and Spain.

Two glasses of sauterne at lunch loosened his tongue, and he spoke with what he believed was some of his former charm about religion, literature, and the threatening aspects of the social order. Mrs. Lawrence seemed genuinely pleased with him, and her interest focused particularly on his intellect; he wanted people to appreciate his mind again—eventually it might become such a pleasant place to inhabit once more.

"Monsignor Darcy still believes that you're his reincarnation, that your faith will eventually become clear."

"Perhaps," he agreed. "I'm quite pagan right now. It's just that religion doesn't seem to have any relevance to life at my age."

When he left her house, he walked down Riverside Drive feeling satisfied. It was enjoyable to discuss topics like the young poet Stephen Vincent Benet or the Irish Republic once again. He had grown completely weary of the Irish question after hearing the bitter accusations from Edward Carson and Justice Cohalan, though there was a time when his own Celtic characteristics had been fundamental to his personal beliefs.

There suddenly seemed to be so much left to experience in life, as long as this renewed passion for old interests didn't mean he was retreating from it once more—withdrawing from life itself.

Restlessness

"I'm extremely old and extremely bored, Tom," said Amory one day, stretching himself comfortably in the cozy window seat. He always felt most at ease when lying down.

"You used to be fun to be around before you became a writer," he went on. "Now you hold back any good idea because you think it might work for something you could publish."

Life had returned to a routine without any grand ambitions. They had figured out that by being careful with money, they could still manage to keep the apartment, which Tom had become attached to with the contentment of an old house cat. The vintage English hunting prints hanging on the walls belonged to Tom, along with the large tapestry that was a leftover from his more extravagant college years, and the countless mismatched candlesticks scattered throughout the room, plus the ornate Louis XV chair that nobody could sit in for longer than a minute without developing serious back pain—Tom insisted this was because you were actually sitting on the ghost of Montespan—but regardless of his explanations, it was Tom's collection of furniture that convinced them to remain in the place.

They rarely went out: occasionally to see a play, or for dinner at the Ritz or the Princeton Club. With prohibition, the great meeting places had been dealt fatal blows; one could no longer drift to the Biltmore bar at noon or five o'clock and discover like-minded companions, and both Tom and Amory had grown beyond their enthusiasm for dancing with Midwestern or New Jersey debutantes at the Club-de-Vingt (nicknamed the "Club de Gink") or the Plaza Rose Room—moreover, even that activity required several cocktails "to come down to the intellectual level of the women present," as Amory had once explained to a shocked society matron.

Amory had recently received several troubling letters from Mr. Barton—the Lake Geneva house was too big to rent out easily; the best rental income they could get right now would barely cover this year's taxes and essential repairs; in reality, the lawyer was suggesting that the entire property had become nothing but a financial burden for Amory. Still, even though it might not bring in a single dollar for the next three years, Amory decided with an unclear sense of nostalgia that for now, at least, he wouldn't sell the house.

This specific day when he told Tom about his boredom had been completely ordinary. He had gotten up at noon, eaten lunch with Mrs. Lawrence, and then ridden home in a distracted state on top of one of his cherished buses.

"Why shouldn't you be bored," Tom yawned. "Isn't that the typical state of mind for a young man of your age and circumstances?"

"Yes," said Amory thoughtfully, "but I'm more than bored; I am restless."

"Love and war destroyed you."

"Well," Amory thought about it, "I'm not certain that the war itself had any major impact on either you or me—but it definitely destroyed the old foundations, basically wiped out individualism from our generation."

Tom looked up in surprise.

"Yes it did," Amory insisted. "I'm not sure it didn't destroy it completely from the entire world. Oh God, what a joy it used to be to imagine I might become a truly great dictator or writer or religious or political leader—and now even a Leonardo da Vinci or Lorenzo de Medici couldn't make a real old-fashioned impact in the world. Life has become too enormous and complicated. The world has grown so massive that it can't even move its own fingers, and I was planning to be such a significant finger—"

"I don't agree with you," Tom interrupted. "There have never been men put in such self-centered positions since—oh, since the French Revolution."

Amory strongly disagreed.

"You're confusing this era where every crazy person claims to be an individualist with a true age of individualism. Wilson has only held power when he's spoken for others; he's had to make compromise after compromise. As soon as Trotsky and Lenin take a clear, unwavering position, they'll become nothing more than brief footnotes in history like Kerensky. Even Foch doesn't have half the importance of Stonewall Jackson. War used to be the most individual pursuit a person could engage in, yet the popular war heroes had neither real authority nor responsibility: Guynemer and Sergeant York. How could a schoolboy possibly idolize Pershing? A truly great man has no time to actually accomplish anything except simply exist and be great."

"Then you don't think there will be any more permanent world heroes?"

"Yes—in history—not in life. Carlyle would have trouble finding material for a new chapter on 'The Hero as a Big Man.'"

"Go ahead. I'm listening well today."

"People desperately want to believe in leaders today, almost pathetically so. But as soon as we find a popular reformer, politician, soldier, writer, or philosopher—whether it's a Roosevelt, Tolstoy, Wood, Shaw, or Nietzsche—conflicting waves of criticism sweep them away. Good God, no one can handle being in the spotlight anymore. It's the fastest way to fade into irrelevance. People grow tired of hearing the same name repeatedly."

"Then you blame it on the press?"

"Absolutely. Look at yourself; you're working for The New Democracy, which is considered the most brilliant weekly magazine in the country, read by the people who make things happen and all that. What's your job? Well, it's to be as clever, as interesting, and as brilliantly cynical as possible about every person, belief system, book, or policy that you're assigned to cover. The more harsh criticism and spiritual controversy you can create around the subject, the more money they pay you, and the more copies people buy. You, Tom d'Invilliers, a damaged Shelley, constantly changing, shifting, clever, and unscrupulous, represent the critical consciousness of our society—Oh, don't argue with me, I know how this works. I used to write book reviews in college; I thought it was great fun to dismiss the latest honest, sincere attempt to present a theory or solution as a 'welcome addition to our light summer reading.' Come on now, admit it."

Tom laughed, and Amory continued triumphantly.

"We want to believe. Young students try to believe in older authors, constituents try to believe in their Congressmen, countries try to believe in their statesmen, but they can't. There are too many voices, too much scattered, illogical, poorly thought-out criticism. The situation is even worse with newspapers. Any wealthy, backward-thinking old party with that particularly greedy, money-grabbing type of mindset known as financial genius can own a newspaper that serves as the intellectual sustenance for thousands of exhausted, rushed men—men too caught up in the demands of modern life to digest anything but pre-processed information. For two cents, the voter purchases his politics, prejudices, and philosophy. A year later, there's a new political group in power or a change in the newspaper's ownership, and the result is more confusion, more contradiction, a sudden flood of new ideas, their modification, their refinement, the backlash against them—"

He stopped just long enough to catch his breath.

"That's exactly why I've promised myself not to write anything down until my thoughts either become clear or disappear completely; I already have plenty of guilt weighing on my conscience without filling people's minds with reckless, superficial sayings; I could end up causing some harmless, well-meaning capitalist to have a crude encounter with a bomb, or get some naive little Bolshevik caught up with a machine-gun bullet—"

Tom was becoming increasingly agitated by this mockery of his association with The New Democracy.

"What does any of this have to do with you being bored?"

Amory believed it had a lot to do with it.

"How will I fit in?" he asked. "What's my purpose? To continue the human race? Based on American novels, we're supposed to believe that the 'healthy American boy' between nineteen and twenty-five is completely without sexual desire. Actually, the healthier he is, the less true that becomes. The only way to avoid being consumed by it is to find some passionate interest. Well, the war has ended; I take the responsibilities of writing too seriously to just write anything right now; and business, well, business explains itself. It has no real connection to anything in the world that has ever interested me, except for a minor, practical link to economics. What I would experience of it, trapped in some clerical job for the next and best ten years of my life, would have about as much intellectual substance as a corporate training film."

"Try fiction," suggested Tom.

"The problem is I get distracted when I begin writing stories—I become afraid that I'm doing this instead of actually living—I start thinking that maybe real life is waiting for me in the Japanese gardens at the Ritz or at Atlantic City or on the lower East Side."

"Anyway," he went on, "I don't have that essential drive. I wanted to be a normal person, but she couldn't understand it from that perspective."

"You'll find another."

"God! Don't even think that. Why don't you tell me that 'if the girl had been worth it, she would have waited for you'? No way, the girl who's truly worth it won't wait around for anyone. If I believed there would be another one like her, I'd lose whatever faith I still have in people. Maybe I'll mess around with others—but Rosalind was the only girl in the entire world who could have kept me interested."

"Well," Tom yawned, "I've been playing the role of confidant for a full hour now. Still, I'm happy to see you're starting to have passionate opinions about something again."

"I am," Amory agreed reluctantly. "But when I see a happy family, it makes me feel sick to my stomach—"

"Happy families try to make people feel that way," Tom said cynically.

Tom The Censor

There were days when Amory would listen. These moments occurred when Tom, surrounded by clouds of smoke, engaged in his brutal criticism of American literature. Words simply escaped him.

"Fifty thousand dollars a year," he would exclaim. "My God! Look at them, look at them—Edna Ferber, Gouverneur Morris,

Fanny Hurst, Mary Roberts Rinehart—not creating among them one story or novel that will survive ten years. This man Cobb—I don't think he's either clever or entertaining—and what's more, I don't believe very many people do, except the editors. He's just drunk on advertising. And—oh Harold Bell Wright oh Zane Grey—"

"They try."

"No, they don't even make the effort. Some of them have writing ability, but they refuse to sit down and produce one genuine novel. Most of them lack writing talent, I'll grant you that. I think Rupert Hughes attempts to present an authentic, complete portrait of American life, but his writing style and viewpoint are crude. Ernest Poole and Dorothy Canfield make the attempt, but they're held back by their complete absence of any comedic sensibility; however, at least they pack substance into their work rather than diluting it. Every writer should approach each book as though he would face execution the moment he completed it."

"Is that a double entendre?"

"Don't hold me back! There are several writers who appear to have cultural knowledge, intelligence, and considerable literary skill, but they simply refuse to write with honesty. They all insist there's no audience for quality work. So why on earth do Wells, Conrad, Galsworthy, Shaw, Bennett, and the others rely on America for more than half their sales?"

"How does little Tommy like the poets?"

Tom was overwhelmed. He let his arms fall until they hung limply at the sides of the chair and made quiet groaning sounds.

"I'm writing a satire about them now, calling it 'Boston Bards and Hearst Reviewers.'"

"Let's hear it," said Amory eagerly.

"I've only finished the last few lines."

"That sounds very contemporary. Let's hear them, if they're amusing."

Tom pulled a folded piece of paper from his pocket and began reading it out loud, stopping periodically so that Amory could tell it was written in free verse:

"So
Walter Arensberg,
Alfred Kreymborg,
Carl Sandburg,
Louis Untermeyer,
Eunice Tietjens,
Clara Shanafelt,
James Oppenheim,
Maxwell Bodenheim,
Richard Glaenzer,
Scharmel Iris,
Conrad Aiken,
I write your names here
So that you might endure
Even if only as names,
Flowing, purple-tinted names,
In the early works
Of my complete collections."

Amory burst out laughing.

"You win the iron pansy. I'll buy you a meal on the arrogance of the last two lines."

Amory didn't completely agree with Tom's harsh condemnation of American novelists and poets. He found pleasure in reading both Vachel Lindsay and Booth Tarkington, and he respected the dedicated, though limited, artistic skill of Edgar Lee Masters.

"What I hate is this idiotic nonsense about 'I am God—I am man—I ride the winds—I look through the smoke—I am the life sense.'"

"It's ghastly!"

"I wish American novelists would stop trying to make business seem romantically fascinating. Nobody wants to read about it unless it involves corrupt dealings. If business were truly an entertaining subject, people would buy biographies of figures like James J. Hill instead of these lengthy office dramas that drone on about the meaning of smoke—"

"And gloom," Tom said. "That's another favorite, though I have to admit the Russians have cornered the market on that one. Our specialty is stories about little girls who break their backs and get taken in by grumpy old men because they smile so much. You'd think we were a nation of happy disabled people and that the typical fate of the Russian peasant was suicide—"

"Six o'clock," said Amory, looking at his wristwatch. "I'll treat you to a fantastic dinner to celebrate the early works in your collected editions."

Looking Backward

July ended with one final week of sweltering heat, and Amory felt another wave of restlessness as he realized it had been exactly five months since he and Rosalind first met. It was already difficult for him to picture the wholehearted young man who had stepped off the transport ship, burning with desire for life's adventures. One night, as the overwhelming and draining heat poured through his bedroom windows, he spent several hours struggling with a vague attempt to capture forever the intense emotion of that period.

> The February streets, cleansed by nighttime winds, are filled with strange moisture that comes and goes, carrying dampness across empty sidewalks where wet snow catches the light under streetlamps, glistening like golden oil from some heavenly machine, during this hour of melting and starlight.

> Strange moisture—filled with the gazes of countless people, crowded with life carried forward in a moment of calm.... Oh, I was young, because I could turn back to you, so limited yet so beautiful, and experience the essence of half-remembered dreams, sweet and fresh upon your lips.

> ... There was a sharp metallic sound in the midnight air—silence had died and sound had not yet awakened—Life split like ice!—one brilliant note rang out

and there, glowing and pale, you stood... and spring had arrived. (The icicles hung short from the rooftops and the transformed city fell into a swoon.)

Our thoughts were like frozen mist along the gutters; our two spirits kissed, high up on the long, tangled wires—strange half-laughter echoes in this place and leaves behind only a foolish sigh for youthful longings; regret has pursued the things she once loved, abandoning the empty shell.

Another Ending

In mid-August, a letter arrived from Monsignor Darcy, who had apparently just discovered his address:

My Dear Boy:—

Your last letter was enough to make me worry about you. It wasn't like you at all. Reading between the lines, I get the impression that your engagement to this girl is making you quite unhappy, and I can see you've lost all the romantic feelings you had before the war. You're making a big mistake if you think you can be romantic without religion. Sometimes I think that for both of us, the secret to success, when we discover it, lies in the mystical element within us: something flows into us that expands our personalities, and when it flows out, our personalities contract; I would describe your last two letters as rather withered. Be careful not to lose yourself in another person's personality, whether man or woman.

Cardinal O'Neill and the Bishop of Boston are currently staying with me, making it difficult for me to find time to write. However, I would love for you to visit here later, even if just for a weekend. I'm heading to Washington this week.

What I'm going to do in the future remains uncertain. Just between you and me, I wouldn't be shocked if I received a cardinal's red hat on my unworthy head in the next eight months. Either way, I'd like to have a house in New York or Washington where you could stop by for weekends.

Amory, I'm really happy that we're both still alive; this war could have easily wiped out a brilliant family. But when it comes to marriage, you're now at the most dangerous time in your life. You might rush into marriage and regret it later, though I don't think you will. Based on what you've written to me about how terrible your financial situation is right now, what you want simply isn't possible. However, if I'm reading you correctly using the methods I typically rely on, I'd say you're going to face some kind of emotional crisis in the coming year.

Do write to me. I feel frustratingly out of touch with what's happening in your life.

With greatest affection,

Thayer Darcy.

Within a week of receiving this letter, their small household suddenly collapsed. The immediate reason was Tom's mother's serious illness, which would likely be ongoing. They put their furniture in storage, arranged for someone to take over their lease, and said their somber farewells at Pennsylvania Station. It seemed like Amory and Tom were constantly having to say goodbye to each other.

Feeling completely isolated, Amory gave in to a sudden urge and headed south, planning to meet up with Monsignor in Washington. They failed to connect by two hours, and choosing to visit an elderly uncle he remembered from long ago, Amory traveled through Maryland's rich farmland into Ramilly County. However, rather than staying for two days, his visit extended from mid-August almost until the end of September, because it was in Maryland that he encountered Eleanor.

Chapter 3. Young Irony

For years afterward when Amory thought of Eleanor, he could still hear the wind crying around him and sending small shivers into the spaces next to his heart. The night they rode up the hill and watched the cold moon drift through the clouds, he lost another piece of himself that nothing could ever bring back; and when he lost it, he also lost the ability to feel sorry about it. Eleanor was, perhaps, the final time that evil came near to Amory disguised as beauty, the last strange mystery that captivated him with fierce attraction and shattered his soul into fragments.

With her, his imagination went wild, and that's why they rode to the highest hill and watched a sinister moon rise high, because they knew then that they could see the devil in each other. But Eleanor—did Amory only dream her? Afterward their spirits haunted each other, yet both of them hoped with all their hearts never to meet again. Was it the endless sadness in her eyes that attracted him, or was it seeing himself reflected in the brilliant clarity of her mind? She will never have another adventure like the one with Amory, and if she reads this, she will say:

"And Amory will never have another adventure like me."

Nor will she sigh, any more than he would sigh.

Eleanor once tried to write it down:

"The fleeting things we only understand
We will have forgotten...
Set aside...
Longings that disappeared with the snow,
And dreams born
Today:
The unexpected sunrises we delighted in welcoming,
That everyone could witness, that no one could possess,
Will be merely sunrises... and if we encounter each other
We will not care.

Beloved... not a single tear will emerge for this...
A short time from now
No sorrow
Will arise for a kiss we remember—
Not even quiet,
When we have met,
Will offer old spirits a place to wander,
Or disturb the ocean's surface...
If shadowy forms float beneath the waves
We will not notice."

They got into a heated argument because Amory insisted that "sea" and "see" couldn't possibly work as a proper rhyme. Then Eleanor had part of another verse that she couldn't figure out how to start:

"... But wisdom fades away... yet the passing years
Will continue to nourish us with wisdom.... Old age will return
To what came before—
Despite all our sorrow
We will remain unknowing."

Eleanor despised Maryland with every fiber of her being. She came from one of the most established old families in Ramilly County and lived in a large, dreary house with her grandfather. She had been born and raised in France.... I realize I'm beginning this story the wrong way. Let me start over.

Amory felt bored, which was typical for him when he was in the countryside. He would take long walks by himself, wandering around while reciting "Ulalume" to the cornfields and praising Poe for drinking himself to death in such an atmosphere of cheerful self-satisfaction. One afternoon he had walked for several miles down a road he'd never been on before, and then entered a forest based on poor directions from a Black woman, getting completely lost. A storm that was passing through decided to unleash itself, and much to his frustration the sky turned pitch black and rain started pattering down through the trees, which suddenly became sneaky and ghostlike. Thunder rumbled with threatening crashes up the valley and echoed through the woods in sporadic bursts. He stumbled forward blindly, searching for an exit, and eventually, through tangles of twisted branches, spotted a gap in the trees where the continuous lightning revealed open countryside. He ran to the forest's edge and then paused, unsure whether to cross the fields and attempt to reach the safety of the small house indicated by a light far down in the valley. It was only five-thirty, but he could barely see ten steps ahead of him, except when the lightning made everything bright and strange across wide areas around him.

Suddenly an unusual sound reached his ears. It was singing, in a quiet, rough voice, a girl's voice, and whoever was singing was very near to him. A year earlier he might have laughed, or shaken with fear; but in his agitated state he simply stood and listened as the words penetrated his awareness:

> "The long sobs
> Of the violins
> Of autumn
> Wound my heart
> With a monotonous
> Languor."

The lightning tore across the sky, but the singing continued without the slightest tremor. The girl was clearly somewhere in the field, and her voice appeared to drift from a haystack roughly twenty feet ahead of him.

Then it stopped: stopped and started again in a strange chant that rose and lingered and dropped and merged with the rain:

> "All suffocating
> And pale when
> The hour strikes
> I remember
> The ancient days
> And I weep...."

"Who the hell is there in Ramilly County," Amory muttered out loud, "who would recite Verlaine in an improvised melody to a drenched haystack?"

"Someone's there!" the voice called out without any fear. "Who are you—Manfred, St. Christopher, or Queen Victoria?"

"I'm Don Juan!" Amory called out suddenly, his voice cutting through the sound of the rain and wind.

A joyful scream erupted from the haystack.

"I know who you are—you're the blond boy who likes 'Ulalume'—I recognize your voice."

"How do I get up?" he shouted from the bottom of the haystack, where he had ended up completely soaked. A head emerged over the edge—it was so dark that Amory could barely distinguish a section of wet hair and two eyes that shone like a cat's.

"Run back!" the voice called out, "and jump and I'll catch your hand—no, not there—on the other side."

He followed the directions and as he climbed up the side, sinking knee-deep in hay, a small, white hand reached out, grasped his, and pulled him up to the top.

"Here you are, Juan," called out the woman with wet hair. "Do you mind if I drop the Don?"

"You have a thumb just like mine!" he exclaimed.

"And you're holding my hand, which is risky when you can't see my face." He let go of it immediately.

As if responding to his prayers, lightning suddenly flashed, and he looked eagerly at the woman standing beside him on the waterlogged haystack, ten feet above the ground. However, she had covered her face, and all he could see was her slender figure, dark wet hair cut in a bob, and her small white hands with thumbs that curved backward just like his own.

"Have a seat," she offered politely as darkness surrounded them. "If you sit across from me in this little depression, you can share half of the raincoat, which I had been using as a waterproof shelter until you so rudely interrupted me."

"I was asked," Amory said happily; "you asked me—you know you did."

"Don Juan always pulls that off," she said with a laugh, "but I won't call you that anymore, since you have reddish hair. You can recite 'Ulalume' instead and I'll be Psyche, your soul."

Amory blushed, thankfully hidden beneath the veil of wind and rain. They sat facing each other in a small depression in the hay with the raincoat covering most of them, while the rain took care of the rest. Amory was desperately trying to see Psyche, but the lightning wouldn't strike again, and he waited restlessly. Good God! What if she wasn't beautiful—what if she was forty and overly academic—dear heavens! What if, just imagine, she was insane. But he knew that last thought was beneath him. Here Providence had sent him a girl for entertainment just as it had sent Benvenuto Cellini men to kill, and he was questioning whether she was mad, simply because she perfectly matched his frame of mind.

"I'm not," she said.

"Not what?"

"Not mad. I didn't think you were mad when I first saw you, so it isn't fair that you should think so of me."

"How on earth—"

As long as they had known each other, Eleanor and Amory could focus on a topic and then stop talking while still thinking about it, only to speak up ten minutes later and discover that their thoughts had traveled down identical paths, leading them both to similar ideas that other people would have considered completely unrelated to their original discussion.

"Tell me," he insisted, leaning forward with excitement, "how do you know about 'Ulalume'—how did you figure out the color of my hair? What's your name? What were you doing here? Tell me everything right now!"

Suddenly the lightning blazed through with a burst of brilliant light and he glimpsed Eleanor, gazing for the first time into her eyes. She was breathtaking—skin pale as marble under starlight, delicate eyebrows, and eyes that sparkled green like emeralds in the dazzling flash. She appeared to be a witch, around nineteen years old he estimated, both watchful and ethereal, with the distinctive white mark above her upper lip that served as both vulnerability and charm. He collapsed back with a sharp intake of breath against the wall of hay.

"Now you've seen me," she said calmly, "and I suppose you're about to say that my green eyes are burning into your brain."

"What color is your hair?" he asked intently. "It's cut short, isn't it?"

"Yes, it's cut short. I'm not sure what color it is," she replied thoughtfully, "so many men have asked me that question. It's somewhere in between, I guess—Nobody ever pays much attention to my hair anyway. But I do have gorgeous eyes, don't I. I don't care what anyone says, I have gorgeous eyes."

"Answer my question, Madeline."

"Don't remember them all—besides my name isn't Madeline, it's Eleanor."

"I should have seen it coming. You remind me of Eleanor— you have that distinctive Eleanor quality about you. You know exactly what I'm talking about."

There was a silence as they listened to the rain.

"It's dripping down my neck, you crazy person," she said at last.

"Answer my questions."

"Well—name is Savage, Eleanor; lives in a big old house a mile down the road; nearest living relative to contact is her grandfather—Ramilly Savage; height is five feet four inches; number on the watch case is 3077 W; nose is delicate and aquiline; temperament is uncanny—"

"And what about me," Amory interrupted, "where did you see me?"

"Oh, you're one of those men," she replied arrogantly, "who always have to drag themselves into every conversation. Well, my boy, I was relaxing behind a hedge in the sunshine one day last week, when a man came walking by, speaking in a pleasant but self-satisfied manner:

"'And now when the night was growing old' (says he) 'And the star dials pointed to morning At the end of the path a melting' (says he) 'And cloudy brightness was born.'"

"So I lifted my eyes above the hedge, but you had already begun running for some reason I couldn't understand, and all I could see was the back of your lovely head. 'Oh!' I said, 'there's a man who could make many of us swoon,' and I went on speaking in my finest Irish accent—"

"All right," Amory interrupted. "Now go back to yourself."

"Well, I will. I'm one of those people who moves through life giving others excitement, but rarely experiencing much myself except what I imagine I see in men on nights like this. I have the confidence to perform on stage, but I lack the drive; I don't have the patience to write books; and I've never met a man I would want to marry. But then again, I'm only eighteen."

The storm was gradually subsiding, and only the wind continued its eerie rushing sound, causing the haystack to sway and slowly shift back and forth. Amory was completely mesmerized. He sensed that each moment held incredible value. He had never encountered a girl like her before—she would never appear quite the same to him again. He didn't feel at all like an actor in a theatrical performance, which would have been the fitting sensation in such an unusual circumstance—rather, he experienced a feeling of returning home.

"I've just made an important decision," Eleanor said after another pause, "and that's why I'm here, to answer another one of your questions. I've just decided that I don't believe in life after death."

"Really! How ordinary!"

"Absolutely," she replied, "but it's depressing in a stale, nauseating way, nonetheless. I came out here to get soaked—like a drenched hen; soaked hens always think with perfect clarity," she finished.

"Go on," Amory said politely.

"Well—I'm not afraid of the dark, so I put on my raincoat and rubber boots and came outside. You see, I was always scared before to say I didn't believe in God—because lightning might strike me down—but here I am and it hasn't happened, of course, but the important thing is that this time I wasn't any more frightened of it than I had been when I was a Christian Scientist, like I was last year. So now I know I'm a materialist and I was getting friendly with the hay when you came outside and stood by the woods, terrified."

"What are you talking about, you little brat—" Amory shouted angrily. "Scared of what?"

"Yourself!" she yelled, and he flinched. She clapped her hands together and burst into laughter. "Look—look! Conscience—destroy it like I did! Eleanor Savage, materialist—no flinching, no startling, arrive early—"

"But I have to have a soul," he protested. "I can't be rational—and I refuse to be molecular."

She leaned toward him, her intense eyes never leaving his, and whispered with a kind of romantic finality:

"I thought so, Juan, I was afraid of that—you're sentimental. You're not like me. I'm a romantic little materialist."

"I'm not sentimental—I'm as romantic as you are. The idea, you know, is that the sentimental person thinks things will last—the romantic person has a desperate confidence that they won't." (This was an old distinction of Amory's.)

"Epigrams. I'm going home," she said sadly. "Let's get off the haystack and walk to the crossroads."

They slowly climbed down from their elevated spot. She wouldn't allow him to assist her descent and waved him away, landing gracefully in a heap in the soft mud where she remained for a moment, laughing at herself. Then she sprang to her feet and slipped her hand into his, and they crept across the fields, leaping and swinging from one dry patch to another. An extraordinary joy seemed to glimmer in every puddle of water, for the moon had come up and the storm had rushed away into western Maryland. When Eleanor's arm brushed against his, he felt his hands turn cold with terrible fear that he might lose the delicate touch with which his imagination was creating marvels of her. He observed her from the corner of his eye as he always did when he walked with her—she was both a delight and a madness, and he wished it had been his fate to sit eternally on a haystack and view life through her green eyes. His wild spirit soared that night, and when she disappeared like a gray ghost down the road, a profound singing emerged from the fields and accompanied his journey home. All night the summer moths flew in and out of Amory's window; all night vast looming sounds swayed in mystical meditation through the silver grain—and he remained awake in the clear darkness.

September

Amory picked a blade of grass and chewed on it thoughtfully.

"I never fall in love in August or September," he offered.

"When then?"

"Christmas or Easter. I'm a liturgist."

"Easter!" She wrinkled her nose in disgust. "Huh! Spring all dressed up and constrained!"

"Easter would bore spring, wouldn't she? Easter has her hair braided, wears a tailored suit."

"Put on your sandals, oh, you who are swiftest.
Over the glory and swiftness of your feet—"

245

quoted Eleanor softly, and then added: "I guess Halloween is a better day for fall than Thanksgiving."

"Much better—and Christmas Eve works perfectly for winter, but summer..."

"Summer doesn't have its moment," she said. "There's no way we could have a summer romance. So many people have attempted it that the phrase has become a cliché. Summer is just spring's broken promise, a fake replacement for those warm, gentle evenings I imagine in April. It's a melancholy time in life with no development.... It doesn't have its moment."

"Fourth of July," Amory suggested jokingly.

"Don't be ridiculous!" she said, looking him up and down with a sharp gaze.

"Well, what could fulfill the promise of spring?"

She paused to think for a moment.

"Oh, I suppose heaven would, if there was one," she said finally, "some kind of pagan heaven—you should be a materialist," she continued without any connection to what came before.

"Why?"

"Because you look a lot like the pictures of Rupert Brooke."

To some extent Amory tried to imitate Rupert Brooke for as long as he knew Eleanor. What he said, his outlook on life, his feelings toward her, his view of himself—all of these were echoes of the dead English poet's literary sensibilities. She would often sit in the grass, a gentle breeze playing with her short hair, her voice rich and throaty as she moved from topic to topic, from Grantchester to Waikiki. There was something deeply passionate about the way Eleanor read aloud. When they read together, they felt closer—not just emotionally, but physically too—than when she was actually in his arms, which happened frequently, since they had fallen halfway in love almost from the very beginning. But was Amory truly capable of love at this point? He could still cycle through all the emotions within half an hour, as he always had, but even as they lost themselves in their fantasies, he understood that neither of them could feel as deeply as he had once felt before— perhaps that's why they turned to Brooke, and Swinburne, and Shelley. Their opportunity was to make everything beautiful and polished and rich and creative; they had to weave delicate golden threads between his imagination and hers, connections that would substitute for the profound, all-consuming love that seemed so close yet remained nothing more than a dream.

One poem they read repeatedly was Swinburne's "Triumph of Time," and four lines from it echoed in his memory later on warm evenings when he watched fireflies flickering among the shadowy tree trunks and listened to the soft humming of countless frogs. During those moments Eleanor seemed to emerge from the darkness and stand beside him, and he could hear her husky voice, with its sound like a muffled drum, reciting:

"Is it worth shedding a tear, is it worth spending an hour,
To dwell on things that have long since passed their time;
On empty shells and fleeting blossoms,
The abandoned dream and the action left undone?"

They were formally introduced two days later, and his aunt shared her background with him. The Ramillys consisted of two people: elderly Mr. Ramilly and his granddaughter, Eleanor. She had lived in France with a restless mother who Amory pictured as being very similar to his own, and after her mother's death, she had come to America to live in Maryland. She had first gone to Baltimore to stay with her bachelor uncle, and there she demanded to make her debut at seventeen years old. She had a wild winter and arrived in the countryside in March, having argued bitterly with all her Baltimore relatives and shocked them into angry objections. A rather wild group had emerged, who drank cocktails in limousines and were carelessly condescending and patronizing toward older people, and Eleanor, with a wit that strongly suggested the boulevards, led many innocent girls still carrying the scent of St. Timothy's and Farmington into paths of bohemian mischief. When the story reached her uncle, a forgetful gentleman from a more hypocritical time, there was a confrontation, from which Eleanor emerged subdued but defiant and angry, seeking refuge with her grandfather who lived quietly in the country on the edge of old age. That's where her story ended; she told him the rest herself, but that came later.

Often they went swimming, and as Amory floated lazily in the water, he closed his mind to everything except dreamy, soap-bubble worlds where sunlight filtered through trees swaying in the breeze. How could anyone possibly think or worry, or do anything other than splash and dive and lounge there at the edge of time while the beautiful months slipped away. Let the days pass by— sadness and memories and pain existed out there in the world, and here, once again, before he had to go face them, he wanted to drift and stay young.

There were days when Amory felt bitter that life had transformed from a steady journey along a clear path that stretched endlessly ahead, with landscapes flowing and merging together, into a series of rapid, disconnected moments—two years of struggle and intensity, that sudden ridiculous urge for fatherhood that Rosalind had awakened; the partly sensual, partly anxious nature of this fall season with Eleanor. He sensed that it would require all the time he had, more than he could ever afford to give, to paste these odd, unwieldy images into the memory book of his existence. It was all like a feast where he sat during this brief period of his youth and attempted to savor exquisite gourmet dishes.

Vaguely, he made a promise to himself that there would come a time when everything would be united as one. For months, it felt as though he had been switching back and forth between being carried along by a current of love or enchantment, or being trapped in a whirlpool, and during those stagnant moments he hadn't wanted to think, but rather hoped to be lifted up by a wave's crest and carried forward once more.

"The hopeless, fading autumn and our love—how perfectly they match!" Eleanor said sadly one day as they lay soaked by the water.

"The Indian summer of our hearts—" he stopped.

"Tell me," she said finally, "was she light or dark?"

"Light."

"Was she more beautiful than I am?"

"I don't know," Amory replied curtly.

One evening they strolled together as the moon climbed higher and cast an overwhelming radiance across the garden, transforming it into an enchanted realm where Amory and Eleanor moved like ghostly figures, embodying timeless beauty through their strange, magical expressions of love. Eventually they stepped away from the moonlight into the shadowed interior of a vine-covered pavilion, where fragrances hung in the air so hauntingly sweet they seemed almost like melodies.

"Light a match," she whispered. "I want to see you."

Scratch! Flare!

The night and the scarred trees resembled stage scenery, and being there with Eleanor, shadowy and dreamlike, felt strangely familiar somehow. Amory reflected on how only the past ever appeared strange and impossible to believe. The match burned out.

"It's completely dark."

"We're just voices now," Eleanor whispered, "small, lonely voices. Light another one."

"That was my last match." Suddenly he caught her in his arms.

"You belong to me—you know you belong to me!" he shouted frantically... the moonlight wound its way through the vines and seemed to listen... the fireflies clung to their whispered words as though trying to draw his attention away from the radiance of their eyes.

The End of Summer

"No wind is stirring in the grass; not one wind stirs... the water in the hidden pools, as glass, fronts the full moon and so inters the golden token in its icy mass," Eleanor recited to the bare trees that formed the skeleton of the night. "Doesn't this place feel haunted? If you can keep your horse quiet, let's go through the woods and find those hidden pools."

"It's past one o'clock, and you'll catch hell," he protested, "and I don't know enough about horses to take care of one in complete darkness."

"Be quiet, you old fool," she whispered without any real connection to what they'd been discussing, and leaning forward, she gave him a casual tap with her riding crop. "You can leave your old horse in our stable and I'll have him sent over tomorrow."

"But my uncle has to drive me to the station with this old car at seven o'clock."

"Don't be a spoil-sport—remember, you have a tendency toward wavering that prevents you from being the entire light of my life."

Amory pulled his horse up right next to hers and leaned over to take her hand.

"Tell me I am—hurry up, or I'll yank you over here and make you ride behind me."

She looked up, smiled, and shook her head with excitement.

"Oh, please do!—or actually, don't! Why do all the thrilling things have to be so uncomfortable, like fighting and exploring and skiing in Canada? By the way, we're going to ride up Harper's Hill. I believe that's scheduled in our program around five o'clock."

"You little devil," Amory growled. "You're going to make me stay up all night and sleep on the train like an immigrant all day tomorrow, going back to New York."

"Quiet! Someone's coming down the road—let's get out of here! Whoo-ee-oop!" And with a yell that likely sent chills down the spine of the late traveler, she steered her horse into the woods and Amory followed at a leisurely pace, just as he had been following her all day for three weeks.

The summer had ended, but he had spent those days observing Eleanor, a graceful and adaptable Manfred, constructing elaborate intellectual and imaginative structures for herself while she delighted in the artificial behaviors typical of moody teenagers, and they composed poetry during dinner.

> When Vanity kissed Vanity, a hundred happy Junes ago, he gazed at her breathlessly, and so that all people might forever know, he compared her eyes to life and death in verse:
>
> "Through Time I'll preserve my love!" he declared... yet Beauty disappeared with his breath, and, along with her lovers, she was dead...
>
> —Always his cleverness and not her eyes, always his art and not her hair:
>
> "Whoever would learn a trick in rhyme, be wise and stop before his sonnet there"... So all my words, no matter how true, might sing you to a thousandth June, and no one would ever know that you were Beauty for an afternoon.

So he wrote one day, when he reflected on how indifferently we regarded the "Dark Lady of the Sonnets," and how little we recalled her as the great man wished her to be remembered. For what Shakespeare must have longed for, to have been capable of writing with such profound anguish, was that the lady should endure... and now we feel no genuine interest in her.... The irony lies in the fact that if he had valued the poem more than the lady, the sonnet would be merely obvious, derivative rhetoric and no one would have read it after twenty years....

This was the final night Amory would ever see Eleanor. He was departing in the morning, and they had decided to take one last long ride together under the cold moonlight. She wanted to have a conversation, she explained—perhaps the final opportunity in her life when she could think clearly (by which she meant she could maintain her facade comfortably). So they had entered the woods and ridden for thirty minutes with hardly any words exchanged, except when she murmured "Damn!" at an annoying branch—murmured it in a way that no other girl could ever manage to murmur it. Then they began climbing Harper's Hill, leading their weary horses on foot.

"Good Lord! It's quiet here!" whispered Eleanor; "much more lonely than the woods."

"I hate forests," Amory said, trembling. "Any type of trees or thick vegetation in the darkness. Out here everything feels so open and peaceful to the soul."

"The long slope of a long hill."

"And the cold moon rolling moonlight down it."

"And you and me, last and most important."

It was quiet that night—the straight road they traveled to the cliff's edge rarely saw any foot traffic. Only the occasional cabin, appearing silver-gray in the moonlight that carved through the rocky landscape, interrupted the long stretch of barren ground; behind them lay the dark border of the forest like black icing on white cake, and ahead stretched the sharp, elevated horizon. The temperature had dropped significantly—so cold that it enveloped them and erased all memories of warm nights from their thoughts.

"The end of summer," Eleanor said quietly. "Listen to the rhythm of our horses' hooves—'tump-tump-tump-a-tump.' Have you ever had a fever and heard every sound break down into 'tump-tump-tump' until you could have sworn that eternity itself was made up of nothing but tumps? That's how I feel right now— old horses just go tump-tump.... I think that's the only thing that sets horses and clocks apart from us. Human beings can't keep going 'tump-tump-tump' without losing their minds."

The wind picked up and Eleanor wrapped her cloak tighter around herself, shivering from the cold.

"Are you very cold?" asked Amory.

"No, I'm thinking about myself—my dark, aging inner self, the true one, with the basic honesty that prevents me from being completely evil by making me acknowledge my own wrongdoings."

They rode close to the cliff's edge, and Amory looked down. A hundred feet below, where the waterfall crashed into the earth, a dark stream cut a distinct line through the landscape, interrupted by small flashes of light dancing on the rushing water.

"This rotten, rotten old world," Eleanor burst out suddenly, "and the most wretched thing of all is me—oh, why am I a girl? Why am I not a stupid—? Look at you; you're more foolish than I am, not by much, but somewhat, and you can wander around and get bored and then wander somewhere else, and you can mess around with girls without getting caught up in webs of emotion, and you can do anything and be justified—and here I am with the intelligence to do everything, yet chained to the sinking ship of future marriage. If I had been born a hundred years from now, that would be fine, but now what lies ahead for me—I have to marry, that's a given. Who? I'm too smart for most men, and yet I have to lower myself to their level and let them talk down to my intelligence just to get their attention. Every year that I don't marry I have less chance of landing a first-rate man. At best I can choose from one or two cities and, naturally, I have to marry into formal society.

"Listen," she leaned in close again, "I'm attracted to intelligent men and handsome men, and naturally, no one values personality more than I do. Oh, only one person out of fifty has any real understanding of what sex actually is. I'm obsessed with Freud and all of that, but it's terrible that every bit of genuine love in the world is ninety-nine percent passion and just a tiny hint of jealousy." She stopped talking as abruptly as she had started.

"Of course, you're right," Amory agreed. "It's quite an unpleasant overwhelming force that operates as part of the underlying machinery of everything. It's like watching an actor who exposes his technique! Give me a moment to work through this...."

He stopped and searched for a comparison. They had rounded the cliff and were now traveling along the road roughly fifty feet to the left.

"You see, everyone needs some kind of cover to wrap around it. The average minds, Plato's second tier, use the leftovers of romantic chivalry watered down with Victorian feelings—and those of us who think we're the intellectuals hide it by acting like it's just another part of who we are, something that has nothing to do with our brilliant minds; we act like the simple fact that we understand it somehow frees us from falling victim to it. But the reality is that sex sits right at the heart of our most refined thoughts, so near that it clouds our judgment.... I can kiss you right now and I will...." He leaned toward her from his saddle, but she pulled back.

"I can't—I can't kiss you right now—I'm feeling more sensitive."

"You're even more foolish then," he said with clear impatience. "Intelligence offers no shield against sexual desire any more than social customs do..."

"What is?" she snapped. "The Catholic Church or the teachings of Confucius?"

Amory glanced up, somewhat surprised.

"That's your cure-all, isn't it?" she shouted. "Oh, you're nothing but an old hypocrite as well. Thousands of frowning priests keeping the corrupt Italians and uneducated Irish feeling guilty with their endless chatter about the sixth and ninth commandments. It's all just disguises, emotion and spiritual makeup and quick fixes. I'm telling you there is no God, not even a clear abstract goodness; so everything has to be figured out by each person for themselves here in brilliant minds like mine, and you're too much of a self-righteous person to accept it." She released her reins and shook her small fists at the stars.

"If there's a God let him strike me—strike me!"

"Talking about God again like atheists do," Amory said harshly. His materialistic beliefs, which had always been a flimsy cover, were completely destroyed by Eleanor's irreverent words.... She was aware of this and it infuriated him that she knew it.

"And like most intellectuals who find faith inconvenient," he went on with cold detachment, "like Napoleon and Oscar Wilde and others of your kind, you'll cry out desperately for a priest when you're dying."

Eleanor pulled her horse to a sudden stop and he brought his horse to a halt beside her.

"Will I?" she said in a strange voice that frightened him. "Will I? Watch! I'm going over the cliff!" And before he could stop her, she had turned and was riding at breakneck speed toward the edge of the plateau.

He spun around and chased after her, his body feeling frozen, his nerves screaming with alarm. There was no way to stop her. The moon had disappeared behind a cloud and her horse would stumble forward blindly. Then about ten feet from the cliff's edge she let out a sudden scream and threw herself to the side— tumbled from her horse and, rolling twice, crashed into a clump of bushes five feet from the edge. The horse plunged over with a desperate cry. Within moments he reached Eleanor's side and noticed her eyes were open.

"Eleanor!" he shouted.

She didn't respond, but her lips trembled and her eyes suddenly welled up with tears.

"Eleanor, are you hurt?"

"No; I don't think so," she said weakly, and then started crying.

"My horse dead?"

"Good God—Yes!"

"Oh!" she cried out. "I thought I was going to fall over. I had no idea—"

He gently helped her to her feet and lifted her onto his saddle. They began their journey home with Amory walking alongside while she leaned forward over the pommel, crying intensely.

"I have a wild side," she stammered, "I've acted like this twice before. When I was eleven, my mother became—lost her mind—completely insane. We were living in Vienna—"

Throughout the entire journey back, she spoke hesitantly about herself, and Amory's love gradually faded as the moon dimmed. When they reached her door, they automatically moved to kiss goodnight, but she couldn't rush into his embrace, nor did his arms reach out to welcome her as they had the week before. For a moment they stood there, despising each other with a painful sorrow. But just as Amory had loved himself through Eleanor, now what he despised was merely his own reflection. Their pretenses lay scattered around the pale dawn like shattered glass. The stars had long since disappeared, leaving only the soft whispers of wind and the quiet spaces between them... but exposed souls are always fragile things, and soon he turned toward home and allowed fresh hope to enter with the rising sun.

A Poem That Eleanor Sent Amory Several Years Later

"Here, Earth-born, over the gentle rhythm of the water,
Murmuring its melody and carrying a burden of light,
Embracing day like a laughing and glowing daughter...
Here we can whisper unheard, unafraid of the night.
Walking alone... was it magnificence, or something else, that bound us,
Deep in the time when summer lets down her hair?
Shadows we cherished and the designs they spread across the ground
Tapestries, mystical, delicate in the still air.

That was the day... and the night tells another story,
Pale as a dream and darkened with sketched trees—
Spirits of the stars passed by who had searched for glory,

Whispered to us of peace in the mournful breeze,
Whispered of ancient dead beliefs that the day had destroyed,
Youth the coin that purchased delight of the moon;
That was the impulse that we understood and the words that counted
That was the price that we paid to the moneylender June.

Here, deepest of dreams, by the waters that carry not
Anything back of the past that we need not know,
What if the light is only sun and the small streams do not sing,
We are together, it appears... I have loved you so...
What did the final night contain, with the summer ended,
Drawing us back to the home in the shifting grove?
What sneered out of the darkness in the spectral clover? God!... until you
moved in your sleep... and were wildly
afraid...

Well... we have moved on... we are history now to the mysterious.
Strange metal from meteors that fell short in the sky;
Earth-born the restless one is stretched by the water, quite tired,
Close to this incomprehensible changeling that is I...
Fear is an echo we followed to Security's daughter;
Now we are faces and voices... and less, too quickly,
Whispering half-love over the gentle rhythm of the water...
Youth the coin that purchased delight of the moon."

A Poem Amory Sent To Eleanor And Which He Called "Summer Storm"

"Gentle winds, and a song growing faint and leaves falling,
Gentle winds, and far away a fading laughter...
And the rain and over the fields a voice calling...

Our gray windblown cloud hurries and rises above,
Glides across the sun and flutters there to carry her
Sisters onward. The shadow of a dove
Falls on the dovecote, the trees are filled with wings;
And down the valley through the crying trees
The body of the darker storm flies; brings
With its fresh air the breath of sunken seas
And slender delicate thunder...
But I wait...

257

Wait for the mists and for the blacker rain—
Heavier winds that stir the veil of fate,
Happier winds that tangle her hair;
Again
They tear at me, teach me, scatter the heavy air
Upon me, winds that I know, and storm.

There was a summer when every rain was rare;
There was a season when every wind was warm....
And now you pass me in the mist... your hair
Rain-blown about you, damp lips curved once more
In that wild irony, that cheerful despair
That made you old when we have met before;
Ghost-like you drift on out before the rain,
Across the fields, blown with the stemless flowers,
With your old hopes, dead leaves and loves again—
Dim as a dream and pale with all old hours
(Whispers will creep into the growing dark...
Tumult will die over the trees)
Now night
Tears from her wetted breast the splattered blouse
Of day, glides down the dreaming hills, tear-bright,
To cover with her hair the eerie green...
Love for the dusk... Love for the glistening after;
Quiet the trees to their last tops... serene...

Gentle winds, and far away a fading laughter..."

———————

Chapter 4. The Supercilious Sacrifice

Atlantic City. Amory walked along the boardwalk as the day came
to an end, soothed by the endless rhythm of the changing waves
and breathing in the bittersweet scent of the ocean breeze. The sea,
he reflected, had preserved its memories more deeply than the
unreliable land. It still seemed to murmur about Viking ships
cutting through the watery world beneath banners decorated with
ravens, about the British battleships, those gray fortresses of
civilization steaming through the mist of a dark July morning into

the North Sea.

"Well—Amory Blaine!"

Amory glanced down at the street below. A sleek, low-slung sports car had pulled up to the curb, and a recognizable, friendly face peered out from behind the steering wheel.

"Come on down, goopher!" shouted Alec.

Amory shouted hello and walked down a set of wooden stairs toward the car. He and Alec had been getting together on and off, but Rosalind's presence always created a wall between them. This bothered him; he didn't want to lose his friendship with Alec.

"Mr. Blaine, this is Miss Waterson, Miss Wayne, and Mr. Tully."

"How are you doing?"

"Amory," Alec said enthusiastically, "if you hop in, we'll drive you to some quiet spot and give you a small shot of bourbon."

Amory thought it over.

"That's an idea."

"Come in—move over, Jill, and Amory will give you a very charming smile."

Amory squeezed into the back seat next to a flashy blonde with bright red lipstick.

"Hello, Doug Fairbanks," she said casually. "Are you walking for exercise or looking for someone to talk to?"

"I was counting the waves," Amory replied seriously. "I'm getting into statistics."

"Don't kid me, Doug."

When they arrived at a quiet side street, Alec parked the car in the deep shadows.

"What are you doing down here during these cold days, Amory?" he asked, as he pulled out a quart of bourbon from under the fur blanket.

Amory sidestepped the question. The truth was, he hadn't had any clear reason for traveling to the coast.

"Do you remember that party we had during our sophomore year?" he asked instead.

"Do I? When we stayed overnight in those pavilions up in Asbury Park—"

"Lord, Alec! It's hard to believe that Jesse and Dick and Kerry are all three dead."

Alec shivered.

"Don't talk about it. These gloomy autumn days depress me enough."

Jill seemed to agree.

"Doug here is kind of gloomy anyway," she remarked. "Tell him to drink deeply—it's good and hard to come by these days."

"What I really want to ask you, Amory, is where you are—"

"Well, New York, I imagine—"

"I mean tonight, because if you haven't found a room yet, you should help me out."

"Glad to."

"Listen, Tully and I have two rooms with a bathroom between them at the Ranier, and he has to return to New York. I don't want to deal with having to move. The question is, would you take one of the rooms?"

Amory was willing, provided he could get in immediately.

"You'll find the key in the office; the rooms are in my name."

Refusing to continue driving or seek any more excitement, Amory got out of the car and walked leisurely back along the boardwalk to the hotel.

He found himself caught in another downward spiral, a profound and sluggish emptiness, with no motivation to work or write, to love or to lose himself in distractions. For the first time in his life, he actually wished for death to sweep over his entire generation, wiping out their trivial anxieties and conflicts and moments of triumph. His youth had never felt so completely gone as it did now, highlighted by the stark difference between the complete isolation of this current visit and that wild, celebratory gathering from four years earlier. Things that had once been the most ordinary parts of his daily existence back then—restful sleep, an appreciation for the beauty surrounding him, any kind of longing—had all disappeared, and the empty spaces they left behind were filled with nothing but the overwhelming apathy of his shattered illusions.

"To hold a man a woman has to appeal to the worst in him." This statement became the central theme of most of his sleepless nights, and he sensed tonight would be another one. His thoughts had already begun spinning endless variations on this idea. Relentless desire, burning jealousy, the urge to own and dominate—these were all that remained of his love for Rosalind; these stayed with him as compensation for losing his youth— harsh medicine disguised beneath the sweet coating of love's euphoria.

In his room he undressed and wrapped himself in blankets to ward off the cold October air, then dozed in an armchair beside the open window.

He recalled a poem he had read months earlier:

"Oh faithful old heart that worked so hard for me all this time,
I'm wasting my years drifting across the ocean—"

Yet he felt no sense of waste, no awareness of the present hope that such waste would suggest. He believed that life itself had turned its back on him.

"Rosalind! Rosalind!" He whispered the words gently into the dim light until it felt as though she filled the entire room; the damp ocean breeze dampened his hair with mist, the edge of the moon burned across the sky and turned the curtains pale and spectral. He drifted off to sleep.

When he woke up, it was very late and quiet. The blanket had slipped partway off his shoulders, and when he touched his skin, he found it was damp and cold.

Then he noticed urgent whispering coming from less than ten feet away.

He became rigid.

"Don't make a sound!" It was Alec's voice. "Jill—do you hear me?"

"Yes—" she whispered very quietly, very scared. They were in the bathroom.

Then he heard a louder noise coming from somewhere down the hallway outside. It was the murmur of men talking and the sound of repeated, muffled knocking. Amory pushed off his blankets and walked over to the bathroom door.

"My God!" the girl's voice came again. "You'll have to let them in."

"Sh!"

Suddenly, a steady and insistent knocking started at Amory's hall door, and at the same time, Alec emerged from the bathroom, followed by the girl with bright red lips. Both of them were wearing pajamas.

"Amory!" an anxious whisper.

"What's the trouble?"

"It's house detectives. My God, Amory—they're just looking for a test case—"

"Well, better let them in."

"You don't understand. They can get me under the Mann Act."

The girl followed him slowly, looking quite miserable and pitiful in the darkness.

Amory attempted to make a plan quickly.

"You make some noise and let them into your room," he suggested nervously, "and I'll get her out through this door."

"They're here too, though. They'll watch this door."

"Can't you give a false name?"

"No way. I signed up using my real name, and on top of that, they could trace the car's license plate number."

"Say you're married."

"Jill says one of the hotel security officers knows her."

The girl had crept to the bed and collapsed onto it; she lay there listening miserably to the knocking that had gradually intensified into heavy pounding. Then came a man's voice, furious and commanding:

"Open up or we'll break the door down!"

When the voice fell silent, Amory became aware that the room contained more than just people... Above and surrounding the figure hunched on the bed, there lingered an atmosphere, delicate as a moonbeam yet corrupted like stale, weak wine—a terror that was already spreading its influence over all three of them... And near the window, among the moving curtains, stood something else, without clear features or definition, yet strangely recognizable.... At that moment, two significant scenarios presented themselves simultaneously to Amory; everything that unfolded in his thoughts took place in less than ten seconds of real time.

The first truth that blazed clearly in his mind was the profound impersonal nature of sacrifice—he understood that what we call love and hate, reward and punishment, had nothing more to do with it than what day of the month it happened to be. He rapidly went through the details of a sacrifice story he had learned about in college: a student had cheated on an exam; his roommate in a moment of emotional impulse had accepted all the blame—because of the disgrace, the innocent person's whole future appeared clouded by regret and failure, made worse by the ungrateful behavior of the actual cheater. He had eventually killed himself—years later the real facts had emerged. When he first heard the story, it had both confused and troubled Amory. Now he grasped the reality; that sacrifice was not a way to buy freedom. It was like a major elected position, it was like inheriting authority—for certain individuals at specific moments an essential indulgence, bringing with it not a promise but a duty, not safety but unlimited danger. Its own force could pull him down to destruction—the end of the emotional surge that made it achievable could leave the person who made it stranded permanently on an island of hopelessness.

Amory understood that later on, Alec would quietly resent him for having helped him so extensively.

All of this unfolded before Amory like an unrolled scroll, while behind him and watching him were those two silent, attentive presences: the delicate atmosphere that surrounded the girl and that recognizable entity by the window.

Sacrifice, by its very essence, was arrogant and impersonal; sacrifice should remain eternally condescending.

Weep not for me but for thy children.

That, Amory thought, would somehow be the way God would speak to him.

Amory experienced a sudden rush of happiness, and then, like an image in a movie, the glowing presence above the bed slowly disappeared; the powerful shadow near the window—that was the closest he could describe it—lingered for just an instant before the wind seemed to carry it quickly out of the room. He clenched his fists in rapid, thrilling excitement... the ten seconds had ended....

"Do what I say, Alec—do what I say. Do you understand?"

Alec stared at him in stunned silence—his face displaying complete anguish.

"You have a family," Amory continued slowly. "You have a family and it's crucial that you get out of this situation. Do you understand me?" He repeated his words clearly. "Do you understand me?"

"I hear you." The voice sounded oddly tense, and the eyes remained fixed on Amory's without looking away for even a moment.

"Alec, you're going to lie down here. If anyone comes in, you act drunk. You do what I say—if you don't, I'll probably kill you."

There was another moment as they looked at each other. Then Amory walked quickly to the dresser and, grabbing his wallet, motioned urgently to the girl. He caught one word from Alec that sounded like "penitentiary," and then he and Jill were in the bathroom with the door locked behind them.

"You're here with me," he said firmly. "You've been with me all evening."

She nodded and let out a small, choked sob.

In an instant, he had opened the door to the other room and three men walked in. Electric light immediately flooded the space and he stood there, blinking.

"You've been playing a little too dangerous a game, young man!"

Amory laughed.

"Well?"

The leader of the three nodded with authority at a stocky man wearing a checkered suit.

"All right, Olson."

"I've got you, Mr. O'May," Olson said with a nod. The other two men took a quick, curious look at their target before backing away and slamming the door shut behind them.

The stocky man looked at Amory with contempt.

"Haven't you ever heard of the Mann Act? Coming down here with her," he gestured toward the girl with his thumb, "with New York plates on your car—to a hotel like this." He shook his head, suggesting that he had wrestled with what to think about Amory but had now given up on him.

"Well," said Amory with some impatience, "what do you want us to do?"

"Get dressed, quickly—and tell your friend to stop making so much noise." Jill was crying loudly on the bed, but when she heard these words she became quietly resentful and, collecting her clothes, went to the bathroom. As Amory put on Alec's underwear he discovered that his feelings about the situation were pleasantly amusing. The offended moral outrage of the large man made him want to laugh.

"Is anyone else here?" Olson asked, attempting to appear sharp and cunning.

"The guy who had the rooms," Amory said casually. "He's completely wasted, though. He's been passed out in there since six o'clock."

"I'll check on him in a moment."

"How did you find out?" Amory asked with curiosity.

"The night clerk saw you go upstairs with this woman."

Amory nodded; Jill emerged from the bathroom, fully dressed though somewhat disheveled.

"Alright then," Olson said, pulling out a notebook, "I need your actual names—none of that fake John Smith or Mary Brown nonsense."

"Hold on," Amory said quietly. "Just drop that tough-guy act. We simply got caught, that's all."

Olson glared at him.

"Name?" he snapped.

Amory provided his name and his address in New York.

"And the lady?"

"Miss Jill—"

"Hey," Olson shouted angrily, "cut it out with the nursery rhymes. What's your name? Sarah Murphy? Minnie Jackson?"

"Oh, my God!" the girl cried out, covering her tear-streaked face with her hands. "I don't want my mother to find out. I don't want my mother to find out."

"Come on now!"

"Shut up!" Amory shouted at Olson.

An instant's pause.

"Stella Robbins," she stammered at last. "General Delivery, Rugway, New Hampshire."

Olson closed his notebook with a sharp snap and gazed at them with great deliberation.

"Legally, the hotel could hand over the evidence to the police and you'd end up in prison, you would, for transporting a girl from one state to another for immoral purposes—" He stopped to let the weight of his words settle in. "But—the hotel is going to let you off the hook."

"It doesn't want to get in the papers," Jill shouted angrily. "Let us off! Yeah right!"

A tremendous sense of relief washed over Amory. He understood that he was out of danger, and only at that moment did he truly grasp the complete magnitude of what he could have faced.

"However," Olson went on, "there's a protective association among the hotels. There's been too much of this kind of thing, and we have an arrangement with the newspapers so that you get a little free publicity. Not the name of the hotel, but just a line saying that you had a little trouble in Atlantic City. See?"

"I see."

"You're getting off easy—damn easy—but—"

"Come on," Amory said briskly. "Let's get out of here. We don't need a farewell speech."

Olson walked through the bathroom and glanced briefly at Alec's motionless body. Then he turned off the lights and gestured for them to follow him. As they entered the elevator, Amory thought about making a bold gesture—but ultimately decided against it. He reached out and tapped Olson on the arm.

"Would you mind removing your hat? There's a lady in the elevator."

Olson's hat came off gradually. There were about two uncomfortable minutes under the bright lobby lights while the night desk clerk and several late-arriving guests watched them with curiosity; the flashily dressed young woman with her head down, the attractive young man with his chin raised defiantly; what was happening between them was pretty clear. Then they stepped into the cold outside air—where the ocean breeze was crisper and sharper with the early signs of dawn approaching.

"You can grab one of those taxis and take off," said Olson, gesturing toward the hazy shapes of two vehicles where the drivers were likely sleeping inside.

"Goodbye," said Olson. He reached into his pocket in a suggestive manner, but Amory snorted with disgust, and, taking the girl's arm, turned away.

"Where did you tell the driver to go?" she asked as they sped through the dimly lit street.

"The station."

"If that guy writes to my mother—"

"He won't. Nobody will ever know about this—except our friends and enemies."

Dawn was breaking over the sea.

"It's getting blue," she said.

"It looks really good," Amory agreed with a critical eye, and then added as an afterthought: "It's almost breakfast time—do you want something to eat?"

"Food—" she said with a cheerful laugh. "Food is what ruined the party. We ordered a big dinner to be delivered to the room around two o'clock. Alec didn't tip the waiter, so I think the little jerk ratted us out."

Jill's sadness appeared to have lifted more quickly than the fading darkness. "Let me tell you," she said with emphasis, "when you want to throw that kind of party, avoid alcohol, and when you want to get drunk, stay away from bedrooms."

"I'll remember."

He suddenly tapped on the glass and they stopped at the entrance of a twenty-four-hour restaurant.

"Is Alec a close friend of yours?" Jill asked as they settled onto the tall stools inside and rested their elbows on the grimy counter.

"He used to be. He probably won't want to be anymore—and will never understand why."

"It was kind of crazy that you took all that blame. Is he pretty important? More important than you are?"

Amory laughed.

"That remains to be seen," he answered. "That's the question."

The Collapse of Several Pillars

Two days later, back in New York, Amory discovered in a newspaper what he had been looking for—a dozen lines that announced to anyone who might be interested that Mr. Amory Blaine, who "gave his address" as, etc., had been asked to leave his hotel in Atlantic City for entertaining a woman in his room who was not his wife.

Then he jumped, and his fingers began to shake, because right above him was a longer paragraph whose opening words were:

"Mr. and Mrs. Leland R. Connage are announcing the engagement of their daughter, Rosalind, to Mr. J. Dawson Ryder, of Hartford, Connecticut—"

He dropped the paper and collapsed onto his bed, feeling a terrifying, hollow sensation deep in his stomach. She was gone—completely and permanently gone. Until this moment, he had unconsciously held onto a secret hope buried in his heart that someday she would need him and call for him, confessing it had all been a terrible mistake, that her heart was breaking from the pain she had inflicted on him. He could never again find even the dark comfort of longing for her—not this version of Rosalind, who had become harder and older—nor any defeated, shattered woman that his mind might conjure at the threshold of his forties.

Amory had loved her youth, the vibrant glow of her spirit and body, the essence that she was now selling away once and for all. As far as he was concerned, the young Rosalind he had known was dead.

A day later, a short and direct letter arrived from Mr. Barton in Chicago, informing him that since three additional streetcar companies had fallen into receivership, he shouldn't expect any more payments for the time being. Finally, on a bewildering Sunday night, a telegram brought news of Monsignor Darcy's unexpected death in Philadelphia five days earlier.

He realized then what he had sensed behind the curtains in that Atlantic City room.

Chapter 5. The Egotist Becomes A Personage

"A fathom deep in sleep I lie
With old desires, restrained before,
To clamor lifeward with a cry,
As dark flies out the greying door;
And so in quest of creeds to share
I seek assertive day again...
But old monotony is there:
Endless avenues of rain.

Oh, might I rise again! Might I
Throw off the heat of that old wine,
See the new morning mass the sky
With fairy towers, line on line;
Find each mirage in the high air
A symbol, not a dream again...
But old monotony is there:
Endless avenues of rain."

Under the glass entrance of a theater, Amory stood watching the first heavy raindrops hit the sidewalk and spread into dark spots. The air turned gray and shimmery; a single light suddenly appeared in a window across the street; then another light; then hundreds more flickered and sparkled into view. Beneath his feet, a thick skylight with iron studs glowed yellow; in the street, the headlights of taxi-cabs cast bright reflections across the already wet pavement. The unwanted November rain had stubbornly stolen the day's final hour and traded it away to that old thief, the night.

The quiet theater behind him suddenly broke with a strange snapping noise, followed by the loud rumbling of people getting up and the overlapping chatter of numerous voices. The afternoon show had ended.

He stepped to the side, moving slightly into the rain to allow the crowd to pass by. A young boy hurried out, breathed in the cool, moist air and pulled up his coat collar; three or four couples followed in a rush; then came another scattered group of people who, as they stepped outside, always looked first at the wet pavement, then at the rain-soaked air, and finally at the gloomy sky above; at the end came a thick, slow-moving crowd that made him feel dejected with its heavy smell—a mixture of men's tobacco smoke and the stale, cloying scent of old powder on the women. Following the dense crowd came more scattered individuals; a random group of five or six people; a man walking with crutches; and finally the clattering sound of folding chairs being put away inside told him that the ushers had begun their cleanup.

New York didn't seem to be waking up so much as simply rolling over in bed. Pale-faced men hurried past, clutching their coat collars tight against the cold; a large group of exhausted department store girls, chattering like magpies, crowded together along the street with bursts of harsh laughter, three of them sharing each umbrella; a formation of marching police officers went by, already somehow equipped with protective oilskin rain capes.

The rain made Amory feel disconnected from everything around him, and all the horrible parts of living in the city without money came flooding into his mind like a parade of threats. There was the awful, reeking crush of people in the subway—the advertisements forcing themselves on you, staring out like tedious people who grab your arm to tell you yet another boring story; the constant anxiety about whether someone might be pressing against you; a man choosing not to offer his seat to a woman and then resenting her for making him feel guilty; the woman despising him for his selfishness; at its worst, a disgusting nightmare of bad breath, worn-out clothing on unwashed bodies, and the odors of whatever food people had eaten—at its best, simply masses of humanity—either too warm or too chilly, exhausted, and anxious.

He imagined the rooms where these people lived—where the peeling wallpaper displayed heavy, repeating sunflower patterns against green and yellow backgrounds, where there were metal bathtubs and dark hallways and barren, indescribable areas behind the buildings; where even love appeared as temptation—a grimy killing just around the corner, forbidden pregnancy in the apartment upstairs. And there was always the cheap stuffiness of indoor winter, and the endless summers, sweaty nightmares between sticky surrounding walls... grimy diners where careless, exhausted people served themselves sugar with their own dirty coffee spoons, leaving crusty brown residue in the container.

It wasn't so terrible when there were only men or only women present; the real awfulness came when they were cruelly crowded together. There was a certain shame that women radiated when men witnessed them exhausted and impoverished—there was a particular revulsion that men felt toward women who were worn down and destitute. This place was filthier than any battlefield he had witnessed, more difficult to bear than any real suffering forged from mud and perspiration and peril, it was an environment where birth and marriage and death became repulsive, hidden matters.

He recalled a day on the subway when a delivery worker had carried in a large funeral wreath made of fresh flowers, and how its fragrance had instantly purified the air and brought a brief sense of warmth to everyone in the train car.

"I can't stand poor people," Amory thought out of nowhere. "I despise them for their poverty. Maybe poverty was once something noble, but now it's disgusting. It's the most repulsive thing imaginable. It's actually more respectable to be wealthy and corrupt than to be poor and virtuous." He could picture again a scene that had once made an impression on him—a well-dressed young man looking out from a club window on Fifth Avenue, speaking to his friend with complete revulsion on his face. Amory figured that what the man had said was probably: "Dear God! People are absolutely awful!"

Never before in his life had Amory thought about poor people. He reflected cynically on how completely he lacked any human compassion. O. Henry had discovered romance, sadness, love, and hatred in these people—Amory saw only vulgarity, physical dirt, and ignorance. He didn't blame himself: he no longer criticized himself for feelings that were natural and genuine. He accepted all his reactions as part of who he was, unchangeable and beyond moral judgment. This issue of poverty, transformed, enlarged, and connected to some greater, more noble perspective might someday even become his own problem; right now it only stirred his deep disgust.

He walked toward Fifth Avenue, weaving through the threatening dark mass of umbrellas, and stopped in front of Delmonico's to flag down a bus. He pulled his coat tight around himself and climbed up to the top deck, where he sat alone in the thin, steady rain, the cool droplets constantly forming on his face keeping him sharp and alert. Somewhere in his thoughts, a conversation started up again, or rather returned to the center of his attention. It wasn't made up of two voices, but just one, which served as both the person asking questions and the one providing answers:

Question.—Well—what's the situation?

Answer.—I have approximately twenty-four dollars to my name.

Q.—You own the Lake Geneva estate.

A.—But I intend to keep it.

Q.—Are you able to live?

A.—I can't imagine not being able to. People make money in books and I've found that I can always do the things that people do in books. Really they are the only things I can do.

Q.—Be specific.

A.—I don't know what I'll do—and I'm not particularly curious about it either. Tomorrow I'm leaving New York for good. It's a terrible city unless you're running the show.

Q.—Do you want a lot of money?

A.—No. I'm simply afraid of being poor.

Q.—Very afraid?

A.—Just passively afraid.

Q.—Where are you drifting?

A.—Don't ask me!

Q.—Don't you care?

A.—Absolutely. I don't want to commit moral suicide.

Q.—Don't you have any interests left?

A.—None. I have no more virtue left to lose. Just like a cooling pot releases heat, throughout our youth and teenage years we give off units of virtue. That's what people call innocence.

Q.—An interesting idea.

That's why a "good man going wrong" draws people in. They gather around and actually warm themselves with the energy of virtue he radiates. Sarah makes a simple, honest comment and the faces light up with condescending smiles—"How innocent the poor child is!" They're basking in her virtue. But Sarah notices those patronizing smiles and never makes that kind of comment again. Only now she feels a little colder afterward.

Q.—Have you used up all your calories?

A.—All of them. I'm starting to find comfort in other people's goodness.

Q.—Are you corrupt?

A.—I think so. I'm not sure. I'm not sure about good and evil at all anymore.

Q.—Is that a bad sign in itself?

A.—Not necessarily.

What would be the test of corruption?

A.—Becoming truly dishonest with myself—telling myself "I'm not such a bad person," believing I missed my lost youth when I really just envy the joy of losing it. Youth is like having a large plate of candy. Sentimental people think they want to return to the pure, innocent state they were in before they ate the candy. They don't. They simply want the enjoyment of eating it all over again. The married woman doesn't want to relive her girlhood—she wants to relive her honeymoon. I don't want to experience my innocence again. I want the pleasure of losing it once more.

Where are you heading?

This conversation blended disturbingly into his mind's most familiar condition—a disturbing mixture of desires, anxieties, external impressions and bodily responses.

One Hundred and Twenty-seventh Street—or One Hundred and Thirty-seventh Street.... Two and three look similar—no, not really. The seat is damp... are my clothes soaking up moisture from the seat, or is the seat drawing dryness from my clothes?... Sitting on wet surfaces causes appendicitis, according to Froggy Parker's mother. Well, he'd gotten it—I'll sue the steamboat company, Beatrice had said, and my uncle owns a quarter share—did Beatrice make it to heaven?... probably not—He embodied Beatrice's eternal spirit, along with the romantic entanglements of countless dead men who certainly had never given him a thought... if it wasn't appendicitis, maybe it was the flu. What? One Hundred and Twentieth Street? That previous one must have been One Hundred and Twelfth. One O Two rather than One Two Seven. Rosalind isn't like Beatrice, Eleanor resembles Beatrice, except she's wilder and more intelligent. The apartments around here cost a fortune—likely a hundred and fifty per month—perhaps two hundred. Uncle had only paid a hundred monthly for that entire enormous house in Minneapolis. The question—were the stairs positioned on the left or right when you entered? In any case, at 12 Univee they ran straight back and to the left. What a filthy river—I want to go down there and check if it's really that dirty— French rivers are all brown or black, and so were the Southern ones. Twenty-four dollars equals four hundred and eighty doughnuts. He could survive on that for three months and sleep in the park. I wonder where Jill was—Jill Bayne, Fayne, Sayne— what the hell—my neck aches, this seat is terribly uncomfortable. No urge to sleep with Jill, what could Alec possibly see in her? Alec had vulgar taste in women. His own taste was superior; Isabelle, Clara, Rosalind, Eleanor, were all genuinely American. Eleanor would probably pitch, likely left-handed. Rosalind belonged in the outfield, an excellent hitter, Clara at first base, perhaps. I wonder what Humbird's body looks like now. If he himself hadn't been a bayonet instructor he would have gone to the front lines three months earlier, probably would have been killed. Where's that damn bell—

The street numbers along Riverside Drive were hidden by the fog and wet trees, making them nearly impossible to see unless you looked very carefully, but Amory had managed to spot one—One Hundred and Twenty-seventh Street. He stepped off and without any clear plan in mind walked along a curving, sloping sidewalk that led him down to face the river, where he found himself looking at a long pier and a scattered collection of small boat yards filled with tiny vessels: little motorboats, canoes, rowboats, and sailboats. He turned north and walked along the shoreline, hopped over a low wire fence and discovered he was now standing in a large, messy yard next to a dock. The frames of numerous boats in different stages of being fixed surrounded him; he breathed in the scents of sawdust and paint along with the barely noticeable stale smell of the Hudson River. A figure came toward him through the thick darkness.

"Hello," said Amory.

"Do you have a pass?"

"No. Is this private?"

"This is the Hudson River Sporting and Yacht Club."

"Oh! I didn't know. I'm just resting."

"Well—" the man began hesitantly.

"I'll go if you want me to."

The man made vague sounds in his throat and moved on. Amory sat down on an upside-down boat and leaned forward in contemplation until his chin came to rest in his hand.

"Bad luck is likely to turn me into a terrible person," he said slowly.

In The Drooping Hours

While the rain drizzled down, Amory looked hopelessly back at the flow of his life, with all its bright moments and murky depths. To start with, he was still afraid—not physically scared anymore, but frightened of people and their judgments, of suffering and endless routine. Yet, buried deep in his bitter heart, he wondered whether he was really any worse than this person or that one. He knew he could cleverly convince himself that his own weakness was simply the product of his circumstances and surroundings; that often when he got angry at himself for being self-centered, something would whisper flatteringly: "No. Genius!" That was one form of fear, that voice which suggested he couldn't be both great and good, that genius was the precise combination of those mysterious patterns and quirks in his mind, that any self-control would reduce it to ordinariness. Probably more than any specific vice or shortcoming, Amory hated his own character—he detested knowing that tomorrow and the thousand days that followed, he would puff up proudly at praise and brood over harsh words like a mediocre musician or a top-tier actor. He felt ashamed that very straightforward and sincere people usually didn't trust him; that he had often been cruel to those who had lost themselves in him— several young women, and a man here and there throughout college, whom he had negatively influenced; people who had followed him into intellectual pursuits from which only he emerged unharmed.

Usually, on nights like this, and there had been many recently, he could escape from this overwhelming self-examination by thinking about children and the endless potential that children possessed—he leaned forward and listened, and he heard a startled baby wake up in a house across the street and add a small whimper to the quiet night. As quick as lightning he turned away, wondering with a hint of panic whether something in the brooding despair of his mood had created a darkness in its small soul. He trembled. What if someday the balance shifted, and he became something that scared children and crept into rooms in the darkness, seeking dim connection with those spirits who whispered mysterious secrets to the insane of that dark continent on the moon....

Amory smiled a little.

"You're too wrapped up in yourself," he heard someone say. And again—

"Get out and do some real work—"

"Stop worrying—"

He imagined a comment he might make in the future.

"Yes—I was probably self-centered when I was young, but I quickly discovered that thinking too much about myself made me unhealthy and depressed."

Suddenly he felt an overwhelming urge to abandon everything—not to leave dramatically as a gentleman should, but to slip away quietly and pleasurably from view. He imagined himself in an adobe house in Mexico, half-lying on a couch covered with rugs, his slender, artistic fingers holding a cigarette while he listened to guitars playing melancholy accompaniments to an ancient lament of Castile and an olive-skinned, red-lipped girl stroked his hair. Here he could live a peculiar existence, freed from right and wrong and from the relentless pursuit of heaven and from every God (except the exotic Mexican one who was quite lenient himself and rather fond of Eastern fragrances)—freed from success and hope and poverty into that long slide of self-indulgence which led, ultimately, only to the artificial lake of death.

There were countless places where someone could indulge in pleasant decline: Port Said, Shanghai, regions of Turkestan, Constantinople, the South Seas—all territories filled with melancholy, haunting melodies and countless fragrances, where desire could become a way of living and self-expression, where the hues of evening skies and sunsets appeared to mirror only feelings of passion: the shades of lips and poppies.

Still Weeding

Once he had possessed the miraculous ability to sense evil the way a horse detects a broken bridge in the darkness, but the strange man with the unusual feet in Phoebe's room had reduced that gift to nothing more than the faint impression he felt around Jill. His instinct could still detect the foul stench of poverty, but it no longer hunted down the more profound evils that lurked within pride and sensuality.

There were no more wise men; there were no more heroes; Burne Holiday had disappeared from view as if he had never existed; Monsignor was dead. Amory had been raised on a thousand books, a thousand falsehoods; he had listened with enthusiasm to people who claimed to understand, who actually knew nothing. The spiritual contemplations of saints that had once inspired him with wonder during the quiet hours of night now left him feeling vaguely disgusted. The Byrons and Brookes who had challenged life from mountaintops were ultimately nothing more than idle wanderers and pretenders, at best confusing the appearance of bravery with genuine wisdom. The grand display of his disappointment formed itself into an ancient parade of Prophets, Athenians, Martyrs, Saints, Scientists, Don Juans, Jesuits, Puritans, Fausts, Poets, Pacifists; like dressed-up graduates at a college reunion they passed before him as their aspirations, characters, and beliefs had successively cast different colored lights upon his spirit; each had attempted to capture the magnificence of existence and the enormous importance of humanity; each had claimed to bring together everything that came before into his own shaky theories; each had relied ultimately on the established stage and the agreement of the theater, which is that man in his craving for belief will nourish his mind with the closest and most accessible sustenance.

Women—from whom he had expected so much; whose beauty he had hoped to transform into artistic expression; whose mysterious instincts, wonderfully inconsistent and unspoken, he had planned to capture through lived experience—had simply become devoted to securing their own future generations. Isabelle, Clara, Rosalind, Eleanor, were all made distant by their very beauty, which attracted crowds of men, leaving them unable to offer anything except a broken heart and a page of confused writing.

Amory built his loss of faith in getting help from others on several broad logical arguments. He accepted that his generation, despite being battered and devastated by this Victorian conflict, represented the inheritors of human advancement. Setting aside minor disagreements in their conclusions—which, though they might sometimes lead to the deaths of millions of young men, could be rationalized—assuming that Bernard Shaw and Bernhardi, Bonar Law and Bethmann-Hollweg were all fellow inheritors of progress, if only because they agreed against drowning suspected witches—ignoring these opposing viewpoints and examining these men individually as they appeared to be the leaders, he found himself disgusted by the inconsistencies and contradictions within the men themselves.

There was, for example, Thornton Hancock, respected by half the intellectual world as an authority on life, a man who had verified and believed in the principles he lived by, an educator of educators, an adviser to Presidents—yet Amory knew that this man had, in his heart, relied on the priest of another faith.

Monsignor, who had the support of a cardinal, experienced periods of bizarre and terrifying uncertainty—something that seemed impossible to explain within a religion that could account for even skepticism through its own beliefs: if you questioned the existence of the devil, it was the devil himself causing you to doubt. Amory had witnessed Monsignor visiting the homes of unimaginative, narrow-minded people, reading mainstream novels with desperate intensity, and immersing himself completely in mundane activities, all in an attempt to flee from that dreadful feeling.

And this priest, who was a little wiser and somewhat purer, had been, Amory knew, not really any older than he was.

Amory found himself completely alone—he had broken free from a cramped prison into an enormous maze. He stood where Goethe had been when he started writing "Faust"; he occupied the same position Conrad had held when he penned "Almayer's Folly."

Amory told himself that there were basically two types of people who, through natural insight or disenchantment, left the safety of conventional thinking and ventured into the maze of deeper understanding. There were individuals like Wells and Plato, who possessed, somewhat unconsciously, an unusual, concealed sense of traditional belief, who would only accept for themselves what could be accepted for everyone—hopeless idealists who never, despite all their attempts, could enter the maze as bare, unadorned spirits; there were, on the other hand, sharp, trailblazing personalities like Samuel Butler, Renan, and Voltaire, who moved much more slowly, yet ultimately traveled much farther, not following the straightforward pessimistic path of theoretical philosophy but engaged in the endless effort to assign a positive meaning to existence....

Amory came to a halt. For the first time in his life, he developed a deep suspicion of all broad generalizations and witty sayings. They were too simple, too risky for the general public's understanding. Still, most ideas typically reached ordinary people after three decades in exactly this kind of format: Benson and Chesterton had made Huysmans and Newman accessible to the masses; Shaw had made Nietzsche, Ibsen, and Schopenhauer more palatable. The average person encountered the insights of brilliant thinkers who had passed away through someone else's clever contradictions and instructional maxims.

Life was a complete mess... like a football game where everyone was offside and the referee had been eliminated—with everyone insisting the referee would have ruled in their favor....

Progress was a maze... people diving in blindly and then racing frantically back, declaring they had discovered it... the unseen ruler—the life force—the driving principle of evolution... composing a book, launching a war, establishing a school....

Amory, even if he hadn't been a self-centered person, would have begun all his questioning by examining himself. He served as his own prime example—sitting there in the rain, a human being driven by desire and ego, denied by fate and his own nature the comfort of love and family, kept alive to contribute to the growing awareness of humanity.

In self-blame and isolation and disappointment he arrived at the entrance of the maze.

Another dawn spread across the river, while a late taxi rushed down the street, its headlights still glowing like fiery eyes in a face pale from a night of heavy drinking. A mournful siren wailed from somewhere far along the river.

Monsignor

Amory couldn't stop thinking about how much Monsignor would have loved his own funeral. It was magnificently Catholic and ceremonial. Bishop O'Neill performed the solemn high mass and the cardinal delivered the final absolutions. Thornton Hancock, Mrs. Lawrence, the British and Italian ambassadors, the papal delegate, and countless friends and priests attended—yet death's relentless blade had severed all the connections that Monsignor had woven together in his lifetime. For Amory, it was a deeply troubling sorrow to see him lying in his casket, hands folded peacefully over his purple robes. His face remained unchanged, and since he never realized he was dying, it bore no trace of suffering or terror. This was Amory's beloved old friend, his and everyone else's—the church overflowed with people whose faces showed bewildered, vacant stares, with those of highest rank appearing the most devastated.

The cardinal, dressed like an archangel in his ceremonial vestments and mitre, sprinkled the holy water; the organ burst into music; the choir began singing the Requiem Eternam.

All these people grieved because they had relied on Monsignor to some degree. Their sorrow went beyond mere sentiment for the "crack in his voice or a certain break in his walk," as Wells described it. These individuals had depended on Monsignor's faith, his ability to discover joy, his way of transforming religion into something filled with brightness and darkness, making all illumination and shadow simply facets of God. People experienced security when he was close by.

From Amory's failed attempt at sacrifice came only the complete understanding of his disappointment, but from Monsignor's funeral emerged the romantic spirit that would accompany him into the maze ahead. He discovered something he desired, had always desired and would always desire—not to be admired, as he had worried; not to be loved, as he had convinced himself; but to be essential to people, to be irreplaceable; he recalled the feeling of safety he had experienced with Burne.

Life burst open with one of its incredible moments of brilliant clarity, and Amory instantly and forever dismissed an old saying that had been drifting aimlessly through his thoughts: "Very few things matter and nothing matters very much."

Amory felt a powerful urge to provide others with a feeling of safety and reassurance.

The Big Man with Goggles

On the day Amory began his walk to Princeton, the sky stretched above like a colorless dome—cool, vast, and holding no promise of rain. It was an overcast day, the most ethereal of all weather conditions; a day meant for dreams, distant hopes, and crystal-clear insights. It was the kind of day naturally linked to those philosophical truths and pure ideals that vanish in bright sunlight or disappear amid cynical laughter under moonlight. The trees and clouds appeared sculpted with classical restraint; the sounds of the rural landscape had blended into a single tone, as metallic as a trumpet's call, as silent as the Grecian urn.

The day had left Amory in such a reflective state that he irritated several drivers who had to slow down significantly or risk hitting him. He was so absorbed in his thoughts that he barely registered that unusual occurrence—friendliness displayed within fifty miles of Manhattan—when a passing car pulled up next to him and someone called out to him. He glanced up and spotted a stunning Locomobile containing two middle-aged men, one small and worried-looking, seemingly like an unnatural appendage to the other who was large, wore goggles, and had an impressive presence.

"Do you need a ride?" asked the seemingly fake-looking person, glancing sideways at the impressive man as if seeking some routine, unspoken confirmation.

"You bet I do. Thanks."

The chauffeur opened the door wide, and Amory climbed in, settling into the center of the back seat. He studied his traveling companions with curiosity. The large man's most striking quality appeared to be an enormous self-assurance combined with complete boredom toward everything surrounding him. The portion of his face visible beneath his goggles could be described as "strong"; dignified layers of fat had gathered around his chin; somewhere higher up sat a broad, thin mouth and what resembled the rough outline of a Roman nose, while below, his shoulders gave way effortlessly to the substantial mass of his chest and stomach. His clothing was impeccable and understated. Amory observed that the man had a tendency to gaze directly at the back of the chauffeur's head, as though he were pondering some puzzling matter related to the driver's hair with steady but futile concentration.

The smaller man stood out only because he had completely lost himself in the other person's personality. He belonged to that lower-level administrative type who, at forty years old, have printed on their business cards "Assistant to the President," and without any regret dedicate the remainder of their lives to copying someone else's mannerisms.

"Going far?" asked the smaller man in a pleasant, detached manner.

"Quite a stretch."

"Hiking for exercise?"

"No," Amory replied briefly, "I'm walking because I don't have the money to take transportation."

"Oh."

Then again:

"Are you looking for work? Because there's plenty of work available," he went on, sounding somewhat irritated. "All this talk about not having enough jobs. The West particularly needs workers." He indicated the West with a broad, sideways gesture. Amory nodded politely.

"Do you have a trade?"

No—Amory had no profession.

"Clerk, eh?"

No—Amory was not a clerk.

"Whatever your field is," said the little man, appearing to agree thoughtfully with something Amory had mentioned, "now is the time for opportunity and business ventures." He looked again toward the big man, the way a lawyer questioning a witness instinctively glances at the jury.

Amory realized he had to say something, but for the life of him, he could only think of one thing to say.

"Of course I want a great deal of money—"

The small man laughed without joy but dutifully.

"That's what everyone wants these days, but they don't want to put in the effort to achieve it."

"A completely natural and healthy desire. Nearly everyone wants to become wealthy without having to work too hard for it—except for the financiers you see in those dramatic plays who are determined to 'force their way to the top.' Don't you want money that comes easily?"

"Of course not," said the secretary indignantly.

"But," Amory went on, ignoring him, "since I'm quite broke right now, I'm considering socialism as something I might be good at."

Both men looked at him with curiosity.

"These bomb throwers—" The small man stopped speaking as words emerged heavily from the large man's chest.

"If I believed you were someone who throws bombs, I'd drag you straight to the Newark jail. That's exactly what I think about Socialists."

Amory laughed.

"What are you," the large man asked, "one of those drawing room Bolsheviks, one of those idealists? I have to say I don't see any difference between them. The idealists sit around doing nothing and write the material that gets the poor immigrants all worked up."

"Well," said Amory, "if being an idealist is both safe and profitable, I might give it a try."

"What's your problem? Did you lose your job?"

"Not exactly, but—well, call it that."

"What was it?"

"Writing copy for an advertising agency."

"There's a lot of money in advertising."

Amory smiled discreetly.

"Oh, I'll admit there's money in it eventually. Talent doesn't starve anymore. Even art gets enough to eat these days. Artists create your magazine covers, write your advertisements, churn out ragtime for your theaters. Through the massive commercialization of printing, you've discovered a harmless, respectable job for every genius who might have created his own unique place. But watch out for the artist who's also an intellectual. The artist who doesn't conform—the Rousseau, the Tolstoy, the Samuel Butler, the Amory Blaine—"

"Who is he?" the little man asked suspiciously.

"Well," said Amory, "he's a—he's an intellectual figure who isn't very well known right now."

The small man let out his careful laugh, then stopped quite abruptly when Amory's intense eyes fixed on him.

"What are you laughing at?"

"These intellectual people—"

"Do you know what it means?"

The small man's eyes flickered with anxiety.

"Well, it typically means—"

"It always means intelligent and well-educated," Amory interrupted. "It means having an active understanding of humanity's collective experience." Amory decided to be extremely rude. He turned toward the large man. "This young man," he said, pointing at the secretary with his thumb, using the phrase "young man" the way someone might say "bellhop," with no actual reference to age, "has the typical confused understanding that comes with all commonly used words."

"You have a problem with the fact that capital controls printing?" said the big man, staring at him through his goggles.

"Yes—and I refuse to do their thinking for them. It struck me that the foundation of all the business activity I witnessed around me involved overworking and underpaying a group of incompetent people who simply accepted it."

"Listen here," said the large man, "you have to acknowledge that the working man is definitely overpaid—five and six hour workdays—it's absurd. You can't get an honest day's work from someone in the labor unions."

"You've brought it on yourselves," Amory insisted. "You people never make concessions until they're forced out of you."

"What people?"

"Your social class; the class I was part of until recently; those who through inheritance or hard work or intelligence or dishonest means have become the wealthy class."

"Do you think that if that road worker over there had the money, he'd be any more willing to give it up?"

"No, but what's that got to do with it?"

The older man thought it over.

"No, I'll admit it hasn't. It does sound like it has though."

"Actually," Amory went on, "he'd be even worse. People from lower social classes are more narrow-minded, less agreeable, and more self-centered on a personal level—definitely less intelligent. But none of that is relevant to what we're discussing."

"What exactly is the question?"

Here Amory had to stop and think carefully about what the question actually was.

Amory Creates a Saying

"When life takes control of an intelligent man with decent education," Amory began slowly, "that is, when he gets married, he becomes, nine times out of ten, a conservative when it comes to existing social conditions. He might be selfless, compassionate, even fair in his own way, but his primary responsibility is to provide and maintain security. His wife pushes him forward, from ten thousand a year to twenty thousand a year, onward and onward, in a confined treadmill without any windows. He's finished! Life has captured him! He's useless! He's a spiritually married man."

Amory stopped and concluded that it wasn't really such a terrible expression.

"Some men," he went on, "break free from that hold. Perhaps their wives don't care about climbing the social ladder; perhaps they've come across a line or two in a 'dangerous book' that struck a chord with them; perhaps they began on the same hamster wheel as I did and got thrown off. Either way, they're the congressmen who can't be bought, the Presidents who aren't just politicians, the writers, speakers, scientists, and statesmen who aren't merely popular collections of expectations for a handful of women and children."

"He's the natural radical?"

"Yes," said Amory. "He can range anywhere from the disillusioned critic like old Thornton Hancock all the way to Trotsky. Now this spiritually unmarried man doesn't have direct power, because unfortunately the spiritually married man, as a side effect of his pursuit of money, has taken control of the major newspapers, the popular magazines, the influential weeklies—so that Mrs. Newspaper, Mrs. Magazine, Mrs. Weekly can own a better limousine than those oil people across the street or those cement people around the corner."

"Why not?"

"It makes wealthy men the guardians of the world's intellectual conscience and, naturally, a man who has money under one set of social institutions simply cannot risk his family's happiness by allowing the demand for another system to appear in his newspaper."

"But it seems," said the big man.

"Where?—in the discredited publications. Trashy cheap-papered weekly magazines."

"All right—go on."

"Well, my first point is that through a combination of circumstances, with family being the primary one, there exist these two types of minds. One type accepts human nature as it is, exploiting its fears, weaknesses, and strengths for personal gain. In contrast stands the person who, being spiritually unattached, constantly searches for new frameworks that will manage or counterbalance human nature. His challenge is more difficult. Life itself isn't complex—it's the effort to direct and manage life that creates complexity. That is his battle. He contributes to progress—the spiritually attached person does not."

The large man pulled out three big cigars and offered them on his enormous palm. The small man took one, while Amory shook his head and reached for a cigarette.

"Keep talking," said the large man. "I've been wanting to hear from one of you guys."

Going Faster

"Modern life," Amory continued, "no longer transforms century by century, but year by year, ten times more rapidly than it ever has before—populations are doubling, civilizations are becoming more tightly connected with other civilizations, economic interdependence is growing, racial issues are emerging, and—we're moving too slowly. My point is that we need to move much more quickly." He put slight emphasis on his final words and the driver unconsciously pressed harder on the accelerator. Amory and the large man burst into laughter; the small man joined in laughing as well, though after a brief delay.

"Every child," Amory said, "should get an equal beginning. If his father can give him a healthy body and his mother can provide some practical wisdom during his early schooling, that should be what he inherits. If the father cannot provide him with a strong constitution, if the mother has wasted the years she should have spent preparing herself to teach her children by pursuing romantic relationships instead, then the child suffers the consequences. He shouldn't be propped up artificially with wealth, shipped off to those awful preparatory schools, forced through university... Every boy deserves to start on equal footing."

"All right," said the big man, his goggles showing neither approval nor disapproval.

"Next, I would want to see a fair test of government ownership of all industries."

"That's been proven a failure."

"No—it simply didn't work. If the government owned these businesses, we'd have the most brilliant analytical minds in government working for something beyond their own interests. We'd have people like Mackay instead of Burleson; we'd have individuals like Morgan in the Treasury Department; we'd have people like Hill managing interstate commerce. We'd have the finest lawyers serving in the Senate."

"They wouldn't give their best efforts for nothing. McAdoo"

"No," said Amory, shaking his head. "Money isn't the only thing that motivates people to do their best, even in America."

"You said a while ago that it was."

"It is, right now. But if it were made illegal to have more than a certain amount, the best men would all flock to the one other reward which attracts humanity—honor."

The large man made a noise that sounded very much like "boo."

"That's the silliest thing you've said yet."

"No, it isn't silly. It's quite believable. If you had gone to college, you would have been amazed by how the men there would work twice as hard for any one of a hundred small honors compared to those other men who were working to pay their way through school."

"Kids—child's play!" his opponent sneered.

"Not by a long shot—unless we're all children. Have you ever watched a grown man trying to get into a secret society—or a family climbing the social ladder whose name is being considered at some exclusive club? They'll jump at the mere mention of it. The notion that you need to dangle money in front of someone's face to make them work is something we've developed over time, not a fundamental truth. We've been doing this for so long that we've forgotten there are other ways to motivate people. We've created a world where this seems necessary. Let me tell you"— Amory grew more passionate—"if there were ten men who didn't have to worry about getting rich or going hungry, and you offered them a green ribbon for working five hours a day and a blue ribbon for working ten hours a day, nine out of ten would be going after that blue ribbon. That competitive drive just needs something to aim for. If the size of their house is what they're competing for, they'll work themselves to exhaustion for it. If it's just a blue ribbon, I'm convinced they'll work just as hard. They have in other times throughout history."

"I don't agree with you."

"I know it," said Amory, nodding sadly. "It doesn't matter anymore though. I think these people are going to come and take what they want pretty soon."

A sharp hiss escaped from the small man.

"Machine-guns!"

"Ah, but you've taught them how to use it."

The large man shook his head.

"In this country there are enough property owners who won't allow that kind of thing to happen."

Amory wished he knew the statistics of property owners and non-property owners; he decided to change the subject.

But the large man was stirred to action.

"When you talk of 'taking things away,' you're on dangerous ground."

"How can they obtain it without seizing it? For years, people have been delayed with promises. Socialism might not represent progress, but the threat of the red flag is undoubtedly the driving force behind all reform. You have to be dramatic to capture attention."

"Russia is your example of a beneficent violence, I suppose?"

"Quite possibly," Amory acknowledged. "Of course, it's spilling over just like the French Revolution did, but I have no doubt that it's truly a significant experiment and completely worthwhile."

"Don't you believe in moderation?"

"You refuse to listen to the moderates, and we're running out of time. The reality is that the public has accomplished one of those shocking and extraordinary things they manage to do perhaps once every century. They've grasped hold of an idea."

"What is it?"

"However much people's intelligence and talents may vary, their basic human needs remain fundamentally the same."

The Little Man Gets His

"If you took all the money in the world," said the little man with great depth, "and divided it up equally—"

"Oh, shut up!" Amory said sharply, and ignoring the little man's furious glare, he continued with his argument.

"The human stomach—" he started; but the large man cut him off somewhat irritably.

"I'm allowing you to speak, you understand," he said, "but please stay away from discussing stomachs. I've been aware of mine all day. In any case, I disagree with half of what you've said. Government ownership forms the foundation of your entire argument, and it's always a hotbed of corruption. People won't work for mere recognition, that's complete nonsense."

When he finished speaking, the little man spoke up with a determined nod, as if he had made up his mind to say everything he wanted to say this time.

"There are certain things which are human nature," he declared with an owl-like expression, "which have always existed and always will exist, which cannot be changed."

Amory glanced helplessly between the small man and the big man.

"Listen to that! That's exactly what discourages me about progress. Just listen to that! I can easily list more than a hundred natural phenomena that human willpower has transformed—a hundred human instincts that civilization has either eliminated or brought under control. What this person just said has been the final retreat of the world's collective narrow-minded thinkers for thousands of years. It dismisses the work of every scientist, political leader, ethicist, reformer, physician, and philosopher who ever dedicated their life to serving humanity. It's a complete rejection of everything valuable in human nature. Anyone over twenty-five who makes that statement with a clear head should lose their right to vote."

The small man leaned back against the seat, his face turning purple with anger. Amory kept talking, directing his comments to the large man.

"These partially educated, narrow-minded individuals like your friend over there, who believe they're thinking clearly, will show you the same confused mess with every issue that arises. At one moment they're condemning 'the cruelty and barbarism of these Prussians'—the next they're declaring 'we should wipe out the entire German nation.' They consistently claim that 'conditions are terrible right now,' yet they 'have no confidence in these idealistic reformers.' One day they dismiss Wilson as 'merely a visionary, completely impractical'—a year afterward they attack him for turning his visions into reality. They lack coherent, rational thoughts on any topic whatsoever, except for their unwavering, stubborn resistance to all progress. They believe uneducated workers shouldn't receive high wages, but they refuse to recognize that if these workers aren't paid well, their children will remain uneducated as well, trapping us in an endless cycle. That— represents the great middle class!"

The large man with a wide smile on his face leaned forward and grinned at the small man.

"You're taking quite a beating, Garvin; how are you holding up?"

The small man tried to smile and behave as though the entire situation was so absurd it didn't deserve attention. However,

Amory wasn't finished.

"The idea that people can govern themselves depends entirely on this individual. If he can learn to think with clarity, precision, and logic, breaking free from his tendency to hide behind empty phrases, biases, and emotional appeals, then I'm a committed Socialist. If he cannot, then I don't believe it makes much difference what becomes of humanity or our political systems, whether now or in the future."

"I find this both interesting and amusing," the large man said. "You're quite young."

"This might simply mean that modern experiences haven't corrupted me or made me fearful. I have the most precious kind of experience—the accumulated wisdom of humanity—because despite attending college, I've succeeded in gaining a real education."

"You speak too casually about serious matters."

"It's not all nonsense," Amory declared with passion. "This is the first time in my life I've debated Socialism. It's the only cure-all I know. I'm restless. My entire generation is restless. I'm tired of a system where the wealthiest man gets the most beautiful woman if he wants her, where the artist without money has to sell his abilities to a button maker. Even if I had no abilities I wouldn't be satisfied to work ten years, doomed either to remaining single or sneaking around for pleasure, just to give some man's son a car."

"But, if you're not sure—"

"That doesn't matter," Amory declared. "My situation couldn't get any worse. A social revolution might actually put me on top. Of course I'm being selfish. It feels like I've been completely out of place in too many outdated systems. I was probably one of only twenty-four guys in my entire college class who actually received a proper education; yet they'd allow any well-coached idiot to play football while I was ruled ineligible, all because some foolish old men believed we should all benefit from studying conic sections.

I hated the army. I despised business. I'm passionate about change and I've destroyed my conscience—"

"So you'll keep complaining that we need to move faster."

"That much is definitely true," Amory insisted. "Reform will never keep pace with what civilization actually needs unless we force it to happen. A hands-off approach is like spoiling a child by telling yourself he'll eventually turn out fine on his own. Sure, he might—but only if someone makes him."

"But you don't believe all this Socialist talk you're spouting."

"I don't know. Until I spoke with you, I hadn't given it serious thought. I wasn't even sure about half the things I said."

"You confuse me," the large man said, "but you're all the same. People say that Bernard Shaw, despite his beliefs, is the most demanding of all playwrights when it comes to his royalties. Down to the very last penny."

"Well," said Amory, "I simply state that I'm the result of a flexible mind in a restless generation—with every reason to align my thoughts and writing with the radicals. Even if, deep in my heart, I believed we were all blind particles in a world as confined as the swing of a pendulum, I and others like me would fight against tradition; attempt, at least, to replace old hypocrisies with new ones. I've believed I was correct about life at different times, but faith is challenging. One thing I understand. If living isn't a search for the grail it might be an incredibly entertaining game."

For a minute neither of them said anything, and then the large man asked:

"What university did you attend?"

"Princeton."

The large man suddenly became interested; the look behind his goggles changed slightly.

"I sent my son to Princeton."

"Did you?"

"Perhaps you knew him. His name was Jesse Ferrenby. He was killed last year in France."

"I knew him very well. In fact, he was one of my close friends."

"He was—a—quite a fine boy. We were very close."

Amory started to notice similarities between the father and his deceased son, and he realized there had been a feeling of recognition all along. Jesse Ferrenby, the man who had claimed the prize in college that Amory had wanted for himself. It all seemed so distant now. What children they had been, striving for those blue ribbons—

The car slowed down at the entrance to a large estate, surrounded by an enormous hedge and a high iron fence.

"Won't you come in for lunch?"

Amory shook his head.

"Thank you, Mr. Ferrenby, but I need to keep moving."

The large man extended his hand. Amory realized that his connection with Jesse far outweighed any negative impression he had made through his views. What strange, ghostlike figures people were to deal with! Even the smaller man insisted on shaking hands.

"Goodbye!" shouted Mr. Ferrenby, as the car turned the corner and started up the drive. "Good luck to you and bad luck to your theories."

"Same to you, sir," Amory called out, smiling and waving his hand.

"Out of The Fire, Out of The Little Room"

Eight hours from Princeton, Amory sat down beside the Jersey roadside and gazed at the frost-covered countryside. Nature, when viewed as a rather crude phenomenon made up mostly of flowers that looked moth-eaten upon close examination, and of ants that constantly crawled across blades of grass, always proved disappointing; nature represented through skies and waters and distant horizons was more appealing. The frost and the approaching promise of winter excited him now, bringing to mind a fierce battle between St. Regis and Groton from long ago, seven years past—and an autumn day in France twelve months earlier when he had lain in tall grass, his platoon pressed flat around him, waiting to tap the shoulder of a Lewis gunner. He viewed these two scenes together with much the same raw excitement—two games he had participated in, different in their degree of harshness, connected in a way that set them apart from Rosalind or the topic of labyrinths which were, ultimately, the real concerns of life.

"I am selfish," he thought.

"This isn't a quality that will change when I 'witness human suffering' or 'lose my parents' or 'help others.'"

"This selfishness isn't just a part of who I am. It's the most vital part of me."

"It is by somehow rising above rather than by avoiding that selfishness that I can bring poise and balance into my life."

"There isn't a single unselfish virtue that I can't put to use. I can make sacrifices, show charity, give to a friend, suffer for a friend, even lay down my life for a friend—all because these actions might be the finest way to express who I am; yet I don't possess even a trace of genuine human compassion."

The problem of evil had crystallized for Amory into the problem of sexuality. He was starting to connect evil with the intense phallic themes found in Brooke and the early works of Wells. Inseparably connected to evil was beauty—beauty, still a persistent rising storm; gentle in Eleanor's voice, in an old melody at night, rushing wildly through life like layered waterfalls, part rhythm, part shadow. Amory understood that every time he had reached for it with longing it had sneered back at him with the twisted face of evil. Beauty of magnificent art, beauty of all happiness, most especially the beauty of women.

After all, it carried too many connections to recklessness and excess. Beautiful things were often fragile, but fragile things were never virtuous. And in this fresh solitude of his that had been chosen for whatever greatness he might accomplish, beauty had to be conditional or, being a harmony itself, it would create only conflict.

In a way, this gradual abandonment of beauty marked the second phase following his complete disenchantment. He sensed that he was abandoning his opportunity to become a particular kind of artist. Being a specific type of person seemed far more significant.

His thoughts suddenly shifted direction, and he found himself contemplating the Catholic Church. He felt strongly that people who needed organized religion possessed some fundamental deficiency, and for Amory, religion meant the Roman Catholic Church. It was entirely possible that it amounted to nothing more than empty ceremony, but it appeared to be the only unifying, traditional defense against moral decline. Until the masses could be taught to develop moral understanding, someone had to declare: "Thou shalt not!" However, any form of acceptance remained impossible for him at the moment. He needed time without external influence or hidden agendas. He wanted to preserve the tree bare of decorations, to fully understand the path and force of this fresh beginning.

The afternoon gradually shifted from the cleansing goodness of three o'clock to the golden splendor of four. Later he walked through the dull pain of a setting sun when even the clouds appeared to be bleeding, and at dusk he arrived at a cemetery. There was a dim, dreamlike fragrance of flowers and the faint outline of a new moon in the sky with shadows cast everywhere. On a sudden urge he thought about attempting to open the door of a corroded iron tomb built into the hillside; a tomb that had been washed clean and was covered with late-blooming, drooping pale blue flowers that could have sprouted from lifeless eyes, sticky when touched with a nauseating smell.

Amory wanted to feel "William Dayfield, 1864."

He wondered why graveyards ever made people think life was meaningless. Somehow he couldn't find anything hopeless about having lived at all. All the broken columns and clasped hands and doves and angels represented love stories. He imagined that in a hundred years he would enjoy having young people wonder whether his eyes had been brown or blue, and he hoped with great intensity that his grave would feel like it belonged to many, many years in the past. It seemed odd that out of a row of Union soldiers, two or three made him think of lost loves and dead lovers, when they looked exactly like all the others, right down to the yellowish moss covering them.

———

Long past midnight, Princeton's towers and spires remained visible, with scattered lights still burning late into the night—and suddenly, from the clear darkness came the sound of bells. It continued like an endless dream; the spirit of the past watching over a new generation, the chosen young people from the confused, undisciplined world, still romantically nourished by the mistakes and half-forgotten dreams of dead politicians and poets. Here was a new generation, shouting the same old battle cries, learning the same old beliefs, through a daydream of long days and nights; destined ultimately to venture out into that dirty gray chaos to pursue love and pride; a new generation devoted even more than the previous one to the fear of poverty and the worship of success; raised to discover all Gods dead, all wars fought, all faith in humanity shaken....

Amory felt sorry for them, but he still didn't feel sorry for himself—whether his path would be art, politics, religion, or whatever medium he might choose, he knew he was safe now, free from all the emotional turmoil—he could embrace what was worth embracing, wander freely, develop, fight against what needed fighting, and sleep peacefully through countless nights....

There was no God in his heart, he understood; his thoughts remained in chaos; the ache of remembrance persisted; the sorrow for his vanished youth lingered—yet the flood of disappointment had settled something within his spirit, a sense of duty and an appreciation for existence, the subtle awakening of former aspirations and unfulfilled hopes. But—oh, Rosalind! Rosalind!...

"It's all a poor substitute at best," he said sadly.

And he couldn't understand why the struggle was worthwhile, why he had decided to use himself and his inheritance from the people who had influenced him to the fullest extent....

He stretched out his arms toward the crystal-clear, brilliant sky.

"I know myself," he cried, "but that is all."

THE END

Thank You For Reading

You've Just Read a Piece of the Greatest Library Ever Rebuilt

Thank you for reading.

This book is one of thousands we're restoring, reimagining, and translating as part of the **Modern Library of Alexandria** — a global movement to preserve and share humanity's most important ideas.

What was once lost to fire and time is now rising again — not just as memory, but as living, breathing knowledge, freely accessible to all.

What You Can Do Next:

* **Keep Reading.**

  Discover more legendary works — in beautiful print, audiobook, or digital form — at LibraryofAlexandria.com.

* **Build Your Own Library.**

  Every title is available as a paperback, hardcover, or collectible boxset — at true printing cost. Craft a personal library worthy of display.

* **Spread the Light.**

  Share this book. Tell others about the movement. Help us translate every timeless work into every language, so no reader is ever left behind.

By finishing this book, you've already taken part in something extraordinary.

Join us at LibraryofAlexandria.com

Together, we're rebuilding the greatest library the world has ever known.

With appreciation,

The Modern Library of Alexandria Team

Visit:
www.libraryofalexandria.com
Or scan the code below: